MW01010573

MYSTERIES UNCOVERED, SECRETS DECLASSIFIED

LOST CITIES

AND

FORGOTTEN

CIVILIZATIONS

MICHAEL PYE AND KIRSTEN DALLEY, EDITORS

ROSEN
PUBLISHING®

New York

OCT - 7 2013

T₀₀ı.9૫

LoSThis edition published in 2013 by:

The Rosen Publishing Group, Inc.
29 East 21st Street
New York, NY 10010

Additional end matter copyright © 2013 by The Rosen Publishing
Group, Inc.

Library of Congress Cataloging-in-Publication Data

Lost cities and forgotten civilizations/[edited by] Michael Pye,
Kirsten Dalley.
     p. cm.—(Mysteries uncovered, secrets declassified)
Includes bibliographical references and index.
ISBN 978-1-4488-9251-8 (library binding)
1. Civilization, Ancient. 2. Geographical myths 3. Civilization—
Extraterrestrial influences. I. Pye, Michael, 1946– II. Dalley, Kirsten.
CB311.L77 2013
001.94—dc23
                                                          2012032332

Manufactured in the United States of America

CPSIA Compliance Information: Batch #W13YA: For further information, contact Rosen Publishing, New York, New York, at 1-800-237-9932.

Published by arrangement with New Page Books, a division of Career Press, Inc. © Michael Pye and Kirsten Dalley

Contents

Preface

Atlantis. Lemuria. Mu. Eden. These famous names always bring to mind fantastic images of sprawling, flourishing civilizations and idyllic, utopian climes. But did they exist? The established archaeological community would be quick to respond with an emphatic no. But more and more experts are coming forward now—in addition to those who have been fighting to make their voices heard for decades—declaring that, yes, these places did, in fact, exist in some form.

The world is forever and always changing. Ocean levels have risen and fallen innumerable times over the millennia. We are just now realizing how even a seemingly miniscule change in sea level can completely alter the way we live. So why is it so difficult to believe that there once existed vast and glorious cultures that, along with their knowledge and histories, were lost to the sands of time or the depthless waters of a great flood? Most people cite a lack of any tangible evidence to support this idea, but what they don't know (or refuse to know) is that there *is* evidence.

This collection delves into many questions concerning these lost civilizations, including their sometimes gigantic and otherworldly inhabitants, their possible contact with advanced beings and aliens, their religions, and other lost knowledge from a past we all share.

With no past, we can have no future. There is more to history if you know how to look at it and where to look. Let these experts show you the way.

—Michael Pye and Kirsten Dalley

October 2011

Archaeological Scandals
By Frank Joseph

Cultural diffusionists believe that seafarers from the ancient Old World visited North America and influenced its prehistory millennia prior to 1492. They contradict official versions of the past upheld by cultural isolationists—mainstream archaeologists who insist that such contact never took place because no credible evidence supporting it exists.

Scott F. Wolter is a university-trained geologist and president of American Petrographic Services in St. Paul, Minnesota. His firm is tasked to analyze construction materials, and has been cited for professional excellence by the American Association for Laboratory Accreditation. The object of Wolter's scrutiny with which we are concerned was a 200-pound (91-kg) sandstone found in September of 1898 by Swedish immigrant farmer Olof Öhman while clearing his land in the largely rural township of Solem, Minnesota. Lying flat and entwined in the roots of a stunted 30-year-old aspen tree, the 30 × 16 × 6-inch (76 x 41 x 15 cm) slab was covered on its face and one side with what resembled runic writing. Öhman brought his find to the nearest town, Kensington, where it was displayed at the local bank. Interested in finding out the truth concerning the stone, Wolter subjected it to rigorous scientific examination in 2000.

Translated from Medieval Swedish, the front of the object reads:

> Eight Götalanders and twenty two Norwegians on [this] reclaiming/acquisition journey far west from Vinland. We had a camp by two [shelters?] one day's journey north from this stone. We were fishing one day. After we came home we found ten men red with blood and death. Ave Maria. Save from evil.

Inscribed on the side of the stone are the words, "There are ten men by the sea to look after our ships fourteen day's journey from this island. Year 1362.[1]

Although archaeologists dismissed it as a transparent hoax, further independent testing by Newton Horace Winchell, a geologist at the Minnesota Historical Society, confirmed that the weathering on the stone's exterior indicated that its inscription was approximately 500 years old. "There was strong support for an authentic Runestone date of 1362," he concluded, "and little reason to suspect fraud."[2] Unfortunately, his 1910 report was obscured by the denunciations of skeptics, who loudly proclaimed that the stone was a ludicrous forgery. More advanced technological methods of examination to either confirm the inscription's medieval authenticity or conclusively debunk it were not developed until the turn of the 21st century, when the object was entrusted to Scott Wolter for analysis. He had actually never heard of the Kensington Rune Stone and was therefore indifferent to the squabbles concerning its provenance.

He began by using photography with a reflected light microscope, core sampling, and a scanning electron microscope. These tools revealed unmistakable signs of sub-surface erosion requiring a minimum of 200 years to develop. In other words, the Kensington Rune Stone was buried for at least a century before Olof Öhman excavated it. Further examination of each individual rune through a scanning electron microscope revealed a series of dots engraved inside three runes for the letter "R." These dotted runes, never before noticed on the stone by anyone, have only been found in one other place: 14th-century headstones in church cemeteries on the island of Götland, off the coast of Sweden. The Kensington Rune Stone is inscribed with a 14th century date, and its text cites eight crewmen from Götland. No less crucially, Wolter pointed out, "the rare, medieval rune called 'the dotted R' was not known to modern scholars until 1935, yet it occurs on the Kensington Rune Stone, found in 1898. Interpretation: The presence of 'the dotted R' indicates the Kensington Rune Stone inscription could only have been carved during medieval times."[3]

The Kensington Rune Stone on display at the Rune Stone Museum, in Alexandria, Minnesota. Photograph courtesy of Ancient American *magazine, used with permission.*

State-of-the-art testing at an award-winning laboratory in a controlled, scientific environment by a university-trained geologist confirmed Olof Öhman's discovery of an authentic 14th-century memorial. One might imagine that Wolter's unequivocal proof of Norse explorers in the Midwest 130 years before the official discovery of America would have provoked newspaper headlines everywhere and been applauded by archaeologists. On the contrary, he received mixed reviews in the local press, while Scott Anfinson, the Minnesota state archaeologist, and Russell Fridley, former head of the Minnesota Historical Society, snubbed his meticulous research, dismissing the Kensington Rune Stone as "a monument to Scandinavian frontier humor."[4]

His pleas for peer review ignored, Wolter turned his attention to another, although entirely different object equally deprecated by the likes of Anfinson and Fridley, in an effort to show that the Kensington Rune Stone was not anomalous, but part of wider evidence for the presence of overseas visitors in pre-Columbian America. The item he selected had been discovered on February 14, 1889, along the Little Tennessee River, near the mouth of Bat Creek, about 40 miles south of Knoxville. At the time, members of the Smithsonian Institution's Bureau of Ethnology's Mound Survey Project were excavating three undisturbed Native American burial structures at the site, dated to circa 100 CE. One of them, 28 feet (8.5 meters) across and 5 feet (1.5 m) high, yielded nine human skeletons, together with a small, congealed mass of metal objects resembling bracelets. Partially hidden under the back part of a male skull, a relatively flat, thin piece of ferruginous (containing iron oxides), reddish-brown siltstone, 4.49 inches (11.4 cm) long by 2.01 inches (5.1 cm) wide, and engraved with an eight-letter inscription, was removed by archaeologist John W. Emmert.

Because it was found and handled under unimpeachably professional circumstances, the Bat Creek Stone was not dismissed or discarded as a fake, the typical fate of such discoveries. Even so, it could not be admitted as evidence of archaeological heresy—that is, evidence of foreign contact in pre-Columbian times—so the Smithsonian archaeologists presumed, once again without proof, that the inscription had been copied from a Cherokee alphabet invented in 1821 by Sequoyah, a *métis* (person of mixed heritage—usually half European, half Amerindian) silversmith. As such, the Bat Creek Stone was featured at the Smithsonian Institution Museum in Washington, D.C., for the next 80 years, until Henriette Mertz, a former code-breaker for the U.S. government's cryptography department, noticed that the object was actually engraved with Hebrew letters and was improperly displayed upside down. She contacted Dr. Cyrus H. Gordon, a renowned scholar of Near Eastern cultures and ancient languages at Brandeis University, who verified the Semitic identity of the script.

Tennessee's Bat Creek Stone with 2nd-century paleo-Hebrew inscription. Photograph courtesy of Ancient American *magazine. Used with permission.*

It reads from right to left: LYHWD (meaning "for Judea"). Gordon noted that a broken letter on the far left was consistent with the Hebrew glyph, *mem*, in which case the word would instead read: LYHWD[M] ("for the Judeans").[5] He recognized the script as similar to characters on Judean coins of the 2nd century, and therefore dated the text, based on its distinctive lettering, from 70 to 135 CE. This time-frame was corroborated by separate testing performed during the mid-1970s, when "researchers also examined sheet-copper bracelets found with the tablet. Their analysis revealed that the bracelets were made from a zinc-copper alloy commonly used in the Roman Empire between 45 BCE and 200 CE."[6] Later, in 1988, wood fragments found with the inscription were carbon-dated to sometime between 32 and 769 CE.

Despite its discovery by the premiere archaeological organization of the day, the Smithsonian Institution, and despite the vaunted academic credentials of everyone involved and the laboratory testing performed by university-trained professionals, the Bat Creek Stone was vigorously condemned as fraudulent by mainstream archaeologists. They even went so far as to sacrifice one of their own on the altar of politically correct expediency, when John Emmert, the Smithsonian Institution archaeologist who found the artifact, was described as an alcoholic who faked the inscription to curry favor with his supervisor (an accusation never made until the 1970s, by the way)—clearly a baseless, mean-spirited attempt to discredit Dr. Gordon's work.[7] They continued to insist that the inscription was Sequoyah's Cherokee syllabary until they were forced to concede in 2004 that the text was indeed 2nd-century Hebrew. However, they still refused to allow its pre-Columbian origins. The Bat Creek Stone, they now argued, must have been engraved by 19th-century Freemasons. Just who these unidentified Freemason experts in 2nd-century paleo-Hebrew were, however, the skeptics were unable to say.

Although any objective person would have by now rejected the official skepticism as wholly irrational, Scott Wolter was determined to subject the Bat Creek Stone to the most rigorous scientific examination of its checkered career. From May 28 to June 29 of 2010, attended by Dr. Barbara Duncan, Education Director at the Museum of the Cherokee Indian, he performed a battery of tests on the artifact, then on indefinite loan to the McClung Museum at the campus of the University of Tennessee in Knoxville. Petrographic observations using reflected light microscopy and microphoto were used to study the stone's surface, followed by scanning electron microscopy (SEM) analysis. An Olympus SZX12 Zoom microscope with a spot digital camera system was also brought into play. As Wolter concluded:

> since we did not observe any orange-colored silty-clay in the grooves of the inscription, and the overall surface of the stone and the edges of the grooves were polished at the time of discovery, the inscription had to have been made prior to the excavation of the mound by John Emmert.... The complete lack of orange-colored, silty-clay residue in any of the characters of the inscription is consistent with many hundreds of years of weathering in a wet earth mound comprised of soil and hard red clay.... The inscribed stone and all other artifacts and remains found in the mound with it can be no younger than when the bodies of the deceased were buried inside the mound [during the 2nd century CE][8]

The Bat Creek Stone's ancient authenticity had been scientifically verified. The skeptics were silenced, but strangely they showed no interest in testing Wolter's findings for themselves, nor did they welcome his work as a new opportunity to perhaps settle an old controversy one way or the other, regardless of its outcome.

If the Norse Kensington Rune Stone and Hebrew Bat Creek Stone hinted at the range of cultures impacting prehistoric America, that diversity came forcefully to light on October 5, 1877, when Chief Joseph of the Wal-lam-wat-kain, a band of Nez Perce Indians, surrendered to units of the U.S. Cavalry near Chinook in the north of what is now Montana. While in custody, a medicine bag hanging around his neck was stolen. The pouch contained several symbolic items, but one that attracted the most curiosity among the soldiers was a 1-inch (2.5 cm)-square baked clay tablet engraved on both sides with an unfamiliar script. When questioned, Chief Joseph explained that "the tablet had been passed down in his family for many generations, and that they had inherited it from their white ancestors. Chief Joseph said that white men had come among his ancestors long ago, and had taught his people many things."[9]

Chief Joseph's Sumerian tablet at New York's West Point Museum. Photograph courtesy of Ancient American *magazine.*

The object was sent to New York's West Point Museum, where it has been warehoused ever since. Around the turn of the last century, an Assyriology professor at the Oriental Institute of the University of Chicago examined Chief Joseph's peculiar heirloom. An editor of the *Journal of Near Eastern Studies*, with a PhD from Johns Hopkins University, Robert D. Biggs readily determined that the script was a cuneiform receipt for a sacrificial lamb to help celebrate the promotion of someone named Enmahgalanna as high priestess of Nanna, god of the Moon.[10] This same lunar deity was worshipped in southern Iraq, where his most famous shrine was the Great Ziggurat of Ur, originally known as E-temen-nigur(u), or the "house whose foundation creates terror."[11] Still fundamentally intact, the monumental step-pyramid made of mud brick was originally 210 feet (64 m) long, 150 feet (46 m) wide, and 110 feet (33.5 m) high. Professor Biggs determined that Chief Joseph's tablet dated to approximately 2042 BCE, when it was inscribed by the Sumerians.

That these disparate events, so profoundly removed from the environs, time, and culture of Chief Joseph, should have been connected with him in a small tablet seems incredible, until we learn that the pouch in which it was found preserved his most sacred possessions. Traditionally, medicine bags "contained items that would remind the warrior of home, of where he came from," which is exactly how Chief Joseph described the cuneiform square.[12] Moreover, as historical writer Mary Gindling points out:

> The mundane nature of the contents of the tablet argues against forgery. Cuneiform had only been deciphered in 1846, and the process was far from complete even in 1877, so a would-be forger would had to have been an extremely well educated individual, familiar not only with the ancient language itself, but with the shape of the tablets created by the ancient scribes.[13]

That being doubtful to the point of impossibility, especially in frontier America, had seafarers from Mesopotamia actually been capable of navigating halfway around the world during our prehistory?

Georgia's Hearn Stone offers a translatable text from 2nd millennium BCE *Sumer. Photograph courtesy of* Ancient American *magazine. Used with permission.*

This question was at least partially answered 33 years ago, when Dr. Thor Heyerdahl commissioned the construction in Iraq of *Tigris*, the faithful re-creation of a reed-boat depicted in Sumerian temple art. He hoped to prove that the Sumerians possessed a martime technology sufficient for passage at least as far as the Indus Valley, where he suspected there were fundamentally important cultural links with Mesopotamia. Baked clay records dating from the late 3rd millennium BCE made ambiguous references to oceanic Sumerian voyages in reed vessels large enough to carry 28 tons of cargo.

In early spring of 1978, Heyerdahl and his international crew maneuvered their re-creation through the Persian Gulf to Pakistan and out into the Red Sea, but due to military clashes throughout the region, they were denied harbor everywhere except Djibouti. Frustrated,

Heyerdahl destroyed *Tigris* by burning her down to the waterline on April 3, even though she was still seaworthy after more than five continuous months afloat. He thus demonstrated the remarkable hardihood of Sumerian reed-boat construction, which would have rendered transoceanic voyages feasible at the time the Indian leader's tablet was inscribed in the mid-21st century BCE. It was this seafaring technology that appears to explain not only his inherited memento, but other examples of ancient cuneiform found in America.

Shortly after the Cherokee artifact came to light, "a Sumerian tablet with cuneiform writing was found beside ancient stone projectile points near Lexington, Georgia," according to archaeologist, Dr. Gunnar Thompson. "The tablet is from Ur-Nammuk, Iraq, and dates to 2040 BCE," the same year of Chief Joseph's object.[14] Cultural diffusionist researcher Gloria Farley told of a similar find made in the same state by a Mrs. Joe Hearn:

> In 1963, while digging a new flower bed on her property in northwestern Georgia, not far from the Chatahoochee River, her shovel had struck a small, pillow-shaped tablet made of lead.... The cuneiform script, according to Dr. Curtis Hoffman, describes how a scribe named Enlila was aware that it was the 37th or 38th year of the reign of King Sulgi of Ur, which by our reckoning, would have been about 2040 BCE It recorded the sale of sheep and goats, which apparently had been transported overseas to America, for sacrifice to Utu, the sun-god, and the goddess, Lama Lugal.[15]

The correct dates of Shulgi's rule were 2029 to 1982 BCE. Nevertheless, Georgia's Hearn artifact and Chief Joseph's tablet—separated by many hundreds of miles and found nearly a century apart—both date to within 11 years of each other, thus underscoring their common authenticity. The period they share throws new light on their appearance in North America. Archaeologists know it as the Third Dynasty of Ur, or Ur III, a 21st- to 20th-century BCE Sumerian ruling dynasty based in the city of Ur after several centuries of Semitic domination. Shulgi promulgated an expansionist policy that included the broadest commercial ties ever extended by Sumer. If ever in that culture's history its mariners had sailed to America, it would have been during that dynasty. Today the Hearn Tablet is in the possession of LaGrange College, Georgia's oldest private college, which was founded in 1831.

Still another cuneiform tablet dating to the Neo-Sumerian Empire was found near Quaker City, Ohio, in 1978 by an amateur Indian arrowhead collector, who submitted his discovery to David Owen, professor of Near Eastern Studies at Cornell University, in Ithaca, New York. Owen established its ancient provenance and determined that the text had been authored "by a man named Ur-e'e in the month of Dumuzi (late June), in the year (circa 2030 BCE) the *ensi* (ruler) of Karzida was elevated."[16] The inscription returns full circle to Chief Joseph's tablet, with its reference to Nanna, because Karzida was the moon-god's second city of worship.

What particularly distinguishes these cuneiform-inscribed items is their unreserved verification by mainstream archaeologists, who freely admit that all three tablets are authentically Sumerian. Amazingly, they also uniformly and automatically assume that the items were brought to North America by modern collectors, because such items simply could not have arrived here any other way. Professor Owen "suggests that we are not to make too much of the [Quaker City] find, since 'tablets of this type were sold throughout the U.S. in the early years of this [20th] Century, and have shown up in various places, including garbage dumps and garage sales.'"[17] But that does not explain Chief Joseph's tablet, which became public knowledge in 1877, more than 20 years before the alleged importation of Sumerian relics, nor the Hearn Tablet, which was dug up on property that had been in the discoverer's family since 1850. The Quaker City tablet was excavated from a depth of some 2 feet (0.6 m) amid a cluster of Indian arrowheads—hardly the setting for a misplaced trinket from the early 20th century.

Moreover, a thorough Internet search by this author has failed to turn up any indication that brisk sales in authentic cuneiform tablets occurred in the United States during the early 1900s, as Professor Owen stated (again, without proof). The very notion that museum-quality artifacts from ancient Sumer would have been sold off in large quantities to the general public, like bubble gum or cheap trinkets, seems absurd. Professor Owen blandly made the astounding revelation that "many such Ur III tablets have been found in the U.S., including some tablets dug up a few years ago from the ruins of an old apartment house in Auburn, New York."[19] His thorough disinterest in these finds was based on the entirely groundless assumption that each one of them was an early 20th-century import. Because his education programmed him to believe that our continent was impervious to all outside influences prior to Columbus, his mind was closed to any other explanations for the appearance of Sumerian tablets in America. But even his facile dismissal of their significance cannot account for wholly different cuneiform inscriptions found in South America.

During 1959, a construction worker accidentally dug up an unusual bowl on the property of the Manjon family, not far from the pre-Inca ruins of Tiahuanaco, the ritual and administrative capital of a major state power 44 miles (71 km) west of La Paz. The chestnut-brown fired ceramic bowl unearthed not far from Tiahuanaco seems unremarkable at first glance. It is 2.4 inches (6 cm) deep and 5 inches (13 cm) wide, engraved overall with zoological motifs and anthropomorphic characters intersecting two different scripts. While one of these scripts is entirely unlike any known written language, the other is identifiably cuneiform, which went unnoticed by members of the Manjon family. *Magna Fuente*, or the "great fountain," refers to an area of the family's property where the artifact was found. The Bolivian archaeologist Don Max Portugal-Zamora confirmed its pre-Inca provenance and completed some minor repairs.

The inner rim of Peru's La Paz bowl features a cuneiform text in ancient Sumerian. Photograph courtesy of Ancient American *magazine.*

For more than 40 years the bowl was mostly forgotten, until a related find was made in December 2001, again near Tiahuanaco, less than four miles (6 km) west of the ruins, at another pre-Inca site known as Pokotia. Inside a pyramidal hill, an excavation team led by professional archaeologist Bernardo Biados dug up a 350-pound (159 kg), 5-foot (1.5 m)-tall, 2-foot (0.6 m)-wide stone statue, broken at the feet and neck and with almost entirely eroded facial features. The male figure stands upright, with its arms at its sides (ribs are indicated by four lines on either side of the chest), a loincloth-like garment about its hips, and simple armbands around both wrists. The puffy headgear atop its head is identical to similar representations found at Tiahuanaco's semi-subterranean court. Inscrutable symbols and cuneiform script spill over its back and onto the fronts of its legs.

When the Pokotia Monolith was removed to La Paz's Museum of Precious Metals (formerly known as the Gold Museum) on Calle Jaén, it was joined by the Magna Fuente object in 2007, when this object's similarly cuneiform text was recalled for comparison. Dr. Alberto Marini, a recognized authority in ancient Mesopotamian languages, determined that the Magna Fuente inscription was Sumerian, and identified the artifact as a libation bowl. Although the wording adorning the colossus has likewise been identified as Sumerian, it is still awaiting proper translation.

The cuneiform evidence supports numerous cultural comparisons between Mesopotamian and Andean civilizations. "Both Sumerians and Peruvians," Dr. Thompson observes, "believed in the existence of a holy mountain with twin peaks, where the Sun rested during the night. Sumerians called their twin peaks *Mashu*; among the Inca, it was known as *Machu* Picchu."[19] The very word *Inca* appears to be derivative of the Sumerian *Enki*; both mean "great lord." The Great Ziggurat of Ur described previously bears an uncanny resemblance to contemporaneous stepped pyramids found at Chicama, along the northwest coast of Peru. "Both Mesopotamian and Peruvian structures," points out Dr. Thompson, "were made from sun-dried bricks."[20] The pre-Inca origins of both the Magna Fuente bowl and the Pokotia Monolith are as authentic as their cuneiform inscriptions. Yet, David Hatcher Childress, president of the World Explorers Club, who visited both finds, wondered if this discovery and decipherment would change the prevailing archaeological attitudes in the Americas, or if mainstream archaeologists—the experts—would just ignore this evidence of transoceanic interaction, as they have done on numerous, other occasions. Perhaps this bowl and statue could not be conveniently destroyed or hidden, but they have been relegated to a fairly obscure museum and summarily ignored for the past eight years.[21]

Combined with these Bolivian revelations, the Ur III tablets—five among possibly dozens more Owens found in the States—should have, at the very least, prompted archaeologists everywhere to reconsider possibilities for Sumerian influences on American prehistory. But none of them had anything to say. What could have been the beginning of an entirely new understanding of our deep past, based on authentic, officially recognized physical evidence, never took place. Instead, the same shop-worn—indeed, obsolete and even erroneous—official version of antiquity is repeated unchanged despite all facts to the contrary. Promulgated for more than 100 years, even up to the present day, by America's educational system, print media editors, and television programmers, this version is accepted by most Americans, who are still kept in the dark regarding the Magna Fuente bowl, the Pokotia Monolith, and the Sumerian tablets.

They would find incredible and outrageous Childress's suggestion that mainstream archaeologists—respected scientists, mind you!—would be capable of deliberately hiding or destroying "subversive" evidence, perhaps even priceless artifacts. At one time, so did Ivan T. Sanderson, an extraordinary naturalist who earned his BA in zoology with honors from Cambridge University, where he later earned MA degrees in botany and geology. His books *Animal Treasure*, *Caribbean Treasure*, and *Living Treasure*, published starting in the late 1930s, are still regarded as classics of nature writing.[22] He wrote 16 books in all about nature and his world travels. In the following decade, he coined the term *cryptozoology* for the scientific investigation of unknown plant and animal life, a discipline he founded. "Sanderson's behavioral observations in the animals' natural environments were invaluable."[23] For more than 30 years, his numerous articles about wildlife were featured in *True, Sports Afield, Argosy,* and the *Saturday*

Evening Post. Beginning in the early 1950s, he was among the first televised zoologists to bring live animals on talk programs, such as *The Johnny Carson Show*, where he was a frequent guest.

Before Sanderson's death in 1973 at 62 years of age, he received a letter from a former Navy Seabee in the U.S. Army Corps of Engineers. During 1943, while stationed on the small Aleutian island of Shemya, he oversaw crewmen clearing land for the construction of a 10,000-foot (3,048 m)-long airstrip, when they bulldozed what they imagined was a series of low hills. About 2 miles (3 km) long, Shemya is the second to last island in the chain of Aleutian Semichi Islands, approximately 200 miles (322 km) from Russian territory, and believed to have never been inhabited. The engineers' work came to a sudden halt, however, after removal of several sedimentary layers exposed a field of human skeletal remains. The engineers realized at once that what they mistook for hillocks were actually burial mounds filled with hundreds of skulls and primarily thigh bones.

Although a remarkable enough find in itself, the inadvertent excavators were amazed to observe that the crania of the skulls measured from 22 to 24 inches (56 to 61 cm) across from base to crown. An adult human male skull normally measures 8 inches (20 cm) from back to front. Closer examination showed that the skulls had been artificially elongated from infancy in a process called *ritual head deformation*, which was known to both the Inca and pharaonic Egyptians. It was used to physically distinguish royalty and aristocracy from the lower orders of society. The engineers also noticed that a neatly cut hole appeared in the upper portion of each skull, the result of *trepanning*, a pre-modern form of brain surgery practiced by physicians in ancient Peru and the Nile Valley.

After the military officers notified their superiors in Washington, D.C., archaeologists from the Smithsonian Institution arrived at Shemya, carefully collected all the bones, and departed without a word of explanation. The letter writer stated that his efforts to learn whatever became of them were unsuccessful, remarking that the bizarre skeletons never received any publicity, and asked the famous zoologist for assistance. Sanderson corresponded with another Army Corps of Engineers veteran of the Shemya discovery, who confirmed the U.S. Navy Seabee's version in every detail. Despite Sanderson's prestige as a world-class scientist, his repeated requests to Smithsonian Institution directors, whom he knew personally for many years, insisted that no wartime collection of unusual human remains in the Aleutians ever took place, and that no records documenting such an undertaking ever existed. He was convinced they were lying, and wondered aloud, "Is it that these people cannot face rewriting all the text books?"[24]

Tragically, the Smithsonian's handling of this most inconvenient evidence at Shemya was not the only such instance of suppression and manipulation of the facts. In 1908, the Institution commissioned G.E. Kincaid to make the first photographic record of the Grand Canyon. Traveling down the length of the Colorado River, Kincaid found more than he bargained for when he entered a massive system of caverns containing military "barracks" stacked with edged weapons and mummified human remains surrounded by hundreds of breastplates, shields, ornaments, and tools. A Buddha-like statue stood atop an altar in its own shrine room, its walls adorned with hieroglyphic script.

Responding to his submitted report, the Smithsonian dispatched S.A. Jordan at the head of expedition team members, who were led by Kincaid to the cavern site. They carted out load after load of artifacts, then sealed the cave entrance with an iron gate. Returning to Yuma, Arizona, Professor Jordan announced at a press conference that another, larger expedition, comprising 30 or 40 archaeologists, geologists, surveyors, and photographers, was being prepared for a major scientific assault on the cave and its contents. The story was headlined by the *Arizona Gazette* as "Explorations in the Grand Canyon. Mysteries of Immense Rich Cavern Brought to Light," on April 5, 1909, and was followed by a series of minor articles. But that was the end of all public discussion of the discovery. Numerous inquiries during the last 100 years have been met with consistent denial by the Smithsonian Institution that such a find was made or such an expedition on its behalf was ever launched. But decades of determined effort undertaken by skeptics to prove that editors of the *Arizona Gazette* engaged in a hoax came to nothing. The alleged cartloads of artifacts removed from the Grand Canyon have disappeared, along with all of G.E. Kincaid's photographs.[25]

A relative misdemeanor in this checkered history of archaeological scandals took place in 1948, when Smithsonian Institution directors ordered that the Kensington Rune Stone—then on loan to the museum—be entirely scrubbed with kerosene, scouring off every trace of original dirt and roots still clinging to it from the day it was found, 50 years prior.[26] Preservation of the artifact's original condition was crucial in affirming the authentic circumstances of its controversial discovery, something Smithsonian Institution scientists would have fully understood.

But even worse than the damaging or suppression of embarrassing evidence has been the destruction of professional careers of nonconforming colleagues by establishment archaeologists. "There used to be more freedom of thought and expression, less worry about what peers said," Michael D. Coe told *Americas* magazine. "Today, there's sort of an academic mafia that runs things. You line up outside these hotel rooms during conferences, wait for a job interview. If you say the wrong thing, you're bad, and you don't get in.... There are reputable publications that won't accept papers written based on anything but stuff dug up by archaeologists."[27]

Coe uttered these words after his retirement in 1996. He is still among the most famous and respected scholars today, the leading figure in Olmec archaeology. During the mid-1960s, his excavation at San Lorenzo (Veracruz) pushed Mesoamerican chronology back 1,000 years, and identified the Olmecs as our continent's first civilizers. He was for 35 years a professor of anthropology at Yale University and curator of the Peabody Museum, in New Haven, Connecticut. His more than a dozen published books influenced a generation of readers and established him as the recognized *doyen* of Olmec studies. "Well, if I were coming up for tenure now, when deconstruction reigns supreme within the entire academic universe," Coe confessed to *Americas* magazine, "I probably wouldn't get in."[28]

During his long years of tenure, he kept his diffusionist opinions to himself. "There are so many resemblances between mental systems of Bali and Mesoamerica, it got to the point I could predict what they [the Balinese] were going to do next from my knowledge of the Maya. Truly amazing! [...] I'm looking at mental systems, cosmological systems, which are almost identical on both sides of the Pacific."[29] Coe's previous training as a CIA operative for the front organization "Western Enterprises" in Taiwan no doubt enabled him to maintain the silence necessary to save his career from premature termination.[30] His experience reflects poorly on the condition of modern archaeology, where a valid line of scientific inquiry—the seminal connections between prehistoric Indonesia and Mesoamerica—was closed by what he termed "an academic mafia that runs things."[31]

As a world class authority on the ancient Near East, Dr. Cyrus Gordon himself knew that "no politically astute member of the establishment who prizes his professional reputation is likely to risk his good name for the sake of a truth that his peers (and therefore the public) may not be prepared to accept for fifty or a hundred years."[32]

Indeed, accredited archaeologists who speak up for cultural diffusion find their reputations ruined and themselves banished from their own profession. During the mid-1970s, Virginia Steen-McIntyre was conducting research at a newly discovered ancient habitation site as part of her PhD dissertation at the University of Idaho. Hueyatlaco (pronounced, "way-at-la-co"), about 70 miles (113 km) southeast of Mexico City, yielded an abundance of prehistoric evidence. Using state-of-the-art radiometric methods and instruments, she and her similarly university-trained colleagues in the Harvard-funded Valsequillo Project competently and repeatedly dated the remains of a man-made fire that had burned a quarter of a million years ago. A sacred tenet in the doctrine of mainstream archaeology holds that the first humans to cross a land-bridge from Siberia into Alaska arrived in Middle America no earlier than 11,000 years ago.

In response, "a branch of the [Mexican] federal government descended on Juan [one of Steen-McIntyre's colleagues at the site], confiscating all his fossils and artifacts, everything discovered during the Valsequillo Project, together with his bone collection at the University of Puebla's anthropology department and all his equipment. Everything was removed to Mexico City. He was forbidden by law to do any more field work, ever. Frustrated, the government-sponsored professionals claimed in print that all the artifacts at Hueyatlaco had been planted by workers."[33]

Her own treatment back in the United States was hardly any better. As Michael Coe predicted, no editor was willing to publish Steen-McIntyre's findings for peer review in any scientific periodical. In the 10 years she struggled without success to get her work into print, she was given no opportunity for further work in her profession, until she could no longer make a living as an archaeologist. Virginia Steen-McIntyre was what conventional scholars label a "rogue professor"— a kind of mad scientist meriting that appelation, because clearly someone like this would have to be crazy not to believe consensus reality! Establishment archaeologists Robert C. Mainfort, Jr., and Mary L. Kwas so categorized Professor Gordon, who dared to assert that Tennessee's Bat Creek Stone had been engraved with a 2nd-century Hebrew inscription. They referred to him as "an archetypical example of what Williams has referred to as 'rogue professors.' Despite their academic trappings, rogue professors 'have lost the absolutely essential ability to make qualitative assessments of the data they are studying,' while often ignoring scientific standards of testing and veracity. Lacking the critical standard of most scholars, rogue professors 'have the opportunity to rogue or defraud the public....'"[34]

After obtaining his PhD at the University of Pennsylvania, Cyrus Gordon was a teacher at Brandeis for 18 years. He served as director of New York University's Center for Ebla Research, spearheading work on that ancient Syrian city. He taught classes and seminars and published work in field archaeology, glyphic art, cuneiform law, the Amarna letters, the Bible, Hebrew language, Ugaritic, Aramaic magic bowls, Nuzi tablets, Minoan Linear A, Homer, Egyptology, Coptic, Hittite, Hurrian, Sumerian, and Classical Arabic. These are the "academic trappings" Mainfort and Kwas stated were used by Cyrus Gordon to "defraud the public" with ideas they found offensive. How their own "academic trappings" might stand up to his could make for a revealing comparison.

In any case, these same skeptics who called him names pounced on other, independent investigators as "cult archaeologists," whose conclusions are worthless because they are not specialists in archaeology. Dr. J. Huston McCulloch, Professor of Economics and Finance at Ohio State University, and translator of international economics papers from their original French language, was thus peremptorily dismissed for championing the Bat Creek inscription's pre-Columbian provenance, because he is not a university-trained archaeologist, even though he is a university-trained scientist and professional linguist. In other words, only accredited archaeologists—and only those who think within the academic box—merit a hearing. Those who doubt official versions of the past are either too eccentric to be taken seriously or unqualified to offer contrary views. Everyone else should just sit down, shut up, and nod in agreement to whatever they are told by the "experts."

How did such a deplorable state of affairs come to pass?

The answer lies with John Wesley Powell, the father of American archaeology. This politically connected, willful director of the Smithsonian Institution's Bureau of Ethnology laid down the law for all professional archaeologists from the late 19th century to the present: "Hence, it will be seen that it is *illegitimate* to use any pictographic matter of a date anterior to the discovery of the continent by Columbus for historic purposes"[35] [emphasis mine]. He insisted that the Americas had been hermetically sealed off from the rest of the outside world by impassable, oceanic barriers until 1492. All apparent evidence for pre-Columbian influences from Europe or elsewhere at work here was henceforward officially forbidden as inadmissible and unworthy of scientific discussion. Any evidence of ancient Old World impact on America could only be either a misinterpretation of the native culture or a deliberate hoax. Therefore, merely considering such evidence was to engage in either folly or fraud. Although Powell's adamantine position assumed the aura of academic law, it was not the outcome of deliberate study or evaluation of evidence, but of religious bigotry.

He had been born and raised the son of a poor, itinerant New York Protestant preacher who ignited in his son a religious fervor that burned for the rest of his life. During the 1840s, when John was still a child, his father raged constantly against the nearby rise of Mormonism, which he condemned as the worst heresy. The boy grew up despising its founder, Joseph Smith, a hatred he nurtured into adulthood. As some indication of the mutual animosity between Powell and the Church of the Latter Day Saints, while he was exploring the Grand Canyon during 1869, he escaped an ambush in which three of his companions were killed in a Wild West–style shoot-out with Mormons.[36] His emphatic denial of any overseas contacts throughout pre-Columbian times was a visceral reaction to everything they believed, including Joseph Smith's contention that waves of immigrants from the Near East had begun arriving in America around 4,000 years ago.

In defending Protestantism from the blasphemous Mormons, Powell embraced the abolitionist movement, which he expanded to include Native American Indians. He felt they had been insulted by the Mormons and other like-minded diffusionists, who falsely attributed the monumental earthworks of prehistory to transoceanic foreigners. Out of his life-long religious hatred arose the doctrine of cultural isolationism, of which he is still its patron saint to establishment archaeologists. Lake Powell, a reservoir on the Colorado River straddling the border between Utah and Arizona, was named in his honor. In 1974, the United States Geographical Survey National Center in Reston, Virginia, was dedicated the John Wesley Powell Federal Building. The USGS's highest recognition of persons outside the federal government is the John Wesley Powell Award.

Far more significant than such official deification is the pervasive influence his Victorian Era doctrine still exerts on the education and outlook of 21st-century American archaeologists. His narrow-minded dogma has stunted their development and deprived them of any original discoveries for more than 100 years. Any meaningful finds have resulted from the efforts of either amateurs wholly disconnected from Academia, or professionals in other disciplines. While conventional scholars kept repeating John Wesley Powell's mantra of no foreigners in America "anterior to the discovery of the continent by Columbus," microbiologists confirmed the existence of DNA from a Near Eastern population group that inhabited the Hills of Galilee in northern Israel 2,000 years ago, among "pure blood" Native American Cherokee Indians.[37] With this revelation, the question of pre-Columbian Hebrews in North America has come full circle from Scott Wolter's independent confirmation of the Bat Creek Stone inscription as authentically ancient. Such a history-altering discovery was beyond the scope of mainstream archaeologists, made instead by professional investigators in different lines of research: genetics and geology.

Thankfully, these ongoing disclosures are severely eroding mainstream archaeology's hitherto unassailable position. Previously, cultural diffusionists hoped that one day the stubborn defenders of John

Wesley Powell would be disabused of his outdated gospel by the sheer weight of persuasive evidence. That strategy has itself been rendered obsolete by an escalating barrage of contrary data fired with devastating effect from other disciplines at Academia's ivory tower. It cannot survive such a lethal pounding, and must collapse of its own exposed weaknesses. From its ruins will ascend the New Archaeology, based, unlike its predecessor, on the forgotten principles of science—namely, that all evidence is at least initially worthy of fair assessment, and that conclusions must be allowed to freely arise only from the facts, minus any interference from bias or preconceived dogma.

The moment Powell declared that any consideration of overseas impact on pre-Columbian America was "illegitimate," he doomed archaeology to its present crisis and imminent demise. As an intelligent man living at a time of swift change, he should have realized that if there is any constant in the history of science, it is that yesterday's theoretical impossibility is the scientific reality of today.

Notes

1. Nielsen, Richard and Scott F. Wolter. *The Kensington Rune Stone.* Minn.: Lake Superior Agate Publishing, 2005.

2. Wolter, Scott F. *The Hooked X.* St. Cloud, Minn.: North Star Press of St. Cloud, Inc., 2009.

3. Ibid.

4. Haga, Chuck. "Rune Stone champion claims more evidence." *LaCrosse Tribune: http://lacrossetribune.com/news/local/article_74e2b1f8-bad6-11de-a12b-001cc4c002e0.html*, accessed October 17, 2009.

5. Gordon, Cyrus R. "Stone Inscription Found in Tennessee." *Ancient American*, vol. 14, #88, September 2010.

6. Thompson, Gunnar. *American Discovery.* Seattle, WA: Argonauts Misty Isles Press, 1994.

7. Wolter, Scott F. and Richard D. Srehly. "Report of Archaeopetrography Investigation on the Bat Creek Stone." *Ancient American*, vol. 14, #88, September 2010.

8. Ibid.

9. Gindling, Mary. *History Mystery: Chief Joseph's Cuneiform Tablet*: *www.stumbleupon.com/su/8Pv0tq/www.helium.com/items/ 1636848-hisdtory-mystery-chief-josephs-cuneiform-tablet*.

10. Ibid.

11. *Explore the ziggurat of Ur*. The British Museum. *www. mesopotamia.co.uk/ziggurats/explore/zig.html*.

12. Gindling, Mary, op. cit.

13. Ibid.

14. Thompson, Gunnar, op. cit.

15. Dr. Curtis Hoffman was chair of the Department of Anthropology at Bridgewater State College, Massachusetts. Farley quoted by Benjamin Daniali in *Native Village Youth and Education News*, Volume 3, February 2010. *www.nativevillage.org/ Archives/2010%20News%20Archives/February%202010/A%20 Common%20History%20of%20Assyrians.htm*.

16. Tiel, William. "Two Enigmatic Stones from Ohio." *Ancient American*, vol. 9, #58, August 2004.

17. Ibid.

18. Ibid.

19. Thompson, Gunnar, op. cit.

20. Ibid.

21. Childress, David. "Sumerians in Tiahuanaco?" *Atlantis Rising*, #88, July 2011.

22. Sanderson, Ivan T. *Animal Treasure*. NY: Viking Press, 1945; *Caribbean Treasure*. NY: Viking Adult, 1939; *Living Treasure*. N.Y., N.Y.: Viking Press, 1941.

23. Grigonis, Richard. "A Tribute to Ivan T. Sanderson." *www. richardgrigonis.com/Ch01%20Prologue%20and%20On%20 the%20Trail%20of%20Ivan%20Sanderson.html*.

24. "Forbidden Knowledge." *www.theforbiddenknowledge.com/ hardtruth/archeological_coverups.htm*.

25. Some skeptics cast doubt on the very existence of G.E. Kincaid, but in 2008, I spoke personally with the photographer's direct descendant, who told me that his great-grandfather's discovery of

artifact-filled caverns in the Grand Canyon was often retold through-out the generations of his family, just as reported by the *Arizona Gazette*. See *www.onelight.com/hollow/giant/canyon.html*.

26. Leutner, Margaret. "Kensington Rune Stone." *Ancient American*, vol. 3, #13, April/May 1996.

27. Bach, Caleb. "Michael Coe: A Question For Every Answer." Washington, D.C.: Interview, Americas, Organization of American States, January/February, 1996.

28. Ibid.

29. Ibid.

30. Weiner, Tim. *Legacy of Ashes: The History of the CIA*. New York: Doubleday, 2007.

31. Ibid.

32. Gordon, Cyrus R., 2010.

33. Steen-McIntyre, Virginia. "Humans in America One-Quarter of a Million Years Ago." In *Discovering the Mysteries of Ancient America*. Franklin Lakes, N.J.: New Page Books, 2006.

34. Mainfort Jr., Robert, C. Kwas and Mary L. Kwas. "The Bat Creek Fraud: A Final Statement." *Tennessee Anthropologist*, Vol. XVIII, # 2, Fall 1993: *www.ramtops.co.uk/bat2.html*.

35. Powell, J.W. "On Limitations to the Use of Anthropological Data." Washington, D.C.: *The Smithsonian Institution Museum Bureau of Ethnology Journal*, pp. 73-86, 1879.

36. Krakauer, Jon. *Under the Banner of Heaven: A Story of Violent Faith*. New York: Anchor, 2004.

37. Yates, Donald N. "Anomalous Mitochondrial DNA Lineages in the Cherokee." DNA Consultants: *http://dnatestingsystems.good-barry.com/BlogRetrieve.aspx?BlogID=4830&PostID=91847*.

Paradises Lost
By Oberon Zell

Atlantis, Lemuria, the Garden of Eden—myths and fantasies of paradise lost, or actual places that have somehow disappeared from the face of the Earth? And what of the famous legends of a great and universal Deluge that are found in so many ancient cultures? Could there really have been a vast global inundation that drowned entire populations and submerged settlements throughout the world, to be enshrined in legend by the few survivors whose descendants repopulated the world?

I've spent my lifetime researching history's mysteries—from mythical monsters and peculiar peoples to arcane artifacts and lost lands. In nearly every case I have found a truth behind the legend—a small yet significant fact like the grain of sand at the heart of a pearl. The great majority of human history (or rather, pre-history) occurred in a world very different from the one we now inhabit. Up until 10,500 years ago, vast amounts of the Earth's waters were frozen into continent-spanning, miles-thick sheets of ice covering much of North America and Northern Europe, and the sea levels were hundreds of feet lower than they are today, exposing as dry lands the vast areas of the continental shelves. This period of time, called the Würm Glaciation, lasted for 59,500 years.

The choice locations for human settlements have always been at the places where rivers empty into the sea. Along with fresh water from the rivers and the abundance of seafood, there are also easy means of transportation—upriver and along the coastline. When the last Ice Age ended 10,500 years ago with the impact of a large comet or asteroid in the Bahamas, the melting ice raised the sea levels 400 feet (122 m), and the new coastlines moved hundreds of miles inland, inundating more than 10 million square miles (16,093,440 sq km) of formerly habitable land. Because all coastal communities were thus drowned, those few people who had survived in the uplands passed down legends of sunken lands, lamenting lost paradises.

Today all such once-prime real estate is now submerged hundreds of feet beneath the oceans' waves, and also under millennia of sediments still being deposited by the rivers that continue to flow inexorably into the seas. Such prehistoric sites are inaccessible to archaeologists of our time, and therefore will have to be excavated by future generations.

Some of these inundated settlements may have been quite significant. Submerged megalithic ruins are being discovered in numerous places that were once dry land. These ruins include such structures as the still-debated Bimini Wall and other rectangular and pyramidal remnants at various offshore locations. In 1985, an enormous temple-like structure was discovered off the coast of the southernmost Japanese island of Yonaguni Jima. It is more than 165 feet (50 m) long and 65 feet (20 m) wide, and its foundation lies 80 feet (24 m) below the surface, with its highest point just 16 feet (5 m) beneath the waves.

A few mysterious ancient monuments—such as the great Sphinx of Egypt's Giza Plateau—are now thought to be far older than was once believed, the origins of some reaching back even further than 10,500 years ago.

Eden

The ancient Sumerians, Babylonians, Assyrians, and Hebrews all told of an Earthly Paradise that had once existed, but had been lost forever. According to the Bible (Genesis 2:8–14):

> [8] Yahweh God planted a garden in Eden, which is in the east, and there he put the man he had fashioned. [9] Yahweh God caused to spring up from the soil every kind of tree, enticing to look at and good to eat, with the Tree of Life and the Tree of the Knowledge of Good and Evil in the middle of the garden.
>
> [10] A river flowed through Eden to water the garden; from there it was separated into four headwaters. [11] The name of the first

is the Pishon; it winds through the entire land of Havilah, where there is gold. [12] The gold of that land is pure; bdellium and onyx stone are also found there. [13] The name of the second river is the Gihon; it winds through the entire land of Kush. [14] The third river is named the Tigris and it flows to the east of Ashur. And the fourth river is the Euphrates. (Jerusalem Bible © 1966)

This seems to indicate a fairly precise geographical location near the confluence of four well-known rivers. The Tigris and Euphrates, of course, are famous to this day, as they form the boundaries of Mesopotamia, "the land between the rivers," and meet at the head of the Persian Gulf. But where are the Pishon and Gihon Rivers? No other rivers flow today through the desert sands to join the Tigris and Euphrates.

Dr. Juris Zarins of Southwest Missouri State University believes that the Garden of Eden now lies submerged under the waters of the Persian Gulf. He cites Landsat satellite images which reveal a "fossil river" that once flowed through northern Arabia and through the now dry ravines (*wadis*), which modern Saudis and Kuwaitis know as the Wadi Rimah and Wadi Batin. Furthermore, according to the book of Genesis, this region was once rich in an aromatic gum resin (called *bdellium*), which can still be found in north Arabia, and gold, which was still being mined in that area in the 1950s. So the now-dry Rimah-Batin river would have once been the Pishon.

Zarins believes the Biblical Gihon is the Karun River, which has its source in Persia (modern Iran) and flows in a southwesterly direction toward the Gulf. The Karun also shows in Landsat images, and contributed most of the sediment forming the delta at the head of the Persian Gulf until it was diverted in 1765 through the Haffar Channel, which had been dug in 986 to facilitate shipping between Ahvaz and Basra.

During the Great Ice Age, vast amounts of water became locked up in continent-spanning ice sheets, and sea levels fell by 400 feet (122 m), so that what is now the Persian Gulf was dry land all the way to the Strait of Hormuz. It was irrigated not only by the still-extant Tigris and Euphrates but also by the lost Gihon, the Pishon, and their tributaries from the Arabian Peninsula and Iran.

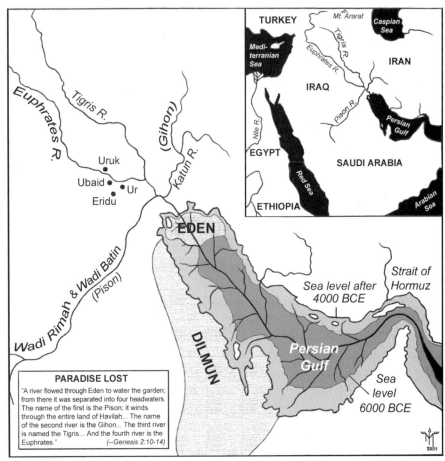

Fig. 1: Eden and Dilmun. Map by the author.

Dilmun

The Sumerians, who invented writing, recorded the legend of a luxuriant and lovely land called Dilmun, located on somewhat higher ground along the eastern coast of Arabia. Dilmun enters the epics in Sumerian creation myths of the third millennium BCE. The by-then-ancient myth of a land of plenty, of eternal life and peace, had lodged firmly in the collective consciousness and a specific locale.

In the Sumerian epic *Enki and Ninhursag*, Enki, as lord of *Ab* (meaning "fresh water"), is living with his wife in the paradise of Dilmun:

The land of Dilmun is a pure place, the land of Dilmun is a clean place,

The land of Dilmun is a clean place, the land of Dilmun is a bright place;

He who is alone lays himself down in Dilmun,

The place, after Enki is clean, that place is bright (Kramer, 2007).

Like the Biblical Garden of Eden, Dilmun was a peaceful place where "the lion killed not, the wolf snatched not the lamb, unknown was the kid-killing dog, unknown was the grain-devouring boar" (Kramer, 2007). Nevertheless, Dilmun had no water, and Enki hears the cries of its Goddess, Ninsikil, and orders the Sun-God, Utu, to bring fresh water from the Earth for Dilmun. As a result:

Her City Drinks the Water of Abundance,

Dilmun Drinks the Water of Abundance,

Her wells of bitter water, behold they are become wells of good water,

Her fields and farms produce crops and grain,

Her city, behold it has become the house of the banks and quays of the land (Kramer, 2007).

Around 6000–5000 BCE came the Neolithic Wet Phase, when rains returned to the Gulf region following a long arid period. The lands of present-day eastern and northeastern Saudi Arabia and southwestern Iran, which had been dry and barren, became green and fertile. Foraging people moved into this paradisial region where the four rivers now ran full. Agriculture began here, as humanity's first "garden" was planted in the lush and fertile valley that we remember as Eden.

But after 5000 BCE, the continued melting of Ice Age glaciers precipitated the sudden rise in global sea level called the Flandrian Transgression. The Gulf began to fill with water, finally reaching its current level around 4000 BCE, having swallowed Eden and all the settlements along the Gulf coast and eventually rising into the southern regions of today's Iraq and Iran. Humankind was driven from the

Garden as Eden disappeared beneath the rising waters. It is interesting to note that this sequence corresponds closely to the 4004 BCE date calculated for the Creation by James Ussher (1581–1656), the Anglican Archbishop of Armagh in Northern Ireland.

The modern world first learned of Dilmun when scholars deciphered cuneiform tablets from the Library of Ashurbanipal in Nineveh, an ancient Assyrian stronghold in modern Iraq, excavated by archaeologist Austen Henry Layard in the 1840s. Some of these tablets comprise a narrative called the *Epic of Gilgamesh,* which describes a great Flood, a mighty Sumerian hero-king, and his search for the Tree of Life.

In the epic, King Gilgamesh goes down from Uruk in Sumer to Dilmun on the Gulf where he is informed by Utnapishtim, the nigh-immortal Sumerian Noah analog who survives the Great Flood, that the Tree of Life still grows beneath the waves, and that a sprig from it would grant immortality. Gilgamesh dives down, finds the Tree (possibly coral, which is associated with immortality), and recovers a sprig. Exhausted from this labor, he collapses on the shore to sleep, whereupon a serpent comes along and steals the sprig, leaving its old skin behind as it disappears into a hole. This story neatly explains why snakes perpetually shed their skins, and why they are thought to live forever.

The Deluge

The *Epic of Gilgamesh* was compiled by a Mesopotamian priest named Sîn-lēqi-unninni ("Sin [the moon god] accepts my prayer") sometime between 1300 and 1000 BCE out of older tales and legends. Tablet XI of the epic includes a detailed account of the Great Deluge as told to Gilgamesh by Utnapishtim. It is taken almost word-for-word from an 18th-century BCE Akkadian epic named after its protagonist, Atrahasis, whose father, Ubara-Tutu, was king of Shuruppak before the flood.

Tablet III of the *Atrahasis Epic* tells how Enki instructs Atrahasis ("extremely wise") to dismantle his house and build a large boat to escape the flood planned by the wind god, Enlil, to destroy the burgeoning human population. This ark is to have a roof and upper and lower decks, and is to be sealed with bitumen. Atrahasis builds the ark, takes his family and livestock aboard, and seals the door. Enlil's storm comes and the land is inundated, frightening even the gods. After seven days the flood subsides, and Atrahasis emerges and offers sacrifices to the gods. Enlil is furious with Enki, but Enki argues, "I ensured the preservation of life." Enki and Enlil agree on other means for controlling the human population in the future.

The very earliest version of the Deluge myth is preserved only fragmentarily in the *Eridu Genesis*, written in Sumerian cuneiform and dating to the 17th century BCE, during the first dynasty of Babylon when Sumerian was still the written language. In this version, it is Ziusudra who is the ark-building hero who saves his family and animals.

Of course, the Western world is most familiar with the Deluge story through the later account of Noah given in the Bible. According to Genesis 6:6–8:

Yahweh regretted having made man on the Earth, and his heart grieved. 'I will rid the Earth's face of man, my own creation,' Yahweh said, 'and of animals also, reptiles too, and the birds of heaven; for I regret having made them.' But Noah had found favor with Yahweh.

So Yahweh instructs Noah to build a great boat—the ark—three decks high with a roof, and to seal it with pitch (bitumen). He tells Noah to take aboard his family and seven of each kind of "clean" animal and bird, and two—a male and a female—of each kind of "unclean" animal. According to Genesis 7:11–12, "In the six hundredth year of Noah's life, in the second month, and on the seventeenth day of that month, that very day all the springs of the great deep broke through, and the sluices of heaven opened. It rained on the Earth for forty days and forty nights...." Verses 18–19 go on to read, "The waters rose and swelled greatly on the Earth, and the ark sailed on the waters. The waters rose more and more on the Earth so that all the highest mountains under the whole of heaven were submerged...." And in verse 24, "The waters rose on the Earth for a hundred and fifty days."

When the waters eventually subside, Noah's ark comes to rest on Mount Ararat, which is located in modern Turkey. Utnapishtim's boat lands on Mount Nisir in Iraqi Kurdistan, only a few hundred miles away. Noah releases a raven once and a dove twice; Utnapishtim releases three birds: a dove, a swallow, and a raven. Noah's youngest son, Ham, has four sons—Cush, Egypt, Put, and Canaan. According to Genesis, their descendants became the Cushites (Africans), Egyptians, Putians (Persians), and Canaanites (Phoenicians), respectively.

Bishop Ussher dated the Deluge of Noah very precisely to the year 2349 BCE, but the historical reign of King Gilgamesh of Uruk is believed to have been much earlier than that, approximately 2700 BCE, by which time the Flood was already a distant legend. So if the Great Deluge did, in fact, occur, when did it happen?

In the epic, Atrahasis is identified as the son of Ubara-Tutu, who was the last antediluvian king in Shuruppak (modern Tell Fara, Iraq) before "the flood swept over" (Lambert and Millard, 1969). Excavations at that site have, in fact, discovered evidence of extensive flooding, which has been radiocarbon dated to ca. 2900 BCE. The flood deposits extend as far north as the city of Kish, interrupting the continuity of settlement. The epic goes on to read: "After the flood had swept over, and the kingship had descended from heaven, the kingship was in Kish," where the next king after the flood was Ngushur. A date for the Deluge of ca. 2900 BCE makes perfect sense in terms of the sequence of Sumerian kings and the accounts in the epics of Gilgamesh and Atrahasis.

Lately, however, a controversial new explanation for the legend of the Great Deluge has been proposed by William Ryan and Walter Pitman, two senior scientists from Columbia University. They postulate that rising sea levels caused a massive transfer of water from the Mediterranean into the Black Sea around 5600 BCE. Funneled through the narrow Bosporus, "[t]en cubic miles of water poured through each day, two hundred times what flows over Niagara Falls.... The Bosporus flume roared and surged at full spate for at least three hundred days" (Ryan and Pitman, 1998). The water level climbed about six inches (15 cm) a day until 60,000 square miles (96,561 sq km) of farmland were inundated. The Black Sea rose hundreds of feet, changing it from a landlocked freshwater lake into a saltwater inland sea connected to the world's oceans.

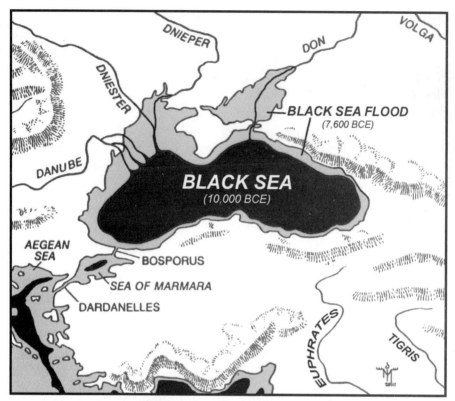

Fig. 2: The Inundation of the Black Sea. Map by the author.

Such flooding would have had a catastrophic effect on the people living around the area of the Black Sea, triggering mass migrations across Europe and the Middle East.

Many researchers now believe that the story of the Great Deluge in the epics of Gilgamesh, Atrahasis, and Noah had its origin in this cataclysmic event. Shells of nine species of saltwater and freshwater mollusks from the Black Sea were radiocarbon-dated by the Woods Hole Oceanographic Institution. They found that the saltwater species ranged in age from 2,800–6,820 years, and the freshwater species ranged from 7,460–15,500 years. Thus the inundation of the Black Sea occurred between 6,820 and 7,460 years ago, or between 4,820 and 5,460 BCE. So rather than confirming the flood of Gilgamesh, Atrahasis, and Noah, this event actually correlates in time more closely to the flooding of Eden by the rising waters of the Persian Gulf during the Flandrian Transgression which, as noted previously, began after 5000 BCE and reached its present level around 4000 BCE.

Bruce Masse, an environmental archaeologist at Los Alamos National Laboratory, has a more radical theory about the Great Flood. Masse and his Holocene Impact Working Group believe that between 2800–3000 BCE, a gigantic comet 3 miles (5 km) in diameter smashed into the Indian Ocean off the coast of Madagascar. The impact site, called Burcle Crater, is about 18 miles (29 km) in diameter, 25 times larger than Meteor Crater in Arizona. Located at 30.865°S, 61.365°E, it is 12,500 feet (4 km) below the surface.

The impact sent 600-foot (183 m)-high tsunamis crashing against the world's coastlines and released plumes of superheated water vapor and particulates high into the atmosphere. Within hours, the blast spawned superhurricanes on the other side of the planet. For about a week, the entire globe was plunged into darkness. Masse believes that up to 80 percent of the world's population perished, making this event the single most lethal catastrophe in human history. In the *Gilgamesh* epic, Utnapishtim sees a pillar of black smoke on the horizon before the sky goes dark for a week. Afterward, a cyclone pummels the Fertile Crescent, causing the legendary Deluge.

Early Spanish explorers in Central and South America were surprised by Indian flood legends that sounded strikingly similar to the story of Noah. Some Spanish priests feared that the Devil planted the stories in the Indians' minds to confuse them. "These stories are all exactly what you would expect from the survivors of a celestial impact," Masse says. "When a comet rounds the sun, oftentimes its tail is still being blown forward by the solar winds so that it actually precedes it. That is why so many descriptions of comets in mythology mention that they are wearing horns." In India, he notes, a celestial fish as "bright as a moonbeam" (Masse, 2007) with a great horn on its head, was said to have warned of an epic Flood that inaugurated a new age of humanity.

Among the 175 flood myths Masse examined, a Chinese version states that the Great Flood occurred at the end of the reign of Empress Nu Wa. Cross-checking historical records with astronomical data, Masse came up with a date for the event of May 10, 2807 BCE. As mentioned previously, excavations at Shuruppak discovered evidence of extensive flooding dated to ca. 2900 BCE, which dovetails with the accounts in the epics of Gilgamesh and Atrahasis. Masse's dating further corroborates his theory that the Deluge of legend was caused by a massive comet impact at that time.

Ancient people variously described comets as heavenly dragons, feathered serpents, celestial fish, or flaming swords. It is thus interesting to note that in the Genesis account of the Fall, Yahweh "banished the man, and in front of the Garden of Eden he posted the cherubs, and the flame of a flashing sword, to guard the way to the Tree of Life" (Genesis 3:24).

Doggerland

Far to the north, another vast inhabited land area was inundated around 8,000 years ago. Now called Doggerland (after the Dogger Bank, known as a hazard to sailors and a boon to fishermen), this area stretched between England and Denmark, where the cold waters of the North Sea now roll. During the last Ice Age, Doggerland was a broad expanse of the continental shelf—a wide, undulating plain with a coastline of salt marshes, mudflats, and lagoons formed by the meandering rivers and lakes fed by melting glacial water from the continental ice sheets further inland. About the size of Great Britain, Doggerland may have been the richest hunting, fowling, and fishing ground in all of Europe during the Mesolithic (Middle Stone Age) cultural era. In recent times, numerous artifacts have been dredged up from the North Sea, confirming human habitation during this time.

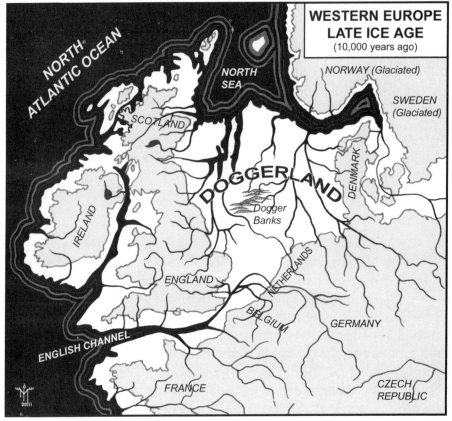

Fig. 3: Doggerland beneath the North Sea. Map by the author.

As sea levels rose after the end of the last glacial period, and continental shelves subsided under the weight of water, Doggerland slowly sank beneath the North Sea. Around 6200 BCE, a massive submarine landslide off the coast of Norway (called the Storegga Slide) caused a catastrophic tsunami which swept over Doggerland and cut through the English Channel, severing the peninsula from the European mainland. Any inhabitants of this forgotten country would have been swept away. The hilly Dogger Bank may have remained as an island until as late as 5000 BCE, when, like Eden and the shores of the Black Sea, it was finally submerged by the Flandrian Transgression.

Lemuria

Lemuria is the name of another submerged land that is hypothesized to have extended from Madagascar through India and throughout Indonesia. The name was coined in 1864 by the zoologist and bio-geographer Philip Sclater, to account for the presence of lemurs in these now widely separated areas. Lemurs (Latin for "ghosts") are charmingly cute primitive primates and our remote ancestors. Proposing that Madagascar and India had once been part of a larger continent, Sclater wrote:

> The anomalies of the Mammal fauna of Madagascar can best be explained by supposing that...a large continent occupied parts of the Atlantic and Indian Oceans...that this continent was broken up into islands, of which some have become amalgamated with...Africa, some...with what is now Asia; and that in Madagascar and the Mascarene Islands we have existing relics of this great continent, for which...I should propose the name Lemuria! (Neild, 2007, pp. 38–39)

Although no "lost continent" ever filled the Indian Ocean basin, it is true that the islands of this region were originally part of a continuous land mass during the Ice Ages, when sea levels were far lower, exposing the continental shelves. The modern islands of Indonesia were once mountains of the vast area now called Sunderland, which extended almost to Australia.

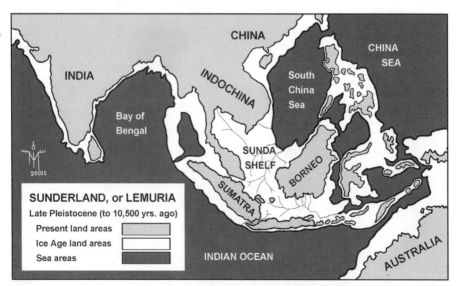

Fig. 4: Lemuria and Sunderland. Map by the author.

The idea of a lost continent in the Indian or Pacific Ocean was picked up by some occult writers, who made it the home of various imagined races and creatures. In the 1880s, Madame Helena Blavatsky (1831–1891) asserted that the gods sunk Lemuria in order to destroy its subhuman inhabitants. In 1894, Frederick Spencer Oliver published *A Dweller on Two Planets*, which claimed that surviving Lemurians were living in a complex of caves and tunnels beneath Northern California's Mount Shasta, and were occasionally seen walking on the mountain in white robes. This belief is still popular today, as can be attested by a visit to any occult bookstore in the town of Shasta.

Mu

Mu is the name of another vast land mass imagined to have once existed in the Pacific Ocean, the remnants of which are New Zealand and Polynesia. This idea was first proposed by Augustus Le Plongeon (1825–1908), who claimed that his (bogus) translations of ancient Mayan writings told of this drowned land, whose survivors were the Mayan Indians of the Yucatan Peninsula. *The Lost Continent of Mu* was later popularized by James Churchward (1852–1936) in a series of rather preposterous books with that title.

According to Churchward, Mu "extended from somewhere north of Hawaii to the south as far as the Fijis and Easter Island." He claimed Mu was the site of the Garden of Eden, and had 64,000,000 inhabitants—known as the *Naacals*. Its civilization, which supposedly flourished 50,000 years ago, was technologically more advanced than that of Churchward's own time, and the ancient civilizations of Mesopotamia, Egypt, India, and the Mayans were merely the degenerate remnants of its colonies. Needless to say, there is no geological basis whatsoever for a submerged Pacific continent.

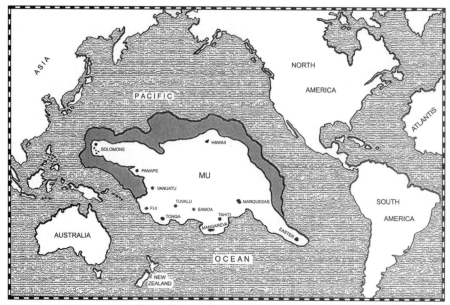

Fig. 5: The Geographical Position of Mu (map adapted from
The Lost Continent of Mu, *1926)*

Atlantis

By far the most famous of all legendary lost civilizations is the fabled island of Atlantis. Its historical existence and location have been debated for more than 2,000 years, but have never been definitively confirmed. It was first mentioned by the Greek philosopher Plato (427–347 BCE), who claimed the story had been passed down in his family from his great-grandfather, who knew Solon (638–558 BCE), a Greek statesman who had learned the account from priests when he visited Egypt in 560 BCE. Plato wrote down Solon's story around 360 BCE in his dialogues *Timaeus* and *Critias*, stating that Atlantis had been destroyed by a volcano, an earthquake, and/or a tsunami about 9,000 years prior to Solon's time, or ca. 9600 BCE:

> [I]n front of the mouth which you Greeks call, as you say, "the pillars of Heracles," there lay an island which was larger than Libya and Asia together; and it was possible for the travellers of that time to cross from it to the other islands, and from the islands to the whole of the continent over against them which encompasses that veritable ocean.... (Plato, *Timaeus* 24-E)

But at a later time there occurred portentous earthquakes
and floods, and one grievous day and night befell them, when
the whole body of your warriors was swallowed up by the
earth, and the island of Atlantis in like manner was swallowed
up by the sea and vanished; wherefore also the ocean at that
spot has now become impassable and unsearchable, being
blocked up by the shoal mud which the island created as it
settled down (Plato, *Timaeus* 25-D).

As the story goes, the paradisial island of Atlantis (meaning "land
of the pillar") belonged to Poseidon, god of the sea. He fell in love
with a mortal woman, Cleito, and built a palace for her on a hill near
the middle of the island, surrounded with "circular belts of sea and
land enclosing one another alternately, some greater, some smaller,
two being of land and three of sea, which he carved as it were out of
the midst of the island; and these belts were at even distances on all
sides, so as to be impassable for man" (Plato, *Critias* 113-D). Cleito
bore five sets of twin boys who became the first rulers of Atlantis.
The island was divided among the brothers with the eldest, Atlas,
becoming the first king of Atlantis. At the top of the hill, a temple
for Poseidon was built. Here the rulers met to discuss laws, pass judg-
ments, and honor Poseidon.

To facilitate travel and trade, a canal was cut through the rings
of land and water running south for five and a half miles (9 km) to
the sea. The populous city of Atlantis extended in an 11-mile (18-km)
circle around the outer ring of water. Beyond the city lay a fertile plain
330 miles (531 km) long and 110 miles (177 km) wide, surrounded by
another canal to bring in water from the mountains.

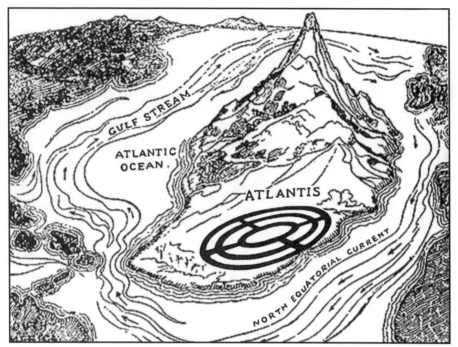

Fig. 6: Map of Atlantis based on Plato's description, originally published in the New York American, Oct. 20, 1912.

Soaring mountains dotted with villages, lakes, rivers, and meadows surrounded the plain to the north. The mild climate allowed two harvests each year. Numerous varieties of herbs, fruits, and nuts grew in abundance. Large herds of animals, including elephants, roamed the island. For generations the Atlanteans lived simple, virtuous lives, but eventually they became corrupted by greed and power. Angered by their immorality, Zeus convened the other gods to determine a suitable punishment. Subsequently, in "one grievous day and night," Atlantis, its people, and its memory were "swallowed by the sea and vanished" (Ibid.).

Where was Atlantis?

Various different locales for Atlantis have been proposed over the years. Plato said that Atlantis had been located "beyond the Pillars of Heracles," which are understood to be the Straits of Gibraltar. This would place Atlantis out in the Atlantic Ocean—most likely around the Azores Islands, about 900 miles west of the Portuguese coast. In *Atlantis: The Antidiluvian World*, published in 1882, Ignatius Donnelly proposed that the Azores were the mountaintops of the sunken continent of Atlantis. These islands rise from a larger foundation called the Azores Plateau, known by mariners as "Dolphin Ridge." About the size of Spain, this region is a discrete block encircled by the Mid-Atlantic Rift. The entire plateau would have been above water during the Ice Age, until an opening of the surrounding Rift evacuated the underlying magma and dropped it into the hole. This happened around 10900 BCE, somewhat earlier than Plato's date.

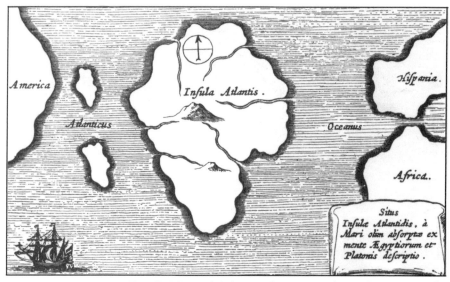

Fig. 7: Map of Atlantis from Mundus Subterraneus *by Athanasius Kircher, Amsterdam, 1665.*

In 2007, planetary geologist Peter Schultz and a team of scientists from Brown University presented evidence that a comet or asteroid exploded over the Earth or slammed into it 12,900 years ago, melting ice sheets, sparking extreme wildfires, fueling hurricane-force winds, and triggering a catastrophic climate change that killed off the mammoths, giant sloths, saber-toothed cats, and other great beasts of the Ice Age. A thin, black layer of carbon sediment dating to 10900 BCE has been found in more than 50 archaeological digs in Canada, California, Arizona, and South Carolina—and even in Belgium. The same black sediment was found at 10 archaeological sites associated with the Clovis people, the earliest humans known in the New World, who disappeared after that date.

Directly beneath the black sediment, researchers found high concentrations of magnetized iridium, charcoal, soot, carbon spherules, fullerenes packed with extraterrestrial helium, and microscopic diamonds that could only have been formed from the intense pressure and heat of an extraterrestrial impact. In this scenario, around 12,900 years ago, a comet or asteroid crossed North America, scattering debris along its route and creating the oval-shaped craters known as the Carolina Bays before smashing into the Atlantic Ocean. The impact site is known as the Nares Abyssal Plain. Its proximity to the Puerto Rico Trench triggered the opening of the Mid-Atlantic Rift, releasing undersea magma and spewing vast amounts of volcanic ash into the atmosphere. The consequent depletion of the magma chamber beneath the Azores Plateau caused the subsidence of that volcanic land mass—identified by Donnelly as the original Atlantis. As a result of this impact, the Earth's geographic axis shifted, so that the North Pole, which had been in the Hudson Bay, moved to its present location in the middle of the Arctic Ocean (the magnetic pole is still catching up, by the way).

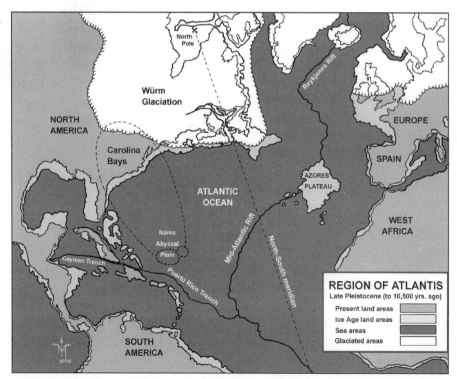

Fig. 8: The Azores Plateau and Ice-Age coastlines of the Atlantic Ocean. Map by the author.

During the Ice Age, large portions of Antarctica were ice-free and temperate. Some serious researchers place Atlantis there. In *Maps of the Ancient Sea-Kings*, published in 1966, Prof. Charles Hapgood of Keene College, New Hampshire, noted that Antarctica appears on ancient nautical charts that long predate the discovery of Antarctica by Capt. James Cooke in 1773–74. Some of these maps appear to show coastal features now hidden beneath the ice. Hapgood proposed that these charts were constructed from ancient source maps originating with a sophisticated seafaring culture existing as early as 7000 BCE, and which had been copied and recopied over many thousands of years. Hapgood pointed out that core samples from the Ross Sea area include pollen, indicating a relatively temperate climate as late as 4000 BCE. He postulated that the ice fully engulfed Antarctica only after the polar shift that occurred around 9500 BCE, coinciding with the end of the last Ice Age. Shultz's findings would correct this dating to 10900 BCE.

Based on Hapgood's theories of a pre-glacial Antarctica and a polar shift at the end of the Ice Age, Canadians Rose and Rand Flem-Ath proposed in their 1995 book *When the Sky Fell* that Plato's Atlantis was actually Antarctica. They pointed out that the polar continent matches Plato's description in the *Timaeus* dialog of "an island which was larger than Libya and Asia together." Furthermore, Antarctica certainly lies "beyond the Pillars of Heracles," as Plato reported. However, the complete absence of any evidence of human structures or habitation in Antarctica pretty well refutes the argument for this location.

Still other researchers place Atlantis in South America, and point to certain geophysical features on the Bolivian Altiplano that match elements of Plato's description, as well as to the ruins of Tiahuanaco—an ancient city considered by many archaeologists to be the oldest in the world. Only 10 percent of its more than 400 acres of ruins have been excavated. In the distant past, Tiahuanaco was a flourishing port at the edge of Lake Titicaca, whose coastline has since receded 12 miles (19 km) and dropped 800 feet (244 m). The lake continues to shrink from evaporation, as no rivers flow into it. In 1980, Hugo Boero Rojo, a Bolivian author and scholar of pre-Columbian cultures, announced the discovery of archaeological ruins 45–60 feet (14-18 m) beneath the lake's surface. Polish-born Bolivian archaeologist Hans Schindler-Bellamy concluded that the Tiahuanaco culture reached back 12,000 years before the present era.

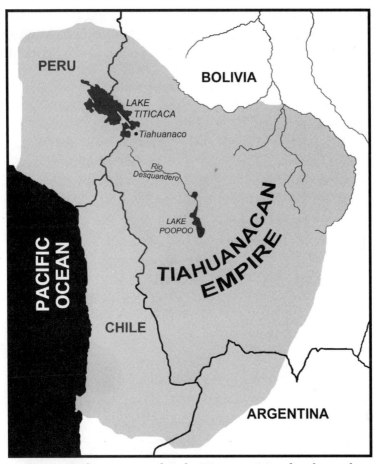

Fig. 9: Tiahuanaco and Lake Titicaca. Map by the author.

Salt deposits indicate that during the Ice Age, this lake was part of a vast inland sea that filled the entire Amazon Basin, so Tiahuanaco would have been a seaport at that time. But after the impact of 10900 BCE, the entire continent of South America tipped eastward as the continent was moved further westward over the Pacific tectonic plate. The west coast rose thousands of feet (the "Andean Upheaval"), spilling the inland sea out into the Atlantic and raising Tiahuanaco to its present height of 13,300 feet (4 km) above sea level. Interestingly, papyrus reeds—otherwise found only in Egypt—grow in profusion along the shores of Lake Titicaca; the local people construct boats from these reeds that are virtually identical to those that have been used in Egypt for millennia. Whether or not Tiahuanaco can be legitimately identified with Plato's Atlantis myth, the site is certainly indicative of an advanced level of civilization during the later Ice Age, perhaps one that that included sufficient seafaring skills to have imported papyrus all the way from Egypt.

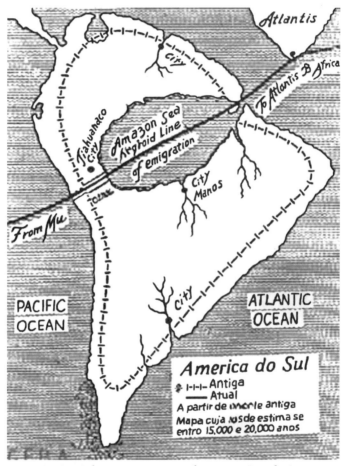

Fig. 10: A 19th-century map of ancient South America.
Courtesy of the Theosophical Society.

The most widely accepted proposed locale for Atlantis is that of Greek archaeologist Spyridon Marinatos, who in 1939 stated that Plato's description of the Atlantean civilization and its cataclysmic destruction seemed very much like that of Bronze-Age "Minoan"[1] Crete, located at the southern edge of the Aegean Sea. Just 70 miles (113 km) north of Crete is a volcanic island once known as Kallisti ("the prettiest one"), now called Thera. In 1628 BCE, an enormous volcanic explosion—10 times the size of the 1883 eruption of Krakatoa in Indonesia—obliterated the entire central area of the island and devastated the magnificent Minoan civilization. The detonation hurled a plume of ash and rock 20 miles (32 km) into the stratosphere, turning day into night over the eastern Mediterranean Sea. Some settlements on Thera were buried under as much as 100 feet (30 m) of ash. Huge tsunamis drowned coastal Greece, Syria, and Egypt, and the volcano below the horizon was visible for hundreds of miles as a "pillar of smoke by day, and fire by night" (Exodus 13:21). This was the event recorded in the Bible as the Exodus; indeed, the 10 plagues that beset Egypt and the so-called parting of the Red Sea (a clear description of a tsunami) were all due to these events.

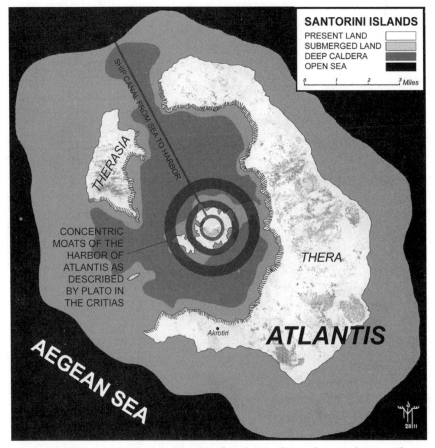

Fig. 11: Thera as Atlantis. Drawn by the author after Galinopoulos.

Marinatos argued that Solon may have confused the Egyptian glyphs for "hundred" and "thousand," and that the destruction of Atlantis should have been read as having occurred 900 years earlier, rather than 9,000. If so, the proper date would have been 1600 BCE—the time of the Thera eruption. Reducing the figures of thousands to hundreds also brings Plato's reported dimensions of Atlantis into accord with those of Thera.

The Flood of Deucalion and Pyrrha

There [in Achaea, i.e. Greece] is a land encircled by lofty mountains, rich in sheep and in pasture, where Prometheus, son of Iapetus, begat goodly Deucalion, who first founded cities and reared temples to the immortal gods, and first ruled over men. This land the neighbors who dwell around call Haemonia [i.e. Thessaly] (*Argonautica*, 3rd century BCE).

According to Greek legend, Lycaon, king of Arcadia, sacrificed a boy to Zeus, king of the Gods. Appalled by this cannibalistic offering, Zeus decided to punish the children of the Titans for their wickedness and impiety by sending a flood to wipe them from the face of the Earth, thus putting an end to the Age of Bronze. The wise Titan Prometheus (whose name means "forethought"), ever defying the tyranny of Zeus, warned his 82-year-old son, Deucalion, the king of Phthia in the southernmost region of Thessaly in ancient Greece. Deucalion then built a large ark, carefully provisioned, in which he and his wife, Pyhhra, the daughter of Prometheus' brother Epimetheus ("afterthought"), rode out Zeus' deluge, which subsequently swept over Greece and drowned all of its other inhabitants. The rivers ran in torrents, and the sea flooded the coastal plain, engulfed the foothills, and washed everything clean. (No animals were saved in this legend.) When the flood waters subsided after nine days, their ark came to rest on Mount Parnassus, where Deucalion was advised by an oracle of Themis to "cover [his] head and throw the bones of [his] mother behind [his] shoulder" (*Argonautica*). Understanding that the oracle was referring to Mother Earth (Gaea), they tossed stones over their shoulders, from which sprang up a new race of humans: men from the rocks thrown by Deucalion, and women from those thrown by Pyhrra. Their eldest son was Hellen, whose descendants became the Hellenes; his sons were Dorus, Xuthus, and Aelous—progenitors of the Greek Dorians, Ionians, and Aeolians, respectively.

Renaissance astronomer Seth Calvisius (1556–1615) gave a date of 1516 BCE for Deucalion's Flood, while Christopher Helvicus (1581–1616), German professor of Greek and Eastern languages at the University of Giessen, offered 1511 BCE. Most researchers agree that the deluge of Deucalion and Pyhrra was contemporary with the Exodus of the Israelites, which can be confidently linked to the eruption of Thera, now dated to 1628 BCE. The flood waters would have been the 50-foot (15-m) high tsunami generated by the collapse of the center of the island, creating the immense caldera that is nearly all that remains of the legendary island we know as Atlantis. Excavations conducted in eastern Crete in 2006 by Greek-born UCLA Earth scientist Costas Synolakis found chaotic debris from the tsunami as high as 90 feet (27 m) above sea level.

Fig. 12: Impact of the Theran tsunami in 1628 BCE. Map by the author.

The controversy begun by Plato 2,350 years ago continues unabated to the present day. Various modern writers have argued compellingly for the location of Atlantis in Bolivia (Jim Allen), Argentina (Doug Fisher), the Bahamas (Edgar Cayce), Mexico (Gene D. Matlock), Ireland (Ulf Erlingsson), Greenland (Mario Dantas), Spain (Georgeos Diaz-Montexano), Morocco (Michael Huebner), Cyprus (Robert Sarmast), Thera (A.G. Galinopoulos), or Antarctica (Rose and Rand Flem-Ath). Because some of these areas were, in fact, inundated at the end of the Ice Age, it may be that *all* locations are valid, and that the original legend of the lost Atlantis is based upon memories of a global maritime civilization whose coastal communities were drowned beneath the waves when sea levels rose 400 feet (122 m) worldwide. As our current global climate change continues warming the seas and melting the remaining ice caps of Greenland and Antarctica, some projections estimate that the global sea levels will rise as much as 18 feet (5.5 m) by the end of the 21st century, and rise another 200 feet (61 m) by the year 3000. How many of our current coastal communities will become the next Atlantis?

Notes:

1. I put "Minoan" in quotes here because it is an erroneous designation for that era of Cretan history. We don't know what the Bronze Age inhabitants called their island. Egyptians called it "Kheftiu," which is our best approximation. Arthur Evans thought he was excavating the palace of King Minos from the legend of Theseus and the Minotaur, so he called the site "Knossos" and named the era "Minoan." But in fact, the destruction of Bronze Age Crete (and Knossos) occurred in 1628 BCE, while the legend of Minos, Theseus, and so on actually derives from a much later period, the Mycenaean, during the 13th century BCE, after the Achaeans had already moved in from Greece and taken over the place. And Knossos wasn't a palace at all—it was a mortuary, necropolis, and temple complex. No signs of habitation (middens, hearths, kitchens, furnishings, eating and drinking implements, and so on) have ever been found there. But the true mystery of Crete would be another whole chapter in a book of history's mysteries!

Resources and References

Allen, J.M. *Atlantis: The Andes Solution.* New York, NY: St Martin's Press, 1998.

———. "Atlantis Bolivia: The Real Atlantis." *http://atlantisbolivia. org/.*

———. "Comparison of the plain of Atlantis with various proposed locations including the Altiplano, Bolivia." *www.atlantisbolivia. org/plaincomparison.htm.*

Ambrose, Stanley H. "Late Pleistocene human population bottlenecks, volcanic winter, and differentiation of modern humans." *Journal of Human Evolution* 34 (6): 1998.

"Atlantis 'Evidence' Found in Spain and Ireland." *National Geographic News,* Oct. 28, 2010. *http://news.nationalgeographic. com/news/2004/08/0819_040819_atlantis_2.html*

"Ballard and the Black Sea: the Search for Noah's Flood." *National Geographic,* May, 1987. *www.nationalgeographic.com/blacksea/ ax/frame.html*

Berlitz, Charles. *The Bermuda Triangle.* Garden City, NY: Doubleday & Co., 1974.

Carney, Scott. "Did a Comet Cause the Great Flood?" *Discover Magazine,* Nov. 2007.

Churchward, James. *The Lost Continent of Mu: Motherland of Man* (1926). Kempton, Ill.: Adventures Unlimited Press, 2007.

Crawford, Harriet. *Sumer and the Sumerians.* Cambridge, UK: Cambridge University Press, 2004.

Daniels, Pat and Horan, Anne, "Atlantis," *Mysteries of the Unknown: Mystic Places.* Alexandria, VA: Time-Life Books, 1987.

Donnelly, Ignatius. *Atlantis: The Antediluvian World* (1882). San Francisco, Calif.: Harper & Row, 1976.

"Extraterrestrial Impact Likely Source of Sudden Ice Age Extinctions." *Science Daily,* Sep. 25, 2007. *www.sciencedaily.com/releases/ 2007/09/070924172959.htm.*

Flem-Ath, Rand, and Rose Flem-Ath. *When the Sky Fell: In Search of Atlantis.* London: Weidenfeld and Nicolson, 1995.

Galanopoulos, A.G., and Edward Bacon. *Atlantis: The Truth Behind the Legend*. Indianapolis/New York: Bobbs-Merrill Co., 1969.

Hadingham, Evan. "Minoan Tsunami: New Clues to the Collapse of the Glorious Culture of Ancient Crete." *Discover Magazine*, Jan. 2008.

Hamblin, Dora Jane. "Has the Garden of Eden been located at last?" *Smithsonian Magazine* 18, No. 2 (May 1987).

Hancock, Graham. *Fingerprints of the Gods*. New York: Three Rivers Press, 1996.

Hapgood, Charles. *Maps of the Ancient Sea Kings*. London, UK: Turnstone Books, 1979.

Jacobsen, Thorkild. "The Sumerian King List." Oriental Institute. *Assyriological Studies 11*. Chicago: University of Chicago Press, 1939.

The Jerusalem Bible, Reader's Edition. Garden City, NY: Doubleday & Co., 1966.

Kramer, Samuel Noah, *Sumerian Mythology: A Study of Spiritual and Literary Achievement in the Third Millennium BC*. Charleston, SC: Forgotten Books, 2007.

Lambert, W.G. and A.R Millard. *Atrahasis: The Babylonian Story of the Flood*. Oxford: Clarendon Press, 1969.

Liddell, Henry George and Robert Scott. *A Greek-English Lexicon*. Oxford: Clarendon Press, 1940.

Masse, Bruce. "The archaeology and anthropology of Quaternary period cosmic impact" in *Comet/Asteroid Impacts and Human Society: An Interdisciplinary Approach*. (Peter Bobrowsky and Hans Rickman, ed.). Berlin: Springer Press, 2007.

The Morien Institute: "The ancient underwater pyramid structure off the coast of Yonaguni-jima, Japan." *www.morien-institute.org/yonaguni_schoch1.html*.

Neild, Ted. *Supercontinent: Ten Billion Years in the Life of Our Planet*. Cambridge, Mass.: Harvard University Press, 2007.

Plato. *The Atlantis Dialogue: Plato's Original Story of the Lost City, Continent, Empire*. Friday Harbor, WA: Shepard Publications, 2001.

Ryan, William, and Walter Pitman. *Noah's Flood: The new scientific discoveries about the event that changed history.* New York, NY: Simon & Schuster, 1998.

Sea Level Rise Explorer. *www.globalwarmingart.com/wiki/Special: SeaLevel.*

Spence, Lewis. *The Problem of Atlantis.* (London: 1924) San Diego, Calif.: Book Tree, 2002

van Mensvoort, Koert. "Doggerland—Mapping a Lost World." Next Nature. *www.nextnature.net/2009/04/mapping-a-lost-world/.*

Zell-Ravenheart, Oberon. *Companion for the Apprentice Wizard.* Franklin Lakes, NJ: New Page Books, 2006. pp. 223-225

Zettl, Helmut. "Tiahuanaco and the Deluge." *Catastrophism and Ancient History: A Journal of Interdisciplinary Study.* Vol. VI, Part 2, July 1984.

The Cosmology of the Afterlife: Hamlet's Mill, the Star-Strewn Path, and the End of Days

By Adrian G. Gilbert

Who when standing before the pyramids of Giza or the lonely megaliths of Stonehenge has not wondered whether the ancients who built them possessed knowledge that we have since lost? The feeling that such monuments must have been built for a lofty purpose is overwhelming. For many, the quest to discover their meaning and purpose can become a lifelong passion. Without a guiding textbook from the past or detailed construction plans to tell us unequivocally why they were built, we can only produce theories of our own retroactively. This is, of course, the scientific approach; it is what archaeologists do all the time. However, even with the best of intentions, we are often hampered by the simple fact that we do not share or understand the worldviews of the people who built these monuments. Unfortunately, because archaeology is an inexact science, and because those who exert the most influence within the discipline do not want to look like fools, there is a tendency to simplify what were probably complex motives on the part of the ancients.

This can lead to naive assumptions, such as that the Great Pyramid of Giza is nothing more than the elaborate tombstone of a megalomaniac pharaoh. At first sight it is difficult to argue with this supposition, especially when we realize that pyramids nearly always contain sarcophagi. However we would not describe a church as a mausoleum just because it contained burials. Although some people choose to be buried inside a church, most church buildings have a greater function than merely to act as a burial chamber.

In order to discover the true meaning and purpose of an ancient monument, one needs tools. One of these tools is metrology, the study of measurements. Close examination reveals that important monuments are nearly always laid out according to some sort of geometrical scheme. By making careful measurements of a monument and its surroundings, it is often possible to discover the units of measurement that were used by its builders. This in itself can be helpful, for knowledge of the units used can often tell us when and by whom it was built.

Another tool, and one that can be used to great effect, is astronomy. It is this tool that primarily concerns us here. In 1969 an extraordinary book was published titled *Hamlet's Mill*. This was not, as the title might suggest, a critique of Shakespeare's play *Hamlet* (although it was the jumping-off point), but rather an investigation into ancient astronomy. What was of interest to the authors, Professors Giorgio de Santillana and Hertha von Dechend (hereafter referred to as "the authors"), was the connection between the traditional story of Hamlet and ancient myths relating to the stars. The Hamlet story itself derives from the *Gesta Danorum* by Saxo Grammaticus, a German author who lived during the 12th and 13th centuries. It seems that Shakespeare had access to this source. However, the authors discovered that the Hamlet story is not original to the *Gesta;* rather, it derives from an earlier, Icelandic saga which has parallels with certain stories in the Finnish classic the *Kalevala*. In the Icelandic version of the saga, the main character's name is Amlodhi, and his adventures are part of a larger cycle. His "mill" (which is not mentioned by Shakespeare) is a mythological machine of gigantic proportions that is used for grinding various substances. First it grinds gold and later salt, but then it is accidentally broken and falls into the sea. Here it continues to grind, turning rocks into sand and making the sea salty. The authors saw in this myth a cosmological meaning. They believed that the turning of Hamlet's (Amlodhi's) mill was a symbol for a cosmological process: a sequence of "world-ages" determined by the day of the equinox shifting backward, over time, through the zodiac. At the end of each age there would then be some sort of cataclysm, as the heavens would apparently become "dislocated" from their position at the start of the age.[1]

The authors eventually found that myths from all over the world told a similar story. They realized that these myths, fragmentary as they were, must have a common source, and that this common source would need to be very old, indeed. For them, Hamlet's mill was a metaphor for the heavenly machine that appears to turn around the earth. The axis—or spindle—of this mill runs from pole to pole. Presently the North Pole is located close to Polaris, the north star, but the authors also recognized that there is another, equally important axis linking the *poles of the ecliptic*, and that it too needed to be considered.

The ecliptic is the name given by astronomers to the imaginary circle or pathway followed by the sun as it appears to move through the zodiac at a rate of roughly one degree per day. In reality, of course, it is the earth that moves around the sun, so that what we term the *axis of the ecliptic* is really the axis of the earth's orbit around the sun.[2] Were the earth oriented in an upright position relative to its orbit, the pole of the ecliptic would be the same as the North Pole. However, because the earth is tipped over (at an angle of roughly 23.5 degrees) from the vertical, this is not the case. In fact, the pole of the ecliptic is situated within the constellation of Draco. Furthermore, because the earth has a slight wobble to its rotation—rather like a spinning top that is running down—the actual position of the north celestial pole is not constant. In fact it moves in a circle around the pole of the ecliptic (which is constant), taking roughly 26,000 years to make a full revolution. The "latitude" of this circle relative to the North Pole of the ecliptic is roughly 23.5 degrees south of it. This wobbling displacement causes the phenomenon we call the *precession of the equinoxes* (see Figure 1). We will return to this subject in more detail later.

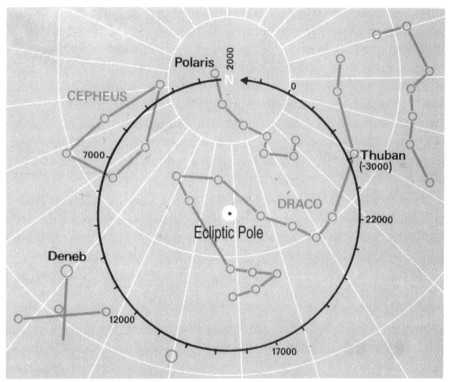

Figure 1. The orbiting of the North Pole, over time, around the pole of the ecliptic. From The Mitchell Beazley Concise Atlas of the Universe *by Patrick Moore. London: Mitchell Beazley Ltd., 1970, p. 141.*

Hamlet's Mill is not an easy book to read. However, when I first came across it in 1975, it was a revelation. Here I found proof for something that I had already known intuitively for years. Astrology— and I use this term in its original sense as the scientific, comprehensive study of the stars, rather than fortune telling—is much older than is generally thought. The idea that many ancient myths are based upon astronomical or astrological realities is obvious to anyone who makes a serious study of these matters. For example, the Greek myths about the 12 labors of Hercules can be understood as metaphors for the annual movement of the sun through the 12 signs of the zodiac. Hercules slaying the Nemean Lion refers to the movement of the sun through the constellation of Leo; and obtaining the girdle of the Amazonian queen is most likely a reference to the sun passing through the constellation of Virgo. We also know from the Greek authors that most of their classic constellations derived their names and identities from my-thology. One has only to think of the story of Perseus and Andromeda who, along with her parents, King Cepheus and Queen Cassiopeia, and the dragon (Draco), which threatened to eat her, are now con-stellations of the northern sky. The real importance of *Hamlet's Mill*, however, is that the authors brought a welcome scientific rigor to the study of astronomy in myths. Extracting deeper meanings from these myths was not always easy, as they were to write in their concluding chapter:

> It is now known that astrology has provided man with his con-tinuing *lingua franca* through the centuries. But it is essential to recognize that, in the beginning, astrology presupposed an astronomy. Through the interplay of these two heavenly con-cepts, the common elements of free literate knowledge were caught up in a bizarre bestiary, whose taxonomy [principles of classification] has disappeared. With the remnants of the system scattered all over the world, abandoned to the drift of cultures and languages, it is immensely difficult to identify the original themes that have undergone so many sea-changes.[3]

It was with such thoughts in mind that in 1984, I set about writing my first book, *The Cosmic Wisdom Beyond Astrology*. The purpose of this book was to explore astrology from four perspectives: scientific, artistic, philosophical, and religious. These perspectives represent the fourfold division of man's being, which can be thought of as body, soul, mind, and spirit, all symbolically linked to the four elements of Earth, Water, Air, and Fire, respectively. I purposely used this ap-proach in order to build bridges between the outlooks of four discrete groups of people: the first type being those who relate to the world pri-marily through the body; the second, through the emotions; the third, through the mind; and the fourth, through intuition. I also made use of the common language of astrology. This *lingua franca* was used extensively during the Middle Ages and even the Renaissance when discussing matters having to do with alchemy, medicine, prognostica-tion, and the occult sciences. Yet the scope of my own book was still limited, for I had not then a sufficient knowledge of either astronomy or ancient religions and mythologies to see the important connections between astronomy, astrology, and prophecy.

In 1992, I made the acquaintance of Robert Bauval, a Belgian engineer who was born in Egypt and had spent many years investigating the pyramids of Giza from the perspective of astronomy. Bauval had a thesis which at its core was very simple: the great pyramids of Giza represent the belt-stars of Orion. Though he had originally arrived at this theory intuitively, he backed it up with extremely detailed research covering both Egyptian ideas relating to the astronomy of the constellation of Orion, the orientation of shafts in the Great Pyramid toward certain stars, and the sacred literature the Egyptians inscribed on the walls of some of their pyramids, the so-called Pyramid Texts. We know from their sacred texts that the ancient Egyptians regarded the constellation of Orion as being the star-form of their favorite god, Osiris. They also believed that after death, the souls of their pharaohs (and perhaps their own, as well) would travel to these very stars. Here they would be united with Osiris, formerly a king of Egypt but now the ruler of the kingdom of the dead. The pyramids of Giza, it seemed, were intended to aid this post-mortem ascent to the stars. All this evidence proved beyond all reasonable doubt—in my opinion, at least—that not only did the pyramids on the ground resemble a three-dimensional representation of Orion's Belt, but that this resemblance was no accident.[4]

I was extremely impressed with Bauval's work and agreed to write a book with him, *The Orion Mystery*. This book contains a lot more than a simple rendition of Bauval's original theories concerning the pyramids and Orion. It also discusses the possibility that the pyramids embodied wisdom far more ancient than even that of Old Kingdom Egypt. In particular, the structures (or rather, the alignments directed through them) seem to mark the passage of a long age. In addition to the three great pyramids, the Giza complex also features two sets of three smaller, satellite pyramids. Although these are often referred to as the pyramids of the queens, there is actually no reason for believing that any queens were ever buried in them. In fact, Robin Cook (who drew the illustrations in the book) made an important discovery. He found that both sets of satellite pyramids were spatially related to the central pyramid of Khafre, rather than the pyramids they stand next to, Khufu and Menkaure. Parallel lines from the Khafre pyramid, all at 30 degrees to the meridian, which could be drawn from significant locations on the Khafre pyramid, would pass through the centers of

The Cosmology of the Afterlife   67

each of the Menkaure satellite pyramids, while similar lines, at 26.5 degrees from the east-west axis, could be drawn through the Khufu satellites.

What was so interesting about this was that the first set pointed toward the setting point of the Belt of Orion—not when the pyramids were built (c. 2500 BCE), but much earlier, around 10500 BCE. This date is significant because at that time, the Belt stars were at their lowest point in a cycle of movement caused by the precession of the equinoxes— the same apparent cyclical movement of the sky that causes the celestial pole to move in a circle around the pole of the ecliptic. Since then, the apparent movement of the Belt stars makes it look as though they are drifting northward; today, they stand just below the celestial equator, which means they rise in the east, directly in front of the Great Sphinx.

Now, remember that the authors' contention is that the rotation of Amlodhi's quern (or Hamlet's mill) is really a metaphor for the cyclical motion of the sky as it appears to rotate around the earth's pole. However, as we have seen, because of the precessional cycle, this pole itself moves—very slowly, it's true—in a circle around the pole of the ecliptic. This is the reason why the mill is broken in the story: its spindle jumps out from the millstone. According to Norse myth, this millstone fell to the bottom of the sea, while the hole in its middle formed a drain through which the waters of the sea above were drawn into a whirlpool. It was this image of water spiralling down a hole, the authors said, that gave rise to another myth, that of the *maelstrom*, the great mythological funnel of water or whirlpool which mariners and map-makers have traditionally placed firmly in the Norwegian Sea. The legendary maelstrom is clearly marked on a map of Scandinavia drawn by Fr. Athanasius Kircher, the late Renaissance Jesuit priest and polymath (see Figure 2). In his map, Kircher shows an imaginary, underground stream that apparently takes water from the North Sea, via the maelstrom drain, and channels it to the northern Baltic. Though no such channel exists in actuality, its pathway on the map more or less follows the Arctic Circle. This, as we shall see, is indeed important if we are to fully understand the myth of the maelstrom and its connection to Hamlet's mill.

Figure 2. Kircher's picture showing the maelstrom. From Mundus
Subterraneus *by A. Kircher, 3rd Ed., 1678.*

The earth's wobbling motion has other effects that are not con-
fined to the northern latitudes. One of these is the so-called precession of the equinoxes. Put simply, what this means is that the degree
on the ecliptic that the sun occupies on the first day of spring changes
over time. In fact it moves backward (*precesses*) along the ecliptic at a
rate of roughly 1 degree every 72 years. If we think of each sign of the
zodiac as containing 30 degrees (one-twelfth of a full circle of 360 degrees), this means it takes approximately 2,160 years to traverse one
sign. Currently, the spring equinox is moving out of the sign of Pisces
and into Aquarius (hence the popular song from the 1960s).

There is another way of studying the precessional cycle that is actually more accurate than looking at the stars of the zodiac. Our sun is but one star in the galaxy we call the Milky Way. Although we know intuitively that this is a typical spiral galaxy, like so many others we can see with our telescopes, because our solar system is contained within it, we don't see it this way. What we do see is a great circle of stars that seemingly rises and falls, first one arc and then the other, as the earth rotates through its 24-hour cycle. We see our galaxy "edge-on," as a flattened disk, but it actually has a median plane with half its stars on one side and the rest on the other. Thus the galactic, median plane is like an equator. Because this "equator" is basically a great circle in the sky, there are two places where it is crossed by that other great circle, the ecliptic. The authors' research revealed that this fact was known to the ancients; in fact, they believed that these two crossing points in the sky—one in the northern hemisphere, at the cusp of Gemini and Taurus, and one in the southern hemisphere, at the cusp of Sagittarius and Scorpio—were gateways through which souls came into and out of our world. One crossing point was a gate of entry, and the other, a gate of exit. Macrobius, in his *Commentary on the Dream of Scipio* (late 4th century CE), though he misidentifies the exact positions where the galactic plane crosses the ecliptic, describes the process of the soul's descent in some detail:

> The Milky Way girdles the zodiac, its great circle meeting it obliquely so that it crosses at the two tropical signs, Capricorn and Cancer.[5] Natural philosophers named these the "portals of the sun" because the solstices lie athwart the sun's path on either side, checking farther progress and causing it to retrace its course across the belt beyond. Souls are believed to pass through these portals when going from the sky to the earth and returning from the earth to the sky.[6]

Because of the precessional cycle, the place occupied by the summer solstice sun has been sliding back through the zodiac, just as the vernal and autumnal equinoxes have. Today the summer solstice takes place with the sun located exactly at the "portal" where the ecliptic crosses over the plane of the Milky Way, directly above the up-stretched hand or club of Orion. Conversely, the winter solstice occurs with the sun positioned at the other portal, the one in Sagittarius.

Interestingly, these portals were not in alignment with the solstices during the time of Macrobius, nor indeed have they been at any other time during the past 13,000 years or so. It seems that, astronomically speaking and in relation to the precessional cycle, we are living at a major turning point.

Now, this is very interesting because it takes us across the Atlantic to the Maya and their Long Count Calendar. As many people are now aware, this calendar runs out[7] at midnight on December 21, 2012. If it is merely a coincidence that the Maya timed their calendar to end with the sun placed at the southern portal on the winter solstice, then it is a very remarkable coincidence, indeed. What seems more likely, especially given their knowledge and indeed obsession with astronomical time cycles, is that this was deliberate. The Maya somehow knew (though we don't know how) that the precessional cycle would reach a turning point on that precise day.

I have written two books on the subject of the Mayan prophecy for the end of the age, and always I am asked the same question: Where do you plan to be on December 21, 2012? Usually the question behind this question is *Where, assuming this is the end of the world as we know it, do you think it will be safest?* Of course I cannot answer this question with any certainty. One might go to a geologically inactive location yet still have the misfortune of being killed by a falling meteorite. So I would therefore rephrase this question from "Where to go to be safe?" to "Where to go that would be a place of significance?"

One possible answer would be Aswan in southern Egypt. Because this town lies on (or very close to) the tropic of Cancer, the sun passes directly overhead at noon on the summer solstice. Conversely, at midnight on the winter solstice, the sun will pass directly below one's feet. As it will then be situated at the southern "portal," or crossing point of the ecliptic and median plane of the Milky Way, and as this lies very close to the galaxy's center, there will be an alignment of the earth, sun, and galactic center taking place directly underfoot. That event, I think, could be interesting.

There is another latitude in the northern hemisphere that might be worth visiting for the duration of the solstice event. This is the location of the fabled maelstrom somewhere off the coast of northern

Norway. To determine exactly where this is, we need to use a little intuition and also make certain assumptions. From *Hamlet's Mill* we already know that the maelstrom, or "millstream," is a coded reference to the pole of the ecliptic. This pole is located in the constellation of Draco, with celestial declination 66 degrees, 33', 38.55". Just as the summer solstice sun passes directly overhead at certain points, such as Aswan, that lie on the Tropic of Cancer, so every other point in the sky has a corresponding latitude on earth over which it passes at the zenith. For example, the star Vega (+38 degrees, 47', 01"), the brightest in the northern hemisphere, culminates at the zenith very close to the latitude of Washington, D.C. (38 degrees, 53' North). By the same reasoning, the pole of the ecliptic has as its corresponding latitude 66 degrees, 33', 38.55" North, which, as it turns out, passes through northern Norway; in fact, it's actually the Arctic Circle. Of course, working out the correct geographical longitude for the mythic maelstrom is not so easy. Doing this involves making a few more assumptions that are not strictly scientific. However, if we assume that in the ancient world, the prime meridian (their equivalent of the Greenwich Meridian) ran through the Great Pyramid of Giza, then the -30 degrees meridian (equivalent to shifting westward one sign of the zodiac) would fall about 1 degree 15' East of the Greenwich Meridian. The point on the Arctic Circle with this longitude would indeed be in the Norwegian Sea, north of eastern England.

From an esoteric perspective this has some interesting ramifications. If one were positioned on this point on the Arctic Circle at exactly midday, local time, on December 21, 2012, the pole of the ecliptic would be positioned directly overhead, with the 12 signs of the zodiac distributed in a circle around the horizon. Directly in the south the sun would appear on the horizon, aligned with the Sagittarius portal; directly in the north, again on the horizon, would be the Gemini portal; and linking the two (though possibly invisible because of the rising sun) would be the great, star-strewn path we call the Milky Way, like a bridge between the two portals (see diagram 5). The ancients called the Milky Way "the Way of the Dead," the road on which souls travelled between lives, from one gate to the other, in preparation for rebirth.

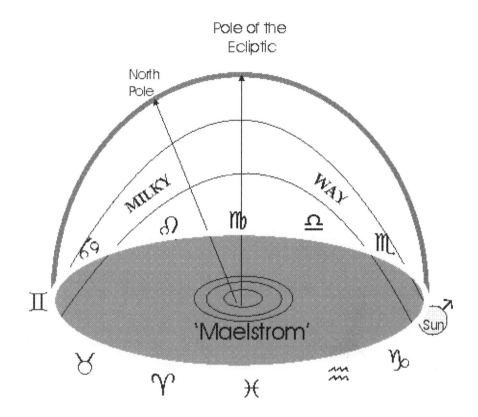

Figure 3. Noon on the arctic circle, winter solstice, 2012.
Copyright Adrian Gilbert, 2011.

It would appear, therefore, that our Norse ancestors, like the Maya priests of Central America, were somehow aware of the significance of the positioning of the Milky Way/ecliptic portals in the measurement of time. When we consider the tableau before us on the date that the Maya Long Count Calendar comes to the end of the present age, the significance of the maelstrom as a measure of time also becomes clear. Standing on the deck of a boat, we would have an image spread around the horizon surrounding the maelstrom that is reminiscent of the 12-gated city of New Jerusalem that is described at the end of the Bible. For looking round from this point, we would see the 12 signs of the zodiac—the gates of New Jerusalem—distributed around the horizon, and directly above, the mast, or tree, of the "boat" on which we would have to stand—the pole of the ecliptic. It would be a magical sight, and I think I would rather like to be there to witness it. Provided the sky was clear of clouds and the sea was calm, observing the star-strewn path from that vantage point and on that auspicious date would make for a most interesting experience.

Notes

1. From de Santillana, Giorgio and Hertha von Dechend. *Hamlet's Mill*. Boston: Gambit, Inc., 1969, p. 2.

2. This assumes that the earth's orbit is circular, which it isn't: it is elliptical. However, this makes little or no difference to the arguments presented here. Seen from the earth, the sun appears to follow a circular pathway through the zodiac.

3. De Santillana, p. 345.

4. Readers who would like to know more about Bauval's work and his thesis concerning Orion and the pyramids are referred to *The Orion Mystery*, the book we subsequently coauthored.

5. Today this is true of the tropical zodiac, which takes no account of the precession of the equinoxes and places the sun on the cusp of Cancer on the summer solstice and of Capricorn on the winter solstice. In actuality the sun is on the cusp of Gemini and Sagittarius, respectively.

6. From Macrobius (W.H. Stahl, trans.). *Commentary on the Dream of Scipio*. New York: Columbia University Press, 1990.

7. Actually this is not strictly true. All that is happening is that it is completing one "age" of 13 *baktuns*—that is, 13 times 144,000 days—before starting the next one.

Atlantis: The Lost Walhalla

By Philip Coppens

Sometime during the 8th century CE, Viking ships left their Scandinavian homeland and set sail for distant shores. By the end of the 11th century, the end of the Viking Age, their long-ships had reached as far west as Iceland and Greenland, as far south as Northern Africa, and as far east as the Volga River and Constantinople. The Viking Age was not remembered for their exploration of the world, however, but for their brutal conquest of Northern Europe. In England, the Vikings ar-rived in 773 CE, when their serpentine boats were first seen off the coast of Sussex. In 787 CE, three Viking ships docked at Dorchester. When the harbor master tried to find out who these visitors were, he and his assistants were swiftly killed. But the fear of the Vikings truly took root on June 16, 793, when they landed at the tidal island of Lindisfarne, roughly on the bor-der between Scotland and England. Lindisfarne was a center for learning that was famous across the Christian world, but the Vikings turned it into a scene of devastation: the monks were killed, thrown into the sea to drown, or carried away as slaves. Throughout the 9th century, the Vikings would at-tack and slowly take control of the British Isles, as well as many other countries in Europe, including France, where they reached Paris by 845 CE. By the year 900, major towns and ab-beys across the continent had been sacked. Vanquished coun-tries would never be the same again, and distant memories of the Viking raids continue to live on in memory and popular legends to this day.

What caused the Vikings to invade so many European countries remains a mystery, though historians have speculated wildly on the subject. Early theories focused on overpopulation and the need to expand the Viking territory. This proposal has now been abandoned, but there is still no consensus as to why the Vikings invaded Europe. Missing from the gamut of possibilities is that they might have gone in search of their mythical homeland, Walhalla, which, according to their legends, was somewhere to the southwest. Walhalla is traditionally described as a hall, but in myth it was inextricably linked with an island, where the gods had supposedly granted its inhabitants the gift of immortality. That the Vikings had indeed left their homeland in search of Walhalla was the conclusion reached by the Belgian historian Marcel Mestdagh. After years of retelling the same traditional story of the Viking conquest of Europe to his students, he realized that there was a method to the Viking madness, in that they first invaded England and then France. Mestdagh had noticed something that no one had seen before.

After their initial conquests, mostly of islands and coastal regions, the Vikings gathered their so-called Great Army. In England, the Great Army was formed in 866, the core of it created by soldiers brought by boat from Denmark. Their mission was to conquer the major towns and cities, a task that was finally accomplished in 879 when the army crossed the Channel to continue their campaign in France. Mestdagh realized that the way in which the Great Army moved about through England was not haphazard, but rather followed a pattern. It was almost as though something in the landscape—something in the topography, perhaps—was leading them from place to place. Whatever it was, it was something that was still present or visible at that time but has long since been lost to us.

Many years and a great deal of research later, Mestdagh realized that this missing clue was still present in the landscape, though we no longer recognized it as such: it was an ancient road network that fanned out from two towns, one in England (Nottingham) and one in France (Sens). Mestdagh was able to show that the network of roads in England centered on Nottingham, but that the Vikings hadn't been able to find there what they were looking for. After the conquest of Nottingham, new recruits came from Denmark, and the Viking Army crossed the Channel into France. There they made use of the same system of roads, whereby all roads led to the French city of Sens, which the Viking Great Army reached in late 886.

Interestingly, Sens was the only city that the Vikings did not sack. Instead, it was taken after a peaceful siege, which lasted only about six months. The history books make special note of the fact that no one was injured or killed during the siege of Sens. When the Great Army arrived, the people of the town had settled on the islands in the river Yonne, fully expecting that they would be brutally invaded like any other town. Some historians have argued that the archbishop of Sens had bought peace with the Vikings, but there is no evidence to support this. In short, there is no known reason why the Vikings would have suddenly changed their MO. But, Mestdagh wondered, was Sens, the former stronghold of the Celtic tribe known as the *Senones* ("elders"), somehow sacred to the Vikings? Was Sens what the Vikings had been looking for and had now found? Could it be that Sens was their mythical Walhalla? Was this why they did not sack the town?

The Vikings were not alone in having a myth of a lost island. The Celts called it Avalon; for the Portuguese, it was Antilia. Indeed, most people in medieval Europe had heard of an island called Ys, which was sometimes linked with the Irish monk and navigator Saint Brendan or with the lost land of Lyonnesse, itself thought to be located off the western coastline of Cornwall. But for the Greeks, it was the lost island of Atlantis, which they had heard about when they visited the Egyptian temples. The multitude of names was due to the fact that the island was originally known merely as "the Island"—everyone knew what was being referred to. Some, like the Goths, focused on the shape of the island when giving it its name (*Oium*, "the egg"). Although some will rightly argue that Sens is not an island, the surrounding region was and continues to be known as Île-de-France—*the island of France*. Is it any real surprise that the origin of a name used every day by millions of people remains a total mystery to historians?

What the Vikings encountered in northern France was an old and long-forgotten system of roads. Mestdagh believed the road network had originally been the work of the Romans, who were known to have been road builders *par excellence*. The notorious Roman conqueror Julius Caesar had chosen Agedincum—Sens—as the town where he stationed his armies, though it became only an administrative center in the late 4th century CE. It soon became clear, however, that the Romans had not constructed this network of road, as they were interlaced with a network of megalithic stones and therefore dated back thousands of years earlier, long before the Romans ever invaded Gaul. Standing stones and other megalithic constructions are known to have been used as boundary markers by the Celts, a people that came from the Eastern parts of Europe in the first millennium BCE. It is well known that the Celts made active use of these megalithic sites, and when places like Stonehenge were analyzed in the 18th century by the likes of William Stukeley, it was thought that the priestly class known as the druids performed elaborate ceremonies inside and amongst these monuments. But Caesar in his conquest of Gaul specifically targeted and hunted down the druids, thus ensuring that nothing of their knowledge survived.

No such extermination had occurred in the Scandinavian countries, which were equally rich in megalithic sites. In fact, Northern Europe had a relatively peaceful transition from megalithic times all the way to the Vikings. This meant that the knowledge associated with these megaliths survived well into the era of the Vikings, which meant that when they landed in Europe they knew far more about these ancient markers than the local people did. The Vikings had effectively maintained an active link to a former world, and by AD 800 CE, when they set out to find their Walhalla, they managed to do so largely on the basis of this link, which, sadly, had been severed, first by the Romans and later by Christianity in England and France. As a consequence, very little of the Viking knowledge was passed down to us, so Mestdagh had to spend years driving through the countryside of northern France, mapping megaliths, road networks, and ancient monuments, as well as cataloguing ancient legends—all of this at a time (the 1970s and '80s) when there was no GPS or the modern miracle that is Google Earth. It was a monumental task that would be a contributing factor to his early death, though not before he could publish the astonishing conclusions his research had revealed to him.

When he looked at the results of his painstaking research, he realized that this network of roads and megaliths was only part of the story. He also discovered a series of tremendously long ditches, which had at one time formed a series of vast, concentric ovals with Sens at its center. No one had ever figured out what these ovals signified.

In fact, the raised sides of the ditches had once been used to construct roads, many of which survived and are still in use to this day. But Mestdagh's on-site investigations showed that enormous ditches had once been located there and that, oftentimes, they could still be descried in the landscape. Because the ditches were made in sand, their integrity had slowly degenerated during the more than 3,000 years that they had not been in use. Detailed analysis revealed that they were actually ditches with raised borders. In the center of each was a depression or trough that had probably contained water at one time. These inner ditches were often connected to rivers and probably functioned as canals; indeed, portions of the concentric ovals that surrounded Sens were comprised of actual rivers—the portion of the river Marne between Meaux and Châlons-sur-Marne, for example.

The true extent of knowledge that Megalithic peoples—the ones responsible for the thousands of megaliths in Western Europe—possessed has not yet been plumbed either by archaeology or history. But in the 1970s, archaeologist Alexander Thom made an amazing discovery. After performing detailed studies of more than 600 megaliths in Britain, Ireland, and Brittany, he realized that all of them had been built with a standard unit of measurement, which he called the Megalithic yard. He also concluded that there was a central form of government, "because there must have been a headquarters from which standard rods were sent out but whether this was in these islands or on the Continent the present investigation cannot determine" (Thom 1976). That headquarters may have been Sens.

Research carried out by English writer John Michell, as reported in *At the Center of the World: Polar Symbolism Discovered in Celtic, Norse and Other Ritualized Landscapes*, demonstrated that someone in pre-Celtic, and hence Megalithic times possessed an extraordinarily detailed knowledge of the geography of northwestern Europe and had been able to accurately locate the geographical center of the British Isles. Interestingly, the Vikings were also privy to this knowledge. This is an important discovery, for before Michell reported on these discoveries in 1994, Mestdagh had realized that the sacred center at Sens had been created in accordance with the cardinal points, by someone with a detailed understanding of geography. The main axis of this geometrical pattern ran east-west, and went through the center of the city of Sens, extending to the east, with the center of the road system located about 1.5 miles (2.4 km) east of the city.

The end result of Mestdagh's investigation was multifold. First, there was a total of 64 roads extending as far as 200 miles (322 km) in either direction. He had found hundreds of miles of this road network still in use in the 1980s, with numerous megaliths and sacred sites along the way. Second, Mestdagh also realized that many of the names of the towns and villages situated along these roads contained the *Marc-* or *Merc-* prefix: literally, "marker." One of the better known sites is located on the southern road, which skirted the Puy-de-Dôme, a famous extinct volcano, which has commonly been regarded as sacred since Celtic times, if not earlier. Its summit holds a temple dedicated to the Roman god Mercury, a further reference to the *merc-* prefix. Is it a coincidence that Mercurius was thought to be the protector of travelers on the road?

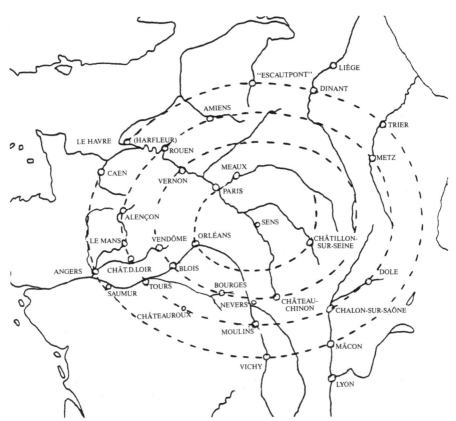

The system of concentric ditches centered on the city of Sens.

This system of four concentric ditches would have required an extraordinary amount of work to construct, for the circumference of Oval I, the first and smallest oval, is already an incredible 400 miles (644 km). Oval IV has axes of 297 and 370 miles (478 and 595 km), and a circumference of 1,106 miles (1,780 km). Staggering dimensions, but definitely still within human capabilities, particularly when we remember that the Great Wall of China stretches for more than 5,500 miles (8,851 km).

On a map of France, Oval III is almost visible to the naked, untrained eye. Take any map from France and find the town of Rouen; follow it down to Le Mans, Tours, and Châteauroux. Further north is a small section between Amiens and Poix; between Poix and Rouen there is a section missing on modern maps, but it is known that there was once a Roman road here. Far from being mere figments of the imagination, these ovals are very real.

When you map the old Celtic tribal boundaries, they coincide with the ovals and the fanlike road network centered on Sens. When we realize that this Megalithic system incorporated standing stones, and that the Celts used these stones as boundary markers, the enigma of why certain standing stones were placed in certain locations is explained. Mestdagh had essentially discovered a Megalithic civilization, a civilization that had once been lost to the sands of time. But had it? There were the clear references to an island, remembered in the name Île-de-France, but could this place really have been the mythical lost island of Atlantis?

Fortunately for the trained historian, Mestdagh did not have to take this on faith. We now know that the story of Atlantis was told to Plato by Solon, who had visited Egypt and heard about the lost city from local temple priests. They had provided Solon with precise dimensions—3,000 stadia (333 miles; 536 km)—of this island, which Plato then incorporated in his account, part of an unfinished work known to us as *Timaeus*. And here is where it gets interesting: Oval IV can be inscribed inside a diamond (as any oval can) comprised of equal sides that are 333 miles (536 km) long. This distance corresponds perfectly with the 3,000 stadia that Plato mentioned as the dimensions of Atlantis. But there is more. Plato locates Atlantis on relatively flat land, and situates it between the mountains and the sea. Oval IV is indeed located on relatively flat land, and sits between mountains (the Alps) and the sea (the Mediterranean). Plato adds that the distance from Atlantis to the sea is 2,000 stadia, or 222 miles (357 km)—precisely the distance from the southernmost point of the diamond to the Mediterranean coastline. Finally, using the system of roads, Mestdagh was able to retrace the "10 Kingdoms of Atlantis" mentioned by Plato, concluding that the area within Oval I was the "middle kingdom" and that the area between Oval I and Oval IV contained the nine other kingdoms. Another Greek philosopher, Proclus, referred to a text of Marcellus, which stated that the width of the middle kingdom of Atlantis was 1,000 stadia, which is actually precisely the width of Oval I! And can it be "just" a coincidence that there is a town named Avalon, the name of a lost mythical land in Celtic tradition, located on this very oval?

Mestdagh also found supporting evidence that the Megalithic civilization was Atlantis from the megalithic era itself. Petit-Mont is a famous *tumulus* (a mound of earth and/or stones over a grave or graves) around the Gulf of Morbihan, a region that is known today mainly for its more than 4,000 standing stones, most of them aligned into rows in and around the town of Carnac. The tumulus dates back to 4600 BCE and is one of the most significant, but also most brutally damaged, cairns in Brittany. Z. Le Rouzic was one of the first French archaeologists who actively investigated and restored the Megalithic monuments of Brittany in the first half of the 20th century. Inside the tumulus, Le Rouzic identified a series of stones that carried inscriptions along the interior walls. Stone M is an ellipse with 18 spokes and is traditionally interpreted as a solar wheel. But Mestdagh contended that this was actually a map of Atlantis, showing the nine-plus-one kingdoms of the lost civilization. An analysis of the carvings around the "solar wheel" added weight to this interpretation, as it showed mountains to the south, the shores of East Anglia and Kent, and the Rhine and Main river system, thus revealing that the "solar wheel"— Atlantis—was situated in a location that makes it a perfect geographical fit with Mestdagh's Megalithic civilization.

The lost civilization of Atlantis had been found. It would have taken our ancestors centuries to build this truly gigantic and sophisticated civilization. We know that the Megalithic city was an island surrounded by an astonishing system of canals, and the etymology of the word *island* provides us with perhaps the best clue as to its shape. For example in Dutch it is *eiland*, which means "egg land" or "the land in the shape of an egg"—an oval. The English word "island" comes from *is-land* or *ys-land*, and it is in Brittany that the story of the drowned land of Ys is recorded. In the story, dykes are used to protect the island from the sea; incredibly, dykes are precisely what Mestdagh found there.

It is my belief that Sens was the capital, the sacred spiritual center, of Atlantis. No doubt this is why its inhabitants were known as the *Senones*, "the elders," in Celtic times. Its sacred nature was also apparent during medieval times, when its archbishops held the prestigious title of Primate of Gaul and Germany, an extraordinary honor which the history books have had great difficulty explaining. The fact that Caesar himself stationed his army in Sens gives further support to the idea that Sens was of great historical importance. Caesar knew that the druids were his most dangerous opponents. He made it his mission to silence and exterminate them, famously giving chase and then cornering them in England on the island of Anglesey. Did Caesar station his army in Sens because it was their French headquarters?

Sens as the center of the Megalithic world might seem odd, given our modern perspective on the history of that area. Today the megaliths in Carnac are far better known. This is something for which the tourism industry is partly to blame. An inventory of all extant French megaliths was established in 1880 and printed in the *Bulletin de la Société d'Anthropologie de Paris*. The report clearly shows that by far the largest concentration of megaliths—261 out of 509 pockets— can be found in and around Sens. Though most of these disappeared by the turn of the last century, due to the encroachment of civilization and the contingencies of our modern age, the area around Sens was once literally littered with megaliths. It was the center of a lost world—Walhalla.

Archaeologists tend to see megalithic monuments in total isolation. For example, the gigantic stone circles of Avebury are located a mere 12 miles (19 km) to the north of Stonehenge, which is probably the best-known megalithic monument in the world. But hardly any research has been undertaken by professional archaeologists to find what common ground, if any, exists between the two structures, even though it's a very straightforward fact that the people of Stonehenge knew of Avebury, and vice versa. Mestdagh's research methodology showed that we should not look at megalithic complexes in isolation—as archaeology tends to do—but as a coherent whole. This idea is also in line with the conclusions drawn by Alexander Thom, that the megalithic civilization had headquarters—a capital—somewhere. That capital has now been identified as Sens. What this means is that from ca. 4500 to 1200 BCE, a major civilization existed in Europe of which we know very little.

What we now call its inhabitants—the Megalithic peoples—shows that we have given primacy to this aspect of their culture, the stone cutting and technology behind it. But Mestdagh's discovery unveiled several more facets of this civilization that was clearly on par with, if not superior to, ancient Egypt. In fact, this is precisely why Solon was told of this city when he visited Egypt. But whereas there are thousands of books about ancient Egypt, there is hardly any knowledge about the Megalithic civilization of Northern Europe. It is missing from the pages of history altogether, and if it had not been for a few Egyptian priests, Solon, and Plato, it might have been lost forever.

When Mestdagh focused his research on Stonehenge and Avebury, he found remnants of an oval road that connected the two sites. The road actually extends beyond the two sites. When traced on a map, he found that two-thirds of this oval still existed and that its dimensions were precisely one-tenth of the dimensions of Oval II in France. With this mathematical information, he had undeniable proof that the megalith builders of France knew of the megalith builders of England. Everything that happened for more than three millennia in Northern Europe was executed according to a plan so great in design that it defies belief. But that is precisely what the lost civilization of Atlantis was.

It is clear that the Ancient Egyptians knew about the lost civilization of Atlantis. By the time Solon arrived in Egypt, the Megalithic civilization of Atlantis was a thing of the past. But ancient Egypt was a thriving civilization when the Megalithic civilization flourished, between 3500 and 1200 BCE. In Egyptian mythology, the Afterlife was identified as an island in the west intersected by canals, and was represented as an enclosed oval formed by the body of Nut, surmounted by Osiris holding aloft the Solar Disk. This Egyptian equivalent of Walhalla was known as the Sekhet-hetep, the Field of Offerings. Egyptologists have interpreted these "myths" as the product of the imaginations of the ancient Egyptians. An alternative interpretation is available, one which clearly shows that Sekhet-hetep was once real and existed in France.

That there was some kind of communication between the Megalithic civilization and Egypt was once accepted in archaeological circles. The Italian anthropologist Guiseppe Sergi recorded finding the sign of the ankh and other hieroglyphic signs on several French dolmens. Professor J. Morris Jones confirmed the suggestion of Sir John Rhys that Celtic languages preserved an Egyptian Hamitic syntax: "The pre-Aryan idioms which still live in Welsh and Irish were derived from a language allied to Egyptian and the Berber tongues" (Rolleston, 2006). French archaeologist Letorneau noted in 1893 in the *Bulletin de la Société d'Anthropologie* that "the builders of our megalithic monuments came from the South, and were related to the races of North Africa." In modern archaeological circles, however, this is a most unpopular opinion; the current politically correct belief is that all cultures developed totally independent of each other, eschewing what is now seen as an outdated colonial perspective that any culture could have been incapable of accomplishing extraordinary feats (such as building the Great Pyramid) on their own. But when it comes to the Megalithic civilization of Atlantis, this stance is turned on its head, and archaeologists argue that there was never any such thing as one monolithic civilization!

Mestdagh's material was only ever made available to a Dutch audience; therefore, follow-up research after his death in 1990 has been limited. Dutch researcher Wim Zitman has studied Mestdagh's conclusions and has noted that the dimensions of the Atlantean civilization contained a series of numbers that are mathematically related to the star Sirius. Sirius is the brightest star in the sky and is sacred in many cultures, but in none more so than in ancient Egypt. Zitman argues that the ancients worked with the notion that time was equal to distance—a concept that is essentially correct, as we now know that time and space are identical—and that when one measures the distances between ancient monuments, one often finds numbers that correspond to certain astronomical measurements. The ancients, he argues, observed the sky and astronomical events, and incorporated them in their earthly constructions to reflect one aspect of the famous maxim "As above, so below"—in this case, what was seen in the skies was reflected on the ground in the sacred layouts of these structures. Zitman, in his book *Egypt: Image of Heaven*, has demonstrated how this occurred in ancient Egypt. But it is clear that for certain astronomical bodies and constellations to be mapped, not everything could be done from Egypt. It is known, for example, that ancient Greek scientists traveled as far north as the Scottish Outer Hebrides, which was the location of the stone circle of Callanish. The location of this megalithic structure was no accident, for it was only at that northern latitude that certain astronomical events (those related to the moon, for example) could be observed.

Similarly, although Mestdagh's discovery of the network of radiating roads emanating from the center like the spokes of a wheel might have been met with incredulity by the archaeologists, it is actually not the only such system of roads in existence, nor is it even the oldest at 5,000 years old. In the 1930s, the French amateur archaeologist Xavier Guichard published the results of his life-long study of the place name *Eleusis*. There is a city that bears that name in both Greece and Egypt. Of the two, the Greek city is the most famous as the home of the Eleusian mysteries. In mythology, we also have the Elysian Fields, which are intimately connected to the Afterlife and can be seen as the Greek equivalent of the Norse Walhalla. Guichard published his findings in a book called *Eleusis Alesia*, a study on the origins of European civilization. Published in 1936, it had a print run of 500 copies, several of which were subsequently lost. When I had a friend check out the copy from the main library in the French city of Lyon in 1997, it had been more than two decades since it had been consulted! According to Guichard, all places named Alesia (or similar) had been given that name in prehistoric times. Not a single location had been so titled in more recent times, meaning that these sites must have been named in extremely ancient times. He believed that the name was derived from an Indo-European root meaning "a meeting point to which people traveled." The majority of these sites can be found in France, where there were once more than 400, while others can be found in Poland and Spain, and as far away as Greece and Egypt. Interestingly, Guichard was unable to find such place names in Britain, which suggests that these cities dated back to the time of the last Ice Age, when Britain was covered with thick sheets of ice and unfit for human habitation.

Guichard, like Mestdagh, made it a point to visit most of these sites in person. He discovered that they all had two characteristic features in common: they were located on a hill overlooking a river, and they were built around a man-made well of saltwater or mineral water. When he mapped their locations, he realized that all the sites lay on lines that radiated, like the spokes of a wheel, from the town of Alaise in eastern France. This is an echo of what Mestdagh discovered at Sens. Guichard believed that 24 equally spaced, radiating lines, plus four lines aligned to the sunrise/sunset at the two equinoxes and the summer and winter solstices, linked the various sites. This yielded a total of 28 lines, showing, perhaps, a lunar connection, and suggesting that our ancestors were somehow able to map the Earth 12,000 years ago. Of course, it was 12,000 years ago that Atlantis sank, at least according to Plato. But all the information we've gleaned so far suggests that it ended sometime around 1200 BCE. So although it is an undeniable fact that the Megalithic civilization of Sens bore the same dimensions and was situated in the same location as Plato's Atlantis, the timing doesn't add up. What are we to make of this?

For Mestdagh the answer lay in the possibility that the number of years that was quoted to Solon did not refer to solar years, but lunar years. If this is true, that would yield an end date of ca. 1200 BCE, which would conform with the information provided to Solon by the Egyptian temple priests. But we cannot be sure that this is the correct approach. If we take Plato's information as gospel, there are several possibilities: someone was confused and in error about the dates of the Atlantean civilization; two separate legends were somehow made one, with another lost civilization somewhere to be found that is 12,000 years old; or the Megalithic civilization of Sens was not, in fact, the real Atlantis. It is clear that the dimensions of Atlantis are identical to those of the Megalithic civilization at Sens. And unless the various analyses of the Megalithic civilizations are wrong, the megaliths of Northwestern Europe do not date back to 12,000 years ago. Which leaves one option, which for the moment needs to be our working hypothesis—namely, that the Megalithic civilization, itself a truly lost civilization, was constructed as a copy, a perfect replica, of *another* civilization that was once lost itself and which was indeed far older. In other words, *the original Atlantis.*

Apart from the time frame, everything about this Megalithic civilization fits into what we know of Atlantis. The dating of the Megalithic civilization itself is by proxy—that is, by the material found on and around the various standing stones. It is my belief that there may have been two discrete phases: the original construction, which occurred about 12,000 years ago, and what was added on later, around 4000 BCE and onward, when people came and repaired the structures, essentially re-creating the lost Atlantis. Of course this is a hypothesis that is currently impossible to validate, but quite often that only means that the truth is out there, just waiting to be discovered.

Bibliography

Rolleston, Thomas William. *Myths and Legends of the Celtic Race.* West Valley City, Utah: Waking Lion Press, 2006.

Thom, Alexander. *Megalithic Sites in Britain.* Oxford, UK: Oxford University Press, 1976.

Temples, Creator-Gods, and the Transfiguration of the Soul

By Freddy Silva

The Earth is populated with persistent legends of men of great intellectual and physical stature and renown who were responsible for constructing places of power—sacred sites, temples, and cities of knowledge. These legends still swirl around such sites as Giza, Tiwanaku, Easter Island, and Teotihuacan like a magnetic mist.

In Egypt, the so-called *Building Texts* (written on the walls of the temple of Edfu) offer us a clue to the motivations of these ancient architects. The records state that after founding the first primeval mound—and later the Academy—at Heliopolis, groups of builder-gods set about locating other mounds at carefully chosen locations that would act as foundations for future temples, the development of which was intended to bring about "the resurrection of the former world of the gods," which had been destroyed long ago by a worldwide flood. They further state that these builder-gods, the *Ahau* (meaning "gods who stand up"), were survivors from an island that had been overwhelmed by a catastrophe that had "inundated [their] former mansions."

The texts place these builder-gods in remote, possibly Palaeolithic times, because the era of dynastic kings supposedly began around 3100 BCE with the Pharaoh Menes, who was considered by the ancient Egyptians to be the first human ruler—that is, a descendant of a purely human bloodline. This era was preceded by the dominion of the *Akhu Shemsu Hor* ("shining ones, followers of Horus"), builder-gods whose lineage was of divine descent. And even earlier in Egyptian prehistory, the texts mention the "Occasion of the First Time,"

89

when the land was ruled by the *Neteru* ("creator-gods"), whose era was brought to a close by the catastrophic global deluge. The advice given to initiates at the temple of Edfu, which we can also read in these texts, offers us a glimpse into what these supernatural builder-gods may have looked like: initiates were instructed to "stand up with the Ahau," who measured 9 cubits tall. That's approximately 15 feet (4.5 m) tall!

Easter Island

Strange as it may seem, these builder-gods reappear much later, during the 18th century, this time on an island in the Pacific ocean. The first European explorer to reach the island of Te Pito o Te Henua ("navel of the world") in the Pacific Ocean was Jacob Roggeveen, who did so in 1722 on Easter Sunday, hence its anglicized name. While stationed there, he faithfully catalogued the islanders' traditions and beliefs, one of which was that their population consisted of two discrete races—the "Short Ears" and the "Long Ears." The term "Short Ears" referred to typical *Homo sapiens*. As for the Long Ears, Roggeveen and his crew claimed they had direct interaction with these giants: "In truth, I might say that these savages are as tall and broad in proportion, averaging 12 feet (3.6 m) in height. Surprising as it may appear, the tallest men on board our ship could pass between the legs of these children of Goliath without bending their head[s]." The islanders believed that the Long Ears' ancestors were magician builder-gods called *Ma'ori-Ko-Hau-Rongorongo* ("masters of special knowledge"), who they believed were responsible for raising the carved stone effigies—the enigmatic *moai* ("images") that punctuate the topography of Easter Island and whose monolithic faces stare longingly at the sky. According to oral tradition, these "masters" moved the colossi with the use of *mana*, a kind of psychic force whereby matter yields to the focused intent of a person skilled in the subtle arts. The natives believed that by the "words of [the gods'] mouths" the statues were commanded to move through the air. Were these divine ancestors of the Long Ears, these master builders, the very same builder-gods mentioned in the ancient Egyptian wall writings? Amazingly, nearly *identical* mythological narratives came out of Tiwanaku in Bolivia and the Pyramid of the Magician at Uxmal, both of which describe temples being created by stones levitated by trumpets, sound, or special vocal commands.

Floods: Mythological and Historical

There are 175 global flood myths that share nearly identical narratives. Many if not most of these come from cultures that supposedly had no contact with one another. Alexander Tollman, an Austrian professor of geology, compared several flood myths that describe the earth being hit by "seven burning suns" before being overwhelmed by floods. He then compared these myths with actual geological anomalies resulting from the molten rock thrown up at meteor impact sites, and conclusively proved that around 10000 BCE, the earth was indeed hit by seven meteor fragments, whose impact generated an increase in radioactive carbon-14, which has been found in fossilized trees dating from that period. Likewise, in 2008 a team of Danish geologists conducted an extensive examination of ice cores in Greenland and settled on a precise date of the catastrophic event of 9703 BCE—barely 100 years later than the date in Plato's well-known account of Atlantis. Startled by the layer of soot in the ice, they remarked that "the climate shift was so sudden that it is as if a button [had been] pressed."

And yet, despite the catastrophe, the ancestral wisdom survived. This knowledge and other important records from men of high learning not only survived the initial catastrophe and ensuing flood but were promulgated by groups of adepts variously called the Seven Sages, the builder-gods, or the Followers of Horus. In the Edfu texts, for example, they were the only divine beings who knew how temples and sacred places of power could be created. In another example, the *Puranas* of the Tamil of southern India mention how Seven Sages visited the sacred hill of Arunachala after the flood to collect knowledge and embark on reconstructing the area between the Indus and the Ganges. And in Andean traditions, the megalithic monument builders are called the *Huari*, a race of white-skinned, bearded giants, the most celebrated of which was a builder-god named Viracocha. Together with seven "shining ones," he set about building the temple complex of Tiwanaku, from whence they set out to promulgate their knowledge throughout the Andes. It is through the efforts of these adepts that we have inherited a legacy of temples and places of veneration all over the globe.

And what a legacy it is. For despite thousands of years of war, the encroachment of modern civilization, and the often suspicious if

not downright hostile stance of organized religion regarding many of
these structures, tens of thousands of sacred sites still stand in just
about every country on Earth. Perhaps not surprisingly, many of these
sites share certain features in common. For example, many were built
using colossal stones, often hauled from hundreds of miles away; many
were aligned to the heliacal rising of specific stars and mirror entire
constellations; and many of them compute with monotonous regular-
ity the solar and lunar calendars, solstices, and equinoxes. And let's
not forget the Herculean effort that was required to build them, seemingly for the mere observation of the heavens. Given all of this, we are
forced to consider the possibility that these temples were likely built
with another purpose in mind, for it is clear that they were built to
last for all eternity, and certainly at least into an age when humanity
would inevitably lose its connection with the divine (today, perhaps?).
It should then come as no surprise that these temples were not only
re-creations of the former world(s) of the gods, but also places where
the individual could be transformed *into* a god. In other words, their
purpose was nothing less than the complete self-realization of the
individual through the transfiguration of the soul.

The Mystery of the Three Steppings of Vishnu

To get an idea of the scale of "spiritual engineering" that these
builder-gods employed to achieve their goals, consider the most
rudimentary of sacred sites, the holy mountain. In virtually every holy
mountain the world over, the exact place of veneration is located in
a spot where the geomagnetic field is more pronounced. Such "landscape temples" are often also accessed by a "spirit road," what the
scientist calls a *telluric current*. These currents are essentially electromagnetic pathways that flow across the face of the earth. During the
course of my research into the way sacred sites are connected to one
another through common narratives, myths, and folklore, I also discovered that they all seem to share an uncannily accurate geometry,
specifically triangles. The triangle is, of course, the geometric representation of the three-fold nature of the Biblical God, the Holy Trinity.
This same idea is also found in Hindu cosmology, in which the god
Shiva appears intertwined with the gods Vishnu and Brahma, all

three representing the concept of *Trimurti*, the three-fold nature of the one divine creative aspect that regulates creation, maintenance, and destruction. Vishnu, whose role it is to protect humans and restore order to the world, is often described in the narrative of the *Rig Veda* as taking three steps:

> I will declare the mighty deeds of Vishnu, of him who measured out the earthly regions...thrice setting down his footstep, widely striding.... He within whose three wide-extended paces all living creatures have their habitation.... Him who alone with triple step hath measured this common dwelling place, long far extended....

And further along in the text, Vishnu strides "widely pacing, with three steppings [sic] forth over the realms of the earth for freedom and for life." Strange behavior indeed for a god. Vishnu is eventually given the attribute *Trivikrama*, meaning "of the three steps." Is it possible that Vishnu, the bringer of order to the world, arranged these holy mountains, these landscape temples, in threes? And are these hills sacred because they are infused with the numinous quality of a creator-god? (Note that *vis-nu* actually means "to enter or infuse" and "all-pervading.") I decided to test my hypothesis.

The Indian subcontinent has many mountains, yet few are sacred, and fewer still are associated with Shiva/Vishnu. The most renowned of these is Mount Kailas, the earthly equivalent of Mount Meru, which itself represents the allegorical structure of the universe as well as the highest spiritual achievement sought by adepts in Hindu, Buddhist, and Jainian cosmologies. Kailas is also the abode of Shiva, a place of "eternal bliss" sacred to five religions. My second contender was the holy hill of Gabbar. Like Kailas, in myth it is the origin of the supreme cosmic power of the universe, and the place where Shiva leaves the heart of his first wife, Sati. The third contender, Maa Sharda, was a conical hill that has been used as a sacred mountain since the Paleolithic era. In the *Reg Vida*, Shiva, mourning over his deceased wife, drops her necklace there. So we have three sites that are connected, through legend, to Shiva, an inextricable aspect of Vishnu. If you link all three sites on a map, it creates a perfect right triangle to within 1 degree of error. Considering that it measures 1,650 miles (2,655 km) along the edges, this is an incredible degree of accuracy, especially as we are dealing with three distinct, naturally occurring features. Vishnu apparently did set down his footsteps three times, "widely striding."

I soon discovered this was by no means a coincidence. Right-angle or isosceles triangles also connect sacred mountains in China, New Mexico, and Japan (including many of Japan's oldest and holiest shrines). This is supported by the fact that temples were later erected near these hot spots, also called "navels of the earth." In the British Isles, for example, three sites more than 600 miles (966 km) apart, yet sharing similar traditions, functions, and age, are connected to each other by a perfect equilateral triangle: Avebury in England, Kealkill in Ireland, and Murchie Moor in Scotland. Similar sites exist throughout the Middle East and in Portugal, as well.

Just how far the Followers of Horus and their later incarnations would go to create these enormous networks of linked power places is in evidence all around the Mediterranean. For example, there exists a demonstrable link between the oracle of Delphi and the Egyptian temple complex at Karnak. Legend states that Karnak is the mother of all oracles, from where all other oracles emanate, and that two doves once flew between Karnak and Delphi; both were dedicated to solar gods (Zeus/Apollo in Greece, and Amun/Ra in Egypt); both once contained notable examples of navel stones; and both were used as places of clairvoyance. It seems that in using the oracles, the adepts were tapping into the power of a connected grid so as to amplify their abilities. The "hill forts" throughout the British Isles were also used for such a purpose. But why did two doves fly between Karnak and Delphi, a distance of 1,070 miles (1,722 km; a figure tantalizingly close to the radius of the moon)? The dove also makes an appearance as a symbol of communication in the story of Noah who, as Ziusudra, is also the central figure of the Sumerian flood myth, as is Manu, the preserver, father of humanity, and institutor of religious ceremonies in the Vedic texts. His progeny call themselves Aryas, meaning "noble," "pure," or "enlightened." In each case, Manu/Ziusudra/Noah is directly instructed by God/the gods to build a boat prior to a flood, and is accompanied in the endeavor by Seven Sages who, after the deluge, go on to teach wisdom to humanity. In other words, they sow the seeds of civilization itself.

Because the ancients were so fond of investing multiple layers of meaning into one symbol, let's take these connections to another level: Karnak, Delphi, and Mt. Ararat (now the proven resting spot of Noah's ark) all share the same dove symbolism, are all associated with tall builder-gods or seven sages, and are all connected by that triple step of Vishnu, the shape of a perfect isosceles triangle. As astonished as I was by this connection, I believed it to be the end of the matter until I calculated that the heart of this particular triangle rests conveniently on the only piece of dry land in that part of the Mediterranean, the island of Cyprus. In fact, the center point rests exactly on the castle of Kolossi, a square-shaped tower reminiscent of the Ka'ba—the Islamic navel stone at Mecca—and the symbol for Mount Meru. In the 13th century, the tower would become the seat of a new generation of sages, the Knights Templar who, ironically, trace their practices to Temple Mount in Jerusalem, whose esoteric origins are echoes of Heliopolis—the original primordial mound from which the Egyptian temple tradition emanated.

Magnetics

A significant factor in the location of these temples and holy sites was the presence of geomagnetic "hot spots." Stories of people being sent flying by an electromagnetic charge in a stone—usually quartz or magnetite—as though touching it somehow grounded its energy, are legion. A study of the Rollright stone circle in England, for example, revealed how the local magnetic field is drawn like a whirlpool into the center of this Neolithic temple. Other studies have shown that the earthen henges surrounding temples such as Stonehenge and Avebury act as conductors of geomagnetism, wherein the stones are used to store and direct the flow of terrestrial energy. At Avebury, the magnetic readings die away at night to a far greater extent than could be accounted for under normal circumstances. When they charge back up at sunrise, the telluric current from the surrounding land is attracted to the chalk henge, and the magnetic fluctuations of the site reach their maximum levels. This may reveal why temple-builders such as the Egyptians often regarded temples as living organisms that sleep at night and awaken at dawn.

An exhaustive survey of the megalithic metropolis of Carnac, France, reveals how the 4,000 stones arranged in up to 13 parallel lines, beginning and ending in egg-shaped stone circles, alternately amplify and release telluric energy throughout the day, with the strongest readings occurring at dawn. The process mirrors the phenomenon known as *electric induction.* The French scientist Pierre Mereux came to the conclusion that the menhirs at Carnac act like accumulators, the dolmens like coils, and the stone circles like concentrators and accumulators. The specially chosen rocks, high in concentrations of quartz, are *piezoelectric,* meaning they generate electricity when compressed or subjected to vibrations. Carnac and its 4,000-plus stones are actually positioned along 31 fault lines on the most active earthquake zone in France, so it is in a nearly constant state of vibration, making the stones electromagnetically active. Clearly the menhirs were not planted here by chance—particularly given the fact that they were transported from 60 miles (97 km) away—because their very presence and orientation is in direct relationship to the terrestrial magnetism. Such measurements alone reveal why the temples were built where they were, and why the degree of work that went into them belies their simple purpose as astronomical markers.

The main beneficiary of the temple is the human body. Every human being on earth is composed of two-thirds water and thus has an electromagnetic charge; virtually every temple is situated above or near water. When the telluric current is located over water, it tends to move in a spiral pattern, and induces a corresponding charge in that most precious of liquids. Samples of water from holy wells and other sacred places show an increase in the vorticular motion of the water as compared to ordinary water. This process actually produces a corresponding effect in the human body. Furthermore, the temple and its charged environment stimulates the iron in the blood, as well as the millions of particles of magnetite suspended inside the human skull. Finally, fluctuations in the local electromagnetic field can influence one's state of awareness, primarily through stimulation of the pineal gland, which in turn can lead to visions/hallucinations and altered states. In other words, a visitor to one of these sites, whether pilgrim or priest, is able to receive information more readily from other levels of reality, which indeed was precisely the purpose of these structures—the transformation of the individual into a god.

Seven Degrees of Perfection

Most people would assume that such sensitive and carefully engineered environments would have been protected from harm, and sure enough, they were. There exists, over the entire face of the globe, a kind of woven, electromagnetic grid. Bearing the name of one of the men who discovered it, Dr. Ernst Hartmann, the Hartmann grid is influenced by underground veins of water as well as magnetic forces emanating naturally from the earth. Could a relationship exist between temples and how this net seems to stretch around them?

I came across a fascinating document by the geo-biologist Blanche Merz, in which she conducted readings at various temples and found that, in each case, the Hartmann net was stretched into 18 lines around the structure, almost like a protective membrane. Because of this, celebrated temples such as those at Saqqara, Karnak, Luxor, and Kom Ombu enjoy an immense "neutral zone," in much the same way that the henge monuments in Britain direct and concentrate the electromagnetic forces *inside* the temples in a controlled manner that is beneficial to the individual. The Edfu *Building Texts* list these Egyptian temples as the original primordial mounds of the gods. Merz went on to find other energy "hot spots" at Chartres, Santiago de Compostela, and a plethora of Indian sacred sites. In Tibet she found that *stupas* (dome-shaped shrines) marked with *nagas* (serpents) identify the places where the lines of the Hartmann net intersect, and that telluric energy is transmitted via the upright stones.

There's more. In the *Funerary Texts* at Saqqara there is a curious passage that states, "Seven degrees of perfection enable passage from earth to heaven." This sentence is widely interpreted as referring to a series of trials that the soul must endure before gaining entry into the afterlife. Because the Egyptians were fond of allegory and metaphor, however, I wondered if the phrase might also be alluding to the doorway or threshold the individual crosses when he/she enters a temple—a "passage from earth to heaven" suggesting a crossing over from the profane, material world into the heavenly otherworld, which neatly defines the purpose of the temple. But that is only one door—where do the "seven degrees" come in?

In Egyptian mythology, the passage of the soul into heaven is made through a place called *Sekhet Ianu*, meaning the "fields of reeds," after which the spirit reaches a paradisiacal land where it spends eternity. We simply know it today as the *Elyssian Fields*. To reach this much-desired land one must pass through a series of gates. During a visit to the temple complex at Saqqara I had the opportunity to study the entrance leading from the profane world into the grand courtyard with its evocative stepped pyramid, engineered by Imhotep, an architect of the gods. This passageway is unique in that it is a colonnade flanked by 18 pillars in the shape of reeds separated by narrow alcoves. Each of the alcoves discharges an alternating (positive and negative) electrical force, which serves as a barrier between the temple and the outside while it influences the body's own electromagnetic "circuitry." In essence, as you walk down this preparatory entrance, you are suitably "en-tranced" prior to making contact with the courtyard of the temple and its mansion of the gods.

The numerical relationship between the 18 stone reeds and the 18 Hartmann lines protecting the perimeter of temples is unmistakable. But for me, the revelation lay in the readings of the alternating energy field found at the entrance and its passageway of reeds, for it consisted of exactly seven positively charged currents. Suddenly an answer to the "seven degrees of perfection" seemed close at hand. Indeed, Merz's own research revealed that at the very wide thresholds preceding the initiatory rooms of the temples, the Hartmann net traverses the entrances with *seven tightly packed grid lines* protecting "the passage from the known to unknown." Seven gates can also be found in the ceremonial chamber at Newgrange, Ireland, where the pilgrim passes seven positively charged lines of force in the chambered passageway before reaching the inner sanctum. This preparation prior to crossing the threshold between the visible and the invisible is reminiscent of what occurs every year at Mecca, as Muslim pilgrims wind seven times in ever-decreasing spirals around the sacred center, the Ka'ba.

Gateways Into Paradise

To help overcome the conditions of the material world that hindered initiates from experiencing a state of oneness with the divine, they would source the energy of such places of power and integrate themselves with the spirit of place, which helped them avoid such negative, limiting emotions as fear, anger, envy, and so forth. Once enlightenment was reached they would attain a state of bliss—or, as many of us describe it, paradise. Interestingly, this simple observation can help us locate that longed-for land. In Avestan—the sacred language of Zoroastrianism—paradise is *pairi daeza*, and literally means "a walled enclosure." According to local traditions, a Jain who has mastered discipline over the physical world and achieved the state of godliness is called a *Jina*. As this word migrated west it became the Arabic *Djinn*, along with its derivative *Allah-Djinn*, or *Aladdin*. Back when Asia Minor was Assyria, a *Djinn* was considered a supernatural being—perhaps not surprisingly, as the root *j-n-n* means "hidden." However, it is also the root of *jannah*, the Islamic concept of paradise. Its derivative in Portuguese—a language brimming with Arabic—is *janela*, meaning "a window, an opening in a wall." If we follow this dizzying etymological trail to its logical conclusion, paradise appears to be a hidden but clearly demarcated space, separated from the ordinary and troublesome world, a "walled enclosure" we can reach through "an opening in the wall."

Every human being longs for some sort of paradise, whether an earthly one in the here-and-now, or one later on, in the afterlife. In creating stone circles, pyramids, and other sacred structures, ancient architects were opting for "the here-and-now" inasmuch as these walled enclosures—temples—demarcated one world from the next. The measurable electromagnetic fields around their perimeters only help to prove the point. The window into these walled enclosures are the literal and figurative *en-trances* through which these deliberately directed electro-magnetic forces flowed, thus entrancing the individual as he or she pierced the veil between this world and the next. In creating these places of power, the ancients created sanctuaries where spiritual transformation was achieved and paradise was experienced here on earth.

Numbers and Knowledge

In ancient texts, temples are often described as cities of knowledge. This is both literally true (they often served as storehouses for texts and bodies of knowledge) and allegorically true, for the temples—with their encoded numerical values, geometries, stellar alignments, and geomagnetic effects—were *themselves* the knowledge. They were designed to correspond to and reflect the perfect laws of nature. The adepts recognized that the fate of the soul while trapped inside the physical body was tied to a cosmos in which geography and the science of the heavens were inextricably bound, and that during its immersion in the material world the soul's unhealthy connection to or over-investment in the body could sever this intimate connection. As the historian Giorgio de Santillana and scientist Hertha von Dechend comment in *Hamlet's Mill*, "Knowledge of cosmic correspondences led up to harmony on an infinite number of levels, and the rigor and absoluteness of number was the instrument with which these correspondences were determined and remembered." In other words, the ancients reduced complex cosmic forces—for example, the 11.060606-year sunspot cycle—down to simple numerical relationships and then applied those relationships to the construction of their temples. For it was believed that by placing the body within an environment of near perfection, the forces present would effect an almost alchemical process on the living organism and return it to a state of perfection.

When examining the design of ancient temples as well as sacred literature, the numerical values 18, 36, 54, 72, 108, and 144 crop up again and again, like handy mnemonic devices. Interestingly, this seemingly haphazard series of numbers actually reflects the core angle of the pentagram—72—as well as its divisors and multiples. Why would the pentagram be important in the structure of temples? Because the pentagram is actually the geometry of all living things. The cells in living organisms are pentagonal, and the proportions of nature's spiral, as expressed by the Golden Ratio, closely follow those of the pentagram. Because temples work through correspondence, by applying the numerical values unique to the pentagram to their design, a correspondence is established between temple, planet, and humanity. If one extends this logic on a global scale by applying the pentagonal numbers as longitudes—using the primordial mound of Heliopolis as 0 degrees—each line of longitude bisects some of the most profound oracles on earth: Easter Island, Angkor, the great *stupa* at Kathmandu, Susa, Nan Madol, Arran, and even the original mound and obelisk at the Vatican.

Another way this sacred knowledge was encoded into temples lies in their designers' use of angles associated with the movement of energy. For example, if you take the other two basic geometric building blocks of life—the tetrahedron and the sphere—and place one inside the other, the angle at which any point of the tetrahedron touches the surface of the sphere is 19.47 degrees. We know that this angle is important in the manifestation of energy because it also happens to be the degree of latitude on the surfaces of many planets where the greatest number of active energy "hot spots" are located: the Mauna Kea volcano on earth, the Olympus Mons volcano on Mars, the great red spot on Jupiter, and so on. The temple builders sought to amplify the power of these sites by relating them to each other at this angle; the circumference of Avebury stone circle, for example, is formed by an angle of 19.47 degrees mapped from the summit of its nearby conical mound, Silbury Hill.

The Angle of Manifestation

The amount of trouble the builder-gods and, later, the fully human architects went to create places of power that intimately connect with and correspond to the human body is easier to understand when you consider the relationship between these sites and the very core of the human body, DNA. When you pile salt on a table it forms a conical mound with a slope angle of 32.72 degrees. The slopes of many ash volcanoes and other soft-particle hills are also defined by this angle. It would seem that gravity causes fine matter to fall this way. There is even a close numerical correspondence between this angle and the speed of gravity, which is 32.17 feet per second.

The mystery of 32.72 is so tantalizingly close to that mystical number 33 that it's worth stopping for a moment to consider the two. The Zoroastrian god, Ahura Mazda, is said to have created the universe with the power of 33 steps. References to this secret process can also be found in the Qabalah. Through the thorough understanding of its 32 principles, one reaches the 33rd degree, or enlightenment. This knowledge would have been a component of the Mystery Schools in Heliopolis, later to become a closely guarded secret within the 33 degrees of Freemasonry, whose roots herald from said academy.

Is 33 just a convenient rounding-off of 32.72? After all, one cannot go around claiming to be a 32.72-degree Mason. If so, why did the United States of America, a country founded by Freemasons, establish its border with Mexico at Yuma where, in the middle of a river, it forms the tip of a pyramid precisely at latitude 32.72 degrees? And why did the Knights Templar, the precursors of the Freemasons, build a castle on the Levant coast at 32.71 degrees, and another at Vadum Iacob, exactly at 33 degrees latitude, both of which, when connected to a third one at Jericho, form a perfect right-angle triangle, a triple step of Vishnu? Stranger still, nearby Mount Carmel, the "vineyard of God," lies at—you guessed it—32.72 degrees, while the transfiguration of Jesus on Mount Tabor occurred at 32.69 degrees. But let's return to the Freemasons for a moment. The true fraternity of Freemasonry is an echo of the Followers of Horus, the falcon god of the sky whose mission was to bring light to humanity. The light of the sky is embodied by the sun, and the solar year (365 days) divided by the sun's cycle (11.060606 years) equals 33. Conversely, the sun defined as a circumference of 360 degrees divided by 11 (the convenient number of the solar cycle) equals 32.72.

All of this brings us back to temples and their corresponding effect on that greatest of structures, the human body. Let's consider the two oldest sacred places on Earth: Stonehenge and Heliopolis. British chronicles dating from the 12th century state that the stones of Stonehenge were brought all the way from Africa by a race of giants. Of course at least part of this story is incorrect since we now know that some of the stones were sourced from a quarry in Preseli, Wales (actually aligned on a pentagonal longitude), and some from the nearby Wiltshire Plain. However, what may have come from Africa is the *knowledge* of temple building, and a sufficient number of giants' graves in this part of the testify to the presence of a race of unusual magician-priests. Stonehenge itself is now carbon-dated to 8000 BCE, placing the original site within the era of those tall builder-gods, the Followers of Horus. So, if we apply the rule of the three steps of Vishnu between Stonehenge (a temple of Light), its Egyptian counterpart of Heliopolis (the city of Light), and the absolute north of the planet (the North Pole), the angle subtending the two places of power is exactly 33 degrees. But where is the explicit connection between the human body the temple? The answer lies with a rather unusual looking pharaoh.

By 1346 BCE, Heliopolis had become a pale shadow of its former glory. In a sudden deviation from norm, the pharaoh Akhenaten moved the capital of Egypt to a site at Til el-Amarna and named it Akhet-aten. His prime motivation was to wrest the temple away from the power of an increasingly corrupt priesthood, which by that time had already usurped control of the rituals and symbols and come to use the temple as a method of crowd control. His secondary motivation was to return the focus of worship to the monotheistic cult of Aten, the sun, which his father, Amenhotep III, had started in Thebes but failed to promulgate due to the prevailing politics. By doing this, Akhenaten revitalized the very concept upon which Heliopolis was founded, for Heliopolis, as a city of the knowledge that transfigures the soul, was the perfect architectural expression of the veneration of Light. It was also home to the Followers of Horus, the falcon god of the sky who seeks to overcome darkness (ignorance) by avenging the death of his father, Osiris, god of light and guardian of the gate into Sekhet Ianu: paradise.

At first glance Akhet-aten seems like a ludicrous place to build a city, let alone a capital. It was remote, 120 miles (193 km) from the nearest complex at Abydos, encircled by desert, and with only the Nile providing an umbilical cord to the rest of the world. But clues suggest a well-conceived plan: for one, in his oblation to the Aten, Akhenaten praises the new capital as "the seat of the First Occasion, which he had made for [Aten] that he might rest in it." To be a "seat of the First Occasion," the site must have been an original primordial mound—in other words, it must stand on ground previously consecrated by the Seven Sages and the builder-gods 8,000 years *prior to* the 14th century BCE. So if we do what Akhenaten did—take the former 33-degree angle marking the relationship between Stonehenge and Heliopolis and move it south to create a new relationship with a new temple of Light at Akhet-aten—the exact angle between the two sites changes to 32.72 degrees. So where does DNA come in?

As I indicated previously, the human body contains a great deal of the one element that benefits most from being inside a temple. It consists of two-thirds water, which turns into ice at exactly 32.72 degrees Fahrenheit (0.4 degrees Celsius). Water actually contains a combination of 33 different substances, offering life to the human body and its spine of 33 bones. Modern research shows that DNA is a remark-ably flexible molecule, and thermal fluctuations can produce bending, stretching, and un-pairing within the structure. In its normal state, the angle of rotation of the bDNA helix is 34.61 degrees, but in a de-hydrated state, it changes into aDNA, and its angle of rotation then becomes—you guessed it—32.72 degrees. *This* is how far the ancients went to situate their sacred sites in order to produce a corresponding effect on the human temple.

108 Degrees West of Heliopolis

If you think that all of this has little bearing on modern life, think again, for the principles that once set the spiritual bar at such a great height continue today in one form or another. Even during the dark times of the decline of ancient Egypt, the rise and fall of the Roman Empire, and the Inquisition, this knowledge continued to be taught, albeit underground (hence the term *occult*, meaning "hidden"). In fact, this is what led to the enlightenment of the classical Greek pe-riod, when notable scholars such as Plato and Pythagoras graduated from the Mysteries Schools of Heliopolis. Indeed, Greek historians such as Herodotus attribute the rise of Greek culture directly to the Egyptians and their fabled temple academy, later to be resuscitated in Alexandria. Groups of adepts persevered under different guises to promulgate the teachings for the next 3,000 years.

The legacy of the temple and the cities of knowledge handed down from the creator-gods before the time of the great flood didn't just seek to benefit the individual within the confines of sacred space, for its effects resonate far beyond, sometimes encompassing an entire city. In Paris, for example, notable buildings, boulevards, and cathedrals have been purposefully modeled over hundreds of years on align-ments mirroring the temple complex of Karnak-Luxor, just as those alignments once mirrored the heliacal rising of Sirius, the star associ-ated with *gnosis* (spiritual knowledge and mystical enlightenment). By this method the temple builders hoped that whole cultures would be maintained in balance indefinitely, the only uncertainty being the ego and the need of individuals to abuse power for narrow ends.

Which brings us to a modern-day correspondence with the tem-ple. One of the sites corresponding to the global pentagonal grid lies in the Bay of Paracas in Peru. Here, on this desert hillside, lies an anomalous, solitary 300-foot (91-m) tall Tree of Knowledge etched deeply into the encrusted sand. The line of longitude on which it rests extends north and marks the capital of one of the world's newest countries, whose Declaration of Independence was created by those new Followers of Horus, the Freemasons, which included George Washington and Benjamin Franklin. Likewise, exactly 108 degrees west of Heliopolis lies the dome of the Capitol in Washington, D.C. The purpose of this building, as Franklin himself stated, "was to be the first temple dedicated to the sovereignty of the people."

In creating an ideal city dedicated to the liberty and freedom of the individual, the restoration of light, and the transformation of the soul, the architects of Washington, D.C. (who were all French or American Freemasons) encoded the very facets of the temple in the orientation of the city's wide boulevards as well as in the relative location of its primary monuments. Thus, in the positions of the White House, the Capitol, the Washington Monument, the Lincoln Memorial, the Pentagon, and even the Grand Lodge of the Freemasons, are encoded the angles 19.47 degrees and 32.72 degrees, the pyramidal angle of 51.49 degrees, and the octave in music. Its main thoroughfare, Pennsylvania Avenue—the avenue of the king—is aligned to the rising of the star of wisdom and the Divine Feminine, Sirius. This is far from a conspiracy or sinister plot; rather, it is, as it has always been, about the use of subtle energy. Energy is neutral: it can benefit the greater good just as it can be abused by the few and used against others. History shows that the vacillation between tyranny and enlightenment has marked the slow, upward trajectory of human development, just as the temples that have endured these changes were once nothing more than simple mounds rising like pregnant bellies out of the land.

Note to readers: All original references are from my book *Common Wealth: The Origin of Sacred Sites and the Rebirth of Ancient Wisdom.*

Our Sonic Past: The Role of Sound and Resonance in Ancient Civilizations

By Marie D. Jones and Larry Flaxman

In a world driven by visual stimulation, sound has often taken a back seat in how we perceive and process stimuli and information and give meaning to our reality: "I'll believe it when I see it," "What you see is what you get," and "Out of sight, out of mind." We generally react more to what we see than what we hear, and we usually give more credence to the actions of others than we do to the words they speak. But ancient civilizations understood the power and influence of sound. Not just any power, but a power that mirrored the creative force, perhaps the same force described in Genesis when God spoke the word, and the world, into existence.

Mysterious Structures

In the country of Bolivia, at 12,900 feet (4 km) above sea level, near the city of Tiahuanaco (also known as Tiwanaku), at the center of the great terrestrial basin of Lakes Titicaca and Aullagas, is a large monument complex called Puma Pumku. The vast complex, now quite deteriorated due to age and exposure to the elements, was once a bustling spiritual and cultural center, along with the nearby temples, the Akapana Pyramid, and other ritual centers that served the people and priests of Tiahuanaco. What remains today are a series of open courtyards, an esplanade, clay platforms, a terraced platform facing megalithic stones, and enormous stone blocks. Some of these massive stone blocks weigh in excess of 100 metric tons. The largest stone slab, a part of the Plataforma Litica, the eastern edge of Puma Punku, weighs 131 metric tons and is carved from red sandstone. Another block at the same site weighs in at "only" 85.21 metric tons. Some of the stones are fitted so precisely that

107

something as thin as a razor blade cannot be wedged between them. The holes bored into the stones are of equal depth, and the cuts are perfectly straight. As if this were not enough of an enigma, factor in the transportation issues that must have been involved. Petrographic and chemical analysis of these blocks by archaeologists indicates that they were somehow transported to the site over a very steep incline from a quarry just over six miles (10 km) away near Lake Titicaca. Other andesite blocks appear to have been transported from quarries about 55 miles (88.5 km) away across the lake. Add all this together and the site becomes a mystery of architectural genius. How did they do it?

Archaeologists suggest the transport of such massive blocks of stone was made possible by a huge labor force working slowly over many, many years. Some suggest that the stone blocks were dragged up the steep incline to the site on ramps. Still others suggest alien intervention, stating that no amount of human labor could have possibly moved these massive megaliths from so far away, and then cut and arranged them with such preternatural precision. It certainly seems improbable that such a complicated endeavor could have been accomplished by an ancient and presumably primitive civilization. Even with today's technology, such a construction would be difficult, to say the very least. It would involve a knowledge of astronomy, masonry, and mathematics, among other things, and would require intense and protracted planning. Yet no records of such knowledge or planning have ever been found at the site. Was this ancient culture truly as primitive as some historians would have us believe?

At the southeastern point of the Polynesian triangle in the Pacific Ocean sits the volcanic island of Rapa Nui, better known as Easter Island. Considered the most remote inhabited island in the world, Easter Island is also home to hundreds of huge stone statues called *moai*, which were carved between 1100 and 1680 CE. There are a total of 887 of these monolithic statues, some with just heads, others with torsos, and a few complete from head to toe. Carved out of solidified volcanic ash, or *tuff*, the moai were formed with stone chisels and sculpted by many people over the period of about a year. According to local legend and lore, the statues represent the deceased ancestral lines of those living on the island. The largest moai weighs 82 tons, and several others come close to that weight. Yet many of these statues—at least a quarter of them—had been moved from the quarry at Rano Raraku, where the ash and tuff they were made from origi-nated. Although theories abound as to how the statues were shaped, carved, constructed, and raised, there is no definitive theory as to how they were moved. Interestingly, the Rapanui myths and traditions say it was *mana*, or a spiritual power, that literally "walked" the moai from the quarry to their various destinations on the island.

The famed site of Stonehenge, a massive stone circle in Wiltshire County, England, is one of many henge monuments built during the Neolithic and Bronze Ages in England. (Henges are Neolithic earth-work sites that contain a ditch and a ring bank exterior to the ditch. Avebury in England is another famed henge site.) Stonehenge may have been an ancient burial site, according to a May 29, 2008, Associated Press article titled "Study: Stonehenge was a burial site for centuries," Cremated remains found at the henge site date back as early as 3000 BCE, and ritual burials may have continued for the next 500 years.

Today, we know that Stonehenge was also a complex astronomical laboratory, in addition to being a site of religious ritual, and it remains a place of reverence even today. Yet there is no definitive theory as to how the builders of Stonehenge moved or constructed the site's blue-stones, which most likely came from the Prescelly Mountains, some 240 miles (386 km) away in Southwestern Wales. The original small bluestones weighed up to 4 tons, and 80 stones in all comprised the henge. Stonehenge was actually built in stages, the last known con-struction occurring in approximately 1600 BCE. It is possible that the Neolithic technology at that time could have created such a structure, but because the original builders left no written records, we still can-not be sure who built it, how they built it, and what they built it for.

Manual labor could have hewn these stones, and certainly erected them, although it would have taken a great deal of time and manpow-er. How the stones managed to get to the henge site from 240 miles (386 km) away is a whole other ballgame. Were they dragged on some kind of rollers, loaded onto barges, sailed up the Rivers Avon and Fromme, and then hauled to the henge site? The large sarsen stones that make up the outer circle weigh up to 50 tons each and may have came from Marlborough Downs, approximately 20 miles (32 km) to the north. How did these massive stones get there?

Perhaps the most widely known and most mysterious of all the stone edifices is the Pyramid at Giza, Egypt. Also known as the Pyramid of

Khufu or the Pyramid of Cheops, it is one of the seven wonders of the ancient world, and a mystery of mysteries for those seeking an understanding of ancient knowledge. The huge pyramid was constructed over a period of 15 to 20 years, ending in 2560 BCE, and may have served as a tomb for the Egyptian pharaoh Khufu. But what makes the structure so awe-inspiring is the fact that the massive pyramid is made up of some 2.3 million limestone blocks transported from nearby quarries, and that the workmanship is said to be so accurate that the four sides of the base have an average error of 2.3 inches (58 mm). The design of the pyramid and its precise measurements have led many Egyptologists and historians to believe it was intended as an homage to the number *pi*.

But there is still controversy and debate over how this pyramid and many others like it—for example, those built by the Mayans and other Mesoamerican civilizations—were built, and who, exactly, built them. In his book *The Great Pyramid: Ancient Egypt Revisited*, John Romer suggests that the materials used to build the pyramid, which included 8,000 tons of granite and 500,000 tons of mortar, were cut and gathered and then carried by boat up and down the Nile River to the site. Laborers may have used the ancient Egyptian technique of hammering wood wedges into the stones and then soaking the stones with water, which would cause the wedges to expand enough to break the stones. Most experts agree the stones were either carried or lifted from the quarries to the site, but precisely *how* they were carried or lifted is unknown. Perhaps the ancients made use of a skill we have long since forgotten or ignored—a skill that involves not hard, grueling, blood-sweat-and-tears labor, pullies, hydraulic lifts, counterweights, or ramps, but something quite different: sound.

A Sound Theory

The concept of using sound to levitate or move solid objects is not a new one. Indeed, we wrote extensively about this in our book *The Resonance Key*: "Quite simply, an acoustic levitator is nothing more than a resonance machine of sorts—a way of introducing two opposing sound frequencies with interfering sound waves, thus creating a resonant zone that allows the levitation to occur. Theoretically, to move a levitating object, simply change or alter the two sound waves and tweak accordingly." We generally don't think of sound as having a tangible or material presence. We can hear it, but certainly we cannot touch it or feel it. But think of the times you've heard a car driving by with the radio blasting, the bass turned up high and booming so loudly that it felt as though the sound were coming from inside your car. Or think of someone going to the doctor to have a kidney stone destroyed by a powerful ultrasound machine. Sound *does* have a physical presence, in the form of the sound waves that can affect the environment and the human body. Scientists have successfully used the properties of sound to cause heavy gases, liquids, and even solid objects (such as spiders, goldfish, and mice) to float in the air. A quick Google search for sonic levitation will turn up a variety of YouTube videos showing water droplets, small critters, and various objects held in suspended animation between two metal objects: a transducer and a reflector. These objects often have concave surfaces to keep the sound waves focused. The sound waves simply move away from the transducer and bounce off of the reflector. When the transducer is placed at the right distance from the reflector, a *standing wave* (a wave that remains in constant position) is created; depending on the orientation of the wave in relation to the pull of gravity, an object in one of the *nodes* of a standing wave—the points where the wave has minimal amplitude—will react as if gravity did not exist and appear to float between the transducer and the reflector.

If sonic levitation is possible for small objects, could it be possible for large objects, as well—even massive stone blocks weighing many tons? There is no proof that this has ever been done, but we do have some eyewitness reports of just such a theory being put into practice. We found one account in the book *The Lost Techniques* by Swedish civil engineer Henry Kjelson. Kjelson writes of the experience of a friend of his, a certain Dr. Jarl, who was asked to go to a remote area of Tibet to tend to a high Lama. While there, he was taken to a field and shown first-hand how the Tibetan monks levitated large objects. The monks began to play trumpet-like instruments while others beat on drums in front of a large stone slab with a hollowed out central cavity, in which a smaller stone had been placed. Nothing happened at first, but as the tempo increased, the stone in the central cavity began to sway, and then hurled itself into the air and landed outside a cave entrance, the exact place the monks had intended it to land. Dr. Jarl watched this process repeated over and over again as the monks moved up to five or six blocks each hour using this method. A similar demonstration was allegedly witnessed by an Austrian filmmaker known only as "Linauer" in the 1930s, this time in a remote part of Northern Tibet. The monks here used a type of gong made up of various metal alloys with a soft gold center. Another metal stringed instrument accompanied it, "played" by the vibrations of the gong. The sound of these instruments was directed toward large screens intended to amplify or direct the sound to move large blocks of stone.

Perhaps the type of stone has a bearing on what kind of sound and frequency is needed. For example, granite is a composite stone, which might make finding a resonant "match" more difficult, while limestone is a much simpler stone. Each type of rock used in the construction of all of these megaliths, pyramids, and other huge structures has its own resonant signature. Even the earth itself has its own resonant frequencies, the most famous of these being the Schumann Resonance of 7.83 Hz. Nikola Tesla used the earth resonances in much of his groundbreaking work in electromagnetic energy and wireless transmission of electricity.

Knowledge of harmonics and sound might have allowed these ancient civilizations to work with exact sound combinations to create the desired result, levitation. In the case of the Great Pyramid at Giza, the earth's own energy field may have played a huge role in not only how the pyramid was built, but its location, as well. The Great Pyramid has interior walls that are constructed of rose granite, which is known for its resonant qualities. Acoustic experiments by engineers in the upper chamber revealed a resonant frequency at 121 Hz, and 117 Hz inside the chamber's granite box. The interactions between the two slightly different frequencies created a frequency that almost matched that of the human heartbeat. Many visitors and researchers at the Giza Pyramid report amazing resonant properties in the King's Chamber in particular, which resonates to an F-sharp chord, and the Chamber Coffer, which resonates to an A, the minor third of F-sharp. Experiments by NASA consultant Tom Danley showed that the *standing frequencies* (frequencies that remain constant when no interference exists) within the five interior rooms came to 16 Hz, an infrasonic level below the threshold of human hearing. Danley then theorized that the pyramid's dimensions, combined with the materials it is made of, intentionally served to amplify sound in the King's Chamber. Again, the frequency pattern matched the tonal structure of the F-sharp chord. In his book *The Giza Power Plant*, Chris Dunn writes about his own research in the chamber, and suggests that the pyramid may have been originally constructed with a sonic purpose. Other pyramid experts propose that this resonant "matching" created a sound-based energy that was used for healing. Perhaps the Pyramid at Giza was a giant sound transmitter and receiver, using earth's resonances outside, and the intricately designed acoustical properties inside.

From Egypt to Florida

A more modern example of how sound may have been used to build a massive stone structure is found in Homestead, Florida, the site of the Coral Castle. Considered the life's work of Latvian immigrant Edward Leedskanin, the Coral Castle is a literal castle made of coral, with massive stones perched upon high walls, a huge 28-ton obelisk, a 9-ton swinging gate, and walls consisting of blocks weighing several tons each. Leedskanin began building the castle in 1920, cutting, transporting, shaping, and arranging more than 1,020 tons of coral himself until he died in 1951. Although some of his neighbors claimed they saw Leedskanin transporting blocks of coral by truck, nobody ever saw him raising the blocks to make the castle. Leedskanin claimed that he had found the key to the building of the pyramids using everyday weights and levers. However, he was also obsessed with magnets and earth energies, and some of his writings contained references to a "magnetic current," and cryptically allude to his ability to levitate objects. The idea that this slight man lifted massive blocks of coral with some type of electromagnetic current or frequency persists to this day.

Even Stonehenge has recently required its own resonant reputation after new research shows that the engineering of the standing stones may have been intended to create the acoustic conditions for amplifying sounds within the henge, possibly even for purposes of putting someone in a trance or altered state of consciousness. In a January 2009 article for *UK Telegraph*, university professor Rupert Till showed that the stones might have been constructed for the purposes of trance dancing, repetitive movements such as whirling or rocking. With a colleague, Dr. Bruno Frazenda, he not only conducted computerized sound experimentation to prove his theory, but actually visited a concrete full-size replica of Stonehenge and used computer-based acoustic analysis software to create sounds and music. He and his colleague walked around the interior of the henge, popping balloons in order to capture the *impulse response* of the stone circle. (An impulse response consists of all the paths taken by a sound between its source and a microphone placed a few yards away, resulting in a kind of acoustic fingerprint.) The result was akin to what happens when you run a wet finger along the rim of a wine glass: it dramatically amplified the original sound in such a way that it might have put those within earshot into a trance state.

In another article for MSNBC.com's January 7, 2008 edition, Rossella Lorenzi writes about the Till experiments, but also discusses previous research by artist and archaeologist Aaron Watson that corroborated Till's findings. Watson specializes in the study of Neolithic monuments and theorized from his own Stonehenge research that "the monument's builders knew how to direct the movement of sound." The standing stones amplify high-frequency sounds such as human voices, whereas low-frequency sounds such as drumming reverberate off of the stones and can then be heard from great distances. It was all designed, as Watson states, to create a "dynamic multisensory experience."

Was this an accidental outcome of the design, or was it intentional? Did these ancient builders truly understand the power of sound, frequency, vibration, and resonance? Another great monument—the El Castillo pyramid at the Maya ruins of Chichen-Itza in Mexico— suggests that many ancient civilizations did understand this power, and knew just how to harness it for ritual purposes. Chichen-Itza is a large pre-Columbian archaeological site located in the northern center of the Yucatán Peninsula. The El Castillo pyramid is a step pyramid of square terraces with stairways up each of the four sides to a temple at the very top. On the spring and autumn equinox, at the rising and setting of the sun, the corner of the structure casts a shadow in the shape of a plumed serpent—Kukulcan, or Quetzalcoatl—along the west side of the north staircase. (Quetzalcoatl was a highly revered Mesoamerican deity, and its iconography has been found throughout the Mayan and Aztec empires.) On these two annual occasions, the shadows from the corner tiers slither down the northern side of the pyramid with the sun's movement to the serpent's head at the base.

Some visitors to El Castillo claim that a handclap produces a strange echo that sounds very similar to the chirping of the Quetzal bird. By 2003, enough attention had been given to this strange echo that it prompted four Belgian researchers to take a more scientific approach to the connection. The resulting study was submitted to the December 2004 issue of the *Journal of the Acoustical Society of America*. The team, led by Nico F. Declercq and Joris Degrieck of the Soete Laboratory at the Department of Mechanical Construction and Production at Ghent University in Belgium, conducted a theoretical study of the special acoustic effects of the El Castillo staircase, where the handclap/bird echo was reported. Though the team already suspected that the bird chirp sound was produced by a normal phenomenon called *Bragg scattering*, no one had ever taken the time to actually demonstrate it at the actual site. Ultimately, the team examined the recorded signals of a direct echo from a delta pulse against a recorded signal of a Quetzal bird in the forest, and a normalized recorded signal of the pyramid echo. Their study involved comparisons with sonograms, measuring frequencies of the various sounds—even the "raindrop effect," which occurs when people climb the pyramid stairs and their shoes produce sound pulses containing all the frequencies. They performed various experiments at the site under different weather conditions to test the relationship between the speed of the sound and temperature variations. Although the experiments bore out the scientists' suspicions regarding Bragg scattering, the fact that they even thought to do this kind of study is indicative of the universal desire to understand and appropriate sound and resonance as a way of effecting physiological and environmental changes. Is it really reasonable to assume that the builders of all these amazing sites came upon these connections by accident?

Cuts Like a Knife

Although we've placed a great deal of emphasis on how sonic levitation might have been used to lift heavy objects, alter human consciousness, or engender trance states, it may have also been used in the stone-cutting process. Consider just how difficult the precise cutting and measuring of these stone blocks would have been for civilizations that lacked the kind of technologically advanced power tools that we take for granted. They may have had access to the most powerful tool of all, a kind of sonic jackhammer that could cut through concrete, stone, asphalt, and hard materials of every sort.

NASA has taken both sonic levitation and sonic positioning (using sound to move solid objects into different positions) seriously enough to develop a real sonic jackhammer, as reported in NASA's May 1, 2005 *Tech Briefs*. A small-scale prototype was actually demonstrated before the public. The jackhammer combines the use of ultrasonic and sonic vibrations to cut through materials, just as a drill would penetrate cement. Though this jackhammer was only a prototype, perhaps those civilizations that came long before us knew how to do this very thing *without* any need of a machine or device. Perhaps the use of music, chanting, drumming, and a general understanding of the earth's electromagnetic field and resonances was enough to allow them to create the most awe-inspiring edifices on earth, all with nothing more than the power of sound.

Bibliography

Declerg, Nico F. and Joris Degrieck, Rudy Briers, Oswald LeRoy. "A theoretical study of special acoustic effects caused by the staircase of the El Castillo pyramid at the Maya Ruins of Chichen-Itza in Mexico." *Journal of Acoustical Society of America.* Issue 116, December 2004.

Dunn, Christopher. *The Giza Power Plant: Technologies of Ancient Egypt."* Rochester, Vt.: Bear & Company, 1998.

Jones, Marie D. and Larry Flaxman. *The Resonance Key: Exploring the Links Between Vibration, Consciousness and the Zero Point Grid.* Franklin Lakes, NJ: New Page Books, 2009.

Kenyon, J. Douglas, Editor. *Forbidden History: Prehistoric Technologies, Extraterrestrial Intervention, and the Suppressed Origins of Civilization.* Rochester, Vt.: Bear & Company, 2005.

———. *Forbidden Science: From Ancient Technologies to Free Energy.* Rochester, Vt.: Bear & Company, 2008.

Romer, John. *The Great Pyramid: Ancient Egypt Revisited.* Cambridge, UK: Cambridge University Press, 2007.

Schmid, Randolph E. "Study: Stonehenge was a burial site for centuries." Associated Press. Retrieved May 29, 2008. *www.usatoday.com/tech/science/2008-05-29-stonehenge-burial-site_N.htm.*

von Däniken, Erich. *Twilight of the Gods: The Mayan Calendar and the Return of the Extraterrestrials.* Franklin Lakes, NJ: New Page Books, 2010.

Oppenheimer's Iron Thunderbolt: Evidence of Ancient Nuclear Weapons

By Micah A. Hanks

The exchange of knowledge between master and student is a timeless expression of the accumulation of human insight. Like some clandestine secret handed from the magi of old down to a new generation of protégés, the wisdom of the ancients is something that many spend their entire lives seeking. This is because they know that this wisdom of the past is of inestimable value to future generations. Whether it be Sun Tzu's treatises on the art of waging war, or the once alchemical agents that form the basis of our modern sciences, we look to the past to learn about ourselves and how to better our existence both today and in the future. The details imparted to us in the particular exchange between master and student that we will be examining here—though obscure at best—will introduce us to unforeseen possibilities that might change our very perspective regarding who we once were, who we are now, and, perhaps most importantly, what we may become.

To begin at what might have been one story's ending, we arrive at the dawn of the atomic age, in the years immediately following World War II. This most dire of modern global conflicts was considered the "war that would end all wars." Of course, ending this conflict came at a horrible cost: the loss of civilian life on a tremendous scale with what all assumed was the first use in Earth's history of nuclear weapons during wartime.

On the morning of August 6, 1945, at approximately 8:15 a.m. Japan time, the Boeing B-29 Superfortress bomber *Enola Gay* had entered airspace directly above Hiroshima, where it dropped a free-fall explosive known to history by the nickname "Little Boy." Within one minute, the bomb detonated over the city at an altitude of approximately 1,900 feet (579 m).[1] No

117

large-scale enemy raid had occurred; a small fleet of U.S. aircraft had been detected and subsequently ignored by early warning radar. For this reason, it was hours before officers from the Japanese General Staff arrived to investigate why all the radio stations in Hiroshima had gone silent.[2] Upon arriving within sight of the city, pilots were stunned to see only a vast pillar of smoke rising over the area. Announcers in broadcasts overheard by Allied sources reported that, "[t]he impact of the bomb was so terrific that practically all living things—human and animal—were literally seared to death by the tremendous heat and pressure set up by the blast. All the dead and injured were burned beyond recognition. Those outdoors were burned to death, while those indoors were killed by the indescribable pressure and heat."[3]

This attack was followed by a similar blast that leveled the city of Nagasaki to the southwest, prompting Japan's surrender and thus ending the Second World War. As has been argued many times with due controversy since the end of the conflict, war always results in death, but killing on the scale seen in the days leading up to Japan's surrender also restored peace to the world...at least for a while. Soon, however, the lingering fear that other countries—especially emerging superpowers such as the Soviet Union—would build their own atomic arsenals presented a terrifying new threat.

Another result of humanity's entry into the atomic age was the utter fascination with which the public regarded these weapons and their development. As information about the Manhattan Project became public knowledge, J. Robert Oppenheimer, dubbed the father of the atomic bomb for his involvement in the project, became something of a celebrity, with his face emblazoned across the covers of American magazines and newspapers. Oppenheimer would also begin lecturing about the scientific merits of this emerging nuclear technology, as well as the necessity for alliances with different countries around the world, from which all could reap the benefit of mutual protection from the threat of nuclear arms in the wrong hands.

Of course, the blasts at Hiroshima and Nagasaki hadn't been the first of their kind. Oppenheimer had been among those at the famous test at Alamogordo, where the first successful detonation of a nuclear weapon (given the nickname "Trinity" by Oppenheimer) had occurred. Much later in 1965, Oppenheimer recalled his feelings from that occasion during a NBC television appearance, saying that, "We knew the world would not be the same. A few people laughed, a few people cried, most people were silent. I remembered the line from the Hindu scripture, the Bhagavad-Gita...'Now, I am become Death, the destroyer of worlds.' I suppose we all thought that one way or another."[4]

Though Oppenheimer was the so-called father of modern nuclear weapons, there are some rather strange circumstances involving this brilliant physicist that have resulted in questions as to whether the test at Alamogordo was indeed the first nuclear detonation in Earth's history. On one occasion, during a seminar Oppenheimer was giving at Rochester University on the development of nuclear weapons, a college student asked if the blast at Alamogordo had been the first of its kind. Oppenheimer replied rather strangely by saying, "Well, yes, in modern times." This statement is troubling for a number of reasons. For one, Oppenheimer seems to be intimating that there had been other nuclear explosions in the past that he knew about. Even if this were indeed found to be the case, where could any such blast have occurred, and who would have been responsible for it? Since Oppenheimer specifically referenced "modern times," it would seem that something akin to the blasts at Alamogordo, Hiroshima, and Nagasaki had once transpired at some point *earlier* in Earth's history.

Logic would tell us, however, that it's very unlikely that an ancient technology ever succeeded in harnessing the power of the atom as we have done in modern times. Some say that Oppenheimer was referencing the mysterious blast that occurred over Tunguska, a remote part of modern-day Russia, in 1908. This explosion, however, was not the result of a man-made device, nor was it even a nuclear blast, as it has since been determined that the concentration of radioactive isotopes in the blast area after the incident did not match the expected levels following a nuclear explosion.[5] So what, then, was Oppenheimer referring to? Did the brilliant physicist really make this unsettling allusion to a student at Rochester during such a lecture? If so, what are the implications? The surprising answers lie hidden deep within some of the late physicist's more esoteric interests, where we begin to see that he may have been referencing an event that occurred much earlier.

It is well known that Oppenheimer was well-versed in the Vedic epics of India, particularly given his propensity to publicly quote Hindu scripture such as the *Bhagavad-Gita*. Oppenheimer was also known to give copies of the *Bhagavad-Gita* to friends as gifts, in addition to keeping a copy of the text on the bookshelf by his desk.[6] According to British journalist Nilesh Prashar, at the funeral of U.S. President Franklin Roosevelt, Oppenheimer read an excerpt from the holy text, which states in part, "Man is a creature whose substance is faith, what his faith is, he is." Oppenheimer also cited the volume as being among his 10 favorite and most influential spiritual books during an interview in 1963.[7]

The *Bhagavad-Gita* is merely one part of the greater epic known as the *Mahabharata*, and one of two manuscripts (along with the Ramayana) that constitute the major Sanskrit epics of India. Of particular relevance to the discussion of nuclear weapons and their potential existence in ancient times, we find mention of something curious in the *Mahabharata*—specifically, during the epic battle said to have taken place between rival nations of the ancient world. If we accept this as a literal account of an armed conflict that took place in ancient times, we are left with the curious mention of a variety of weapons which seem to resemble modern firearms, advanced aircraft, and even explosives with devastating potential that resemble nuclear armaments. The late Alexander Gorbovsky, who served as an expert at the Russian Munitions Agency, wrote about this in his 1986 article "Riddles of Ancient History," where he mentions references to a "terrible weapon" in the *Mahabharata*. "Regrettably, in our age of the atomic bomb, the description of this weapon exploding will not appear to be an exaggeration."[8] Following is the passage to which Gorbovsky is referring. Despite having been authored almost 3,000 years ago, it seems to describe something all too familiar to us today:

[A] blazing shaft possessed of the effulgence of a smokeless fire (was) let off.... This makes the bodies of the dead unidentifiable.... The survivors lose their nails and hair, and their food becomes unfit for eating. For several subsequent years the Sun, the stars and the sky remain shrouded with clouds and bad weather.

The weapon described here, variously referred to in the text as the Weapon of Brahma, the Flame of Indra, or the Iron Thunderbolt, causes various kinds of ailments to living beings, in addition to atmospheric damage. During the early 1960s, it was shown that high-altitude testing with megaton nuclear explosives resulted in the creation of artificial belts of radiation in space. Although it is uncertain whether such radiation belts would cause the "clouds and bad weather" described in the *Mahabharata*, great concern about long-term atmospheric effects have been expressed by the likes of Sir Bernard Lovell, the director of the Radio Astronomy Laboratories at Jodrell Bank Center for Astrophysics.[9] The late Herman Hoerlin, a leading expert on the physics of high-altitude nuclear detonations, also noted in a 1976 study that "recent studies of a possible relationship between certain auroral displays in the north and weather do not exclude the hypothetical possibility of artificial weather-modification by nuclear energy releases."[10] On a greater scale, however, it was thought that the effects of a full-blown nuclear holocaust could result in a *nuclear winter*, in which the smoke and soot filling the air following the detonation would block sunlight, thus reducing temperatures over large areas or even worldwide. Citing a 2006 study on the potential devastation following a nuclear winter, *Science Daily* reported that "even a small-scale, regional nuclear war could produce as many direct fatalities as all of World War II and disrupt the global climate for a decade or more, with environmental effects that could be devastating for everyone on Earth.[11]

The descriptions of this massive weapon in the *Mahabharata* are thought to indicate some kind of projectile, perhaps lending to its description as a "bolt" that strikes locations from above:

> [It was] a single projectile charged with all the power of the Universe. An incandescent column of smoke and flame as bright as the thousand suns rose in all its splendor...it was an unknown weapon, an iron thunderbolt, a gigantic messenger of death, which reduced to ashes the entire race of the Vrishnis and the Andhakas.

Soldiers then "throw themselves into streams to wash themselves and their equipment."[12] Interestingly, this line is reminiscent of individuals attempting to ward off the effects of radiation poisoning. According to the Merck Manual online medical library, initial treatment for exposure to radiation involves careful removal and storage of the individual's clothing (to aid in preventing further contamination), followed by bathing wounded areas and then the rest of the skin.[13]

This portion of the *Mahabharata* appears to describe an event that bears more than a passing resemblance to what we now know of modern nuclear weapons and their attendant dangers. But is it reasonable to infer that ancient nuclear wars were indeed occurring on Earth prior to civilization as we know it today, based solely on the descriptions given in an ancient Sanskrit holy text? Arguably, some portions of the *Mahabharata*, much like the epics of other ancient cultures, are necessarily comprised of fantastical narratives that incorporate the mythologies, values, cultures, and imaginations of its author, all presented as direct reportage. Take, for instance, the remarkable flying craft known as *vimanas* that were described in some detail in many of the Sanskrit legends. These craft resemble everything from modern aircraft to popular depictions of flying saucers and UFOs. Could there be any factual basis for such things existing thousands of years ago, especially when descriptions of their capabilities seem to exceed what modern avionics has achieved? Remarkably, the intricacies pertaining to the design and mechanics of these craft are described at various times throughout the Vedas, with mention of "engines" that consist of an iron enclosure housing mercury or a similar substance that, when stimulated in some way (electrically, perhaps), could cause a vortex to occur within the swirling liquid metal, thus manifesting a strange energy source capable of propelling these flying vehicles to great altitudes at tremendous speeds.

Though remarkable and imaginative, these sorts of descriptions—replete with details that appear to describe a technologically advanced society—have prompted many a modern researcher to consider whether the *Vedas* do indeed contain evidence of some ancient, advanced society. Imagine if they were the last remaining written accounts of some even older civilization which, though forgotten today, was remembered well enough thousands of years ago that attempts were made at cataloguing its various innovations. Perhaps this monumental task was undertaken by people who themselves had only a vague remembrance of these earlier exploits—and even less knowledge of the technology they were attempting to document.

One researcher who has carefully and exhaustively examined the technology depicted in the *Vedas* is Peter Thomson, an instructor at Napier University in Edinburgh who has authored books and articles on everything from green energy, holistic diets, and computer systems that integrate biological life forms, to attempts at finding credible evidence for ancient civilizations and prehistoric nuclear weapons. In his article "Unexplained Flying Vehicles" on his Web site, Thomson describes his research into what he calls a *charged sheath vortex*, a device inspired by and designed to operate based on the aforementioned descriptions of a "swirling mercury engine" from the Sanskrit epics. (Incidentally, this is very similar to the "implosion technology" developed by Austrian inventor Viktor Schauberger in the 1920s and '30s, which itself was based on tornado-like *fluidic vortices*, or whirlpools, and similar vortex movements found in nature.[14]) Regarding the appearance of such advanced concepts in ancient texts, Thomson states the following:

> There is simply too much consistent and working technology in [the Vedas]. These stories can only be fragments of history from the distant past. Twisted, altered, misremembered, but still enough technology remains in these accounts to say with a lot of certainty, we are not the first technological civilization on this planet.[15]

Granted, it may require a suspension of disbelief for anyone to assume that the *Vedas*, as Thomson writes, "can only be fragments of history from the distant past." After all, the *Vedas* could certainly be discussing other things just as easily, especially in the absence of any scientific evidence of ancient technological innovations on par with modern atomic weaponry. However, according to Thomson, the finest evidence for advanced technology exists not in these fascinating descriptions of aviation and engineering innovations in the *Vedas*, but instead in our planet's archaeological, geological, and climate data.

For instance, the ability to manipulate our environment using technology involves the acquisition and practical use of essential metals such as copper, lead, tin, and iron. Thomson notes that mining for such metals, along with the ensuing smelting and processing of usable quantities, resulted in traces that could be observed in glacial deposits around the globe, relative to the time period when such industrialization began. Thomson argues in his article that the industrial development of ancient Greek and Roman societies left a clear signature out, stating that nuclear fission could also be traced in such a way. Any evidence of a nuclear war and the ensuing period of nuclear winter would likely be found within the cores of coral reefs, formed out of calcium carbonate secreted by marine organisms over the centuries, and in the beds of rivers and lakes left undisturbed for long periods of time.[16] Other evidence that would be observable in the geological record might include the extinction of large swaths of animal populations in various regions and habitats, as well as stone and sand melted by the sudden, intense heat at the site of an explosion, resulting in the formation of glass, called *trinitite*. If we were to find evidence of such conditions spanning a relatively short period of time in geological history, we might indeed have a case not only for ancient civilizations, but also, given the right sort of evidence, perhaps even for a clearly traceable nuclear event—or even several of them—in prehistory.

Remarkable though it may seem, many of these criteria *have* been found, most coinciding with the end of the last Ice Age. Thomson notes evidence of expected increases in traces of metals such as iron and copper; of the extinction resulting from an intelligent species proliferating and encroaching on the habitat of megafauna in the locale; of uranium concentrations in coral; and even of the presence of glasslike fused sand and stone at a number of ancient sites. This information serves as the rationale for a bold emerging hypothesis that perhaps a technologically advanced civilization did exist in ancient times. Thomson argues that

[this civilization] mined and smelted copper, lead, tin and almost certainly iron...and destroyed all the megafauna predators from all continents.... It developed a nuclear capability and then destroyed itself in a nuclear holocaust...followed by a nuclear winter that returned the world to an ice age for a further 1000 years.[17]

Speaking more specifically, physical evidence for a nuclear event, or possibly a series of them, exists, as well. A paper written by scientists William Topping and Richard B. Firestone states that anomalous radiocarbon readings were recovered from the Great Lakes region of North America: "The entire Great Lakes region (and beyond) was subjected to particle bombardment and a catastrophic nuclear irradiation that produced secondary thermal neutrons from cosmic ray interactions."[18] Granted, the event to which the authors refer took place in Paleo-Indian times. Moreover, because conventional wisdom holds that nuclear devices simply couldn't have existed so long ago, the authors propose instead the theory that a supernova was likely to blame: "The size of the initial catastrophe may be too large for a solar flare," they say, although a "significantly powerful nearby supernovae or cosmic ray jet could account for it."[19] Obviously, this is only a theory, and as such it does not definitively prove that such natural phenomena caused a nuclear event in ancient times. But left to consider the troubling alternative—namely, that ancient humans may have possessed a greater degree of technical proficiency—what are we to think of explanations that point to the existence of ancient nuclear weapons? Despite the controversy that rages between these two polar opposite positions, one thing is obvious: a nuclear event or events apparently *did* take place in ancient times, and proof of this *does* exist. Regarding a technological *primum movens* behind the nuclear event(s) in question, however, there may indeed be evidence that brings us to an even more unsettling conclusion involving our ancient ancestors and what dreadful technology they may have possessed— despite what conventional history has taught us for so long.

The excavations of the ancient cities in the Indus River Valley have for years hinted at evidence of something curious and potentially frightening. The cities of Harrappa and Mohenjo-Daro in particular (both in modern-day Pakistan) boast a number of anomalies, beginning with their curiously advanced technologies. Of Mohenjo-Daro the late professor Ahmad Hasan Dani said that the city, at the peak of its development more than 3,000 years ago, was likely the most developed and highly advanced city in all of South Asia.[20] And yet, the cities in this region seemed to have suffered a rather sudden catastrophe at some point in their history. Despite the kind of innovation and success they had once seen, something managed to destroy them while they were in their prime. Theories of their demise focused primarily on flooding of the Indus River. Even as recently as 2010, devastating floods that resulted from several months of heavy rain resulted in widespread destruction and the deaths of more than 2,000 people throughout the region.[21] But flooding, even of this magnitude, might not account for the other sorts of anomalies found at Mohenjo-Daro and Harrappa.

For instance, researcher Philip Coppens has written about radioactivity in the region that was purportedly high enough even in modern times that birth defects and cancer have seen a much higher incidence in parts of the region, prompting the Indian government to impose restricted access to certain areas. Some of this might be due in part to negligence at a power facility in the region, from which contaminated wood was brought into the surrounding community and burned, thereby causing at least some of the radioactivity. What cannot be argued, however, is that "a layer of radioactive ash was indeed found in Rajasthan, India," as Coppens notes, covering a far wider area than isolated incidents of contamination would account for. In fact, Coppens states specifically that the radioactivity "covered a three-square mile (5-sq km) area, ten miles (16 km) west of Jodhpur."[22]

But heightened levels of radioactivity in the region are only one indicator of what may have occurred around Harrappa and Mohenjo-Daro thousands of years ago. Alexander Gorbovsky also mentioned the discovery of human remains that contained unusual levels of radiation at the Mohenjo-Daro site. This idea, among others, has been examined by explorer and researcher Jonathan Gray, who discussed such things in his book *Dead Men's Secrets*. The excavations of early Mohenjo-Daro revealed skeletons of people who, curiously, were found lying in the streets in a similar fashion to the casualties of Pompeii. Gray suggests that the skeletons, some of which were allegedly found holding hands, "are still among the most radioactive that have ever been found, on a par with those of Hiroshima and Nagasaki."[23] Gray also notes that the Mohenjo-Daro site boasts a 150-foot (46-m) epicenter, where "everything was crystallized, fused or melted," and that "180 feet (55 m) from the center the bricks are melted on [only] one side, indicating a blast."[24] What has been described here is the sort of sudden melting of solid matter, a process known as *vitrification*, which, as we surmised earlier, is something we'd expect to find at an ancient blast site. It is no surprise to learn that the vitrification of solids occurred not only at Hiroshima and Nagasaki, but also at the earlier explosion site where Oppenheimer and his associates witnessed the famous Trinity blast. Thus, our understanding of the name given to the "Alamogordo Glass" residue found in the aftermath of such explosions—*trinitite*—is made clear. What is not clear, however, is what the source of radioactivity and similar vitrification at ancient sites was. Some have suggested that the impact of a large meteorite might have caused the vitrification process if an explosion occurred in the aftermath; but if we recall the famous Tunguska blast of 1908 (the cause of which was likely a meteorite), we see that the levels of isotopic radioactivity following the blast were far too low to be consistent with a nuclear explosion. What the evidence found at these ancient sites seems to point to is not only a blast with tremendous destructive potential, like that at Tunguska, but also something that clearly resulted from a nuclear event, and which, curiously, seems to have been directed at specific targets such as Mohenjo-Daro. But even if a compelling case for ancient nuclear explosions and technology that involved atomic weaponry exists, as seems to be the case, we still must ask why so little evidence of the ancient civilizations that produced them remains today. If a highly advanced civilization existed thousands of years before our own, it seems reasonable to assume there would at least be *some* remnants of their technology still known about or in use somewhere in the world today, in the form of ancient structures, roadways, monuments, and/or other traceable evidence. This assumption may not be entirely accurate, either. In his book *The World Without Us,* journalist Alan Weisman ponders just how the great mark of civilization left by humanity would look as it disappeared, given a hypothetical situation in which there were no longer any people around to develop and maintain technology and infrastructure.[25] Weisman theorizes that most residential neighborhoods would be overtaken by flora, returning to the forested state that predated them by 500 years. By the time a few thousand years had passed, "the world would mostly look as it did before humanity came along—like a wilderness."[26] In his 2005 *Discover Magazine* article, titled "Earth Without People," Weisman presented a number of scenarios that showed just how quickly the forces of nature would erase evidence of civilization:

> The new wilderness would consume cities, much as the jungle of northern Guatemala consumed the Mayan pyramids and megalopolises of overlapping city-states. From 800 to 900 CE, a combination of drought and internecine warfare over dwindling farmland brought 2,000 years of civilization crashing down. Within 10 centuries, the jungle swallowed all.[27]

Weisman's research places the longevity of our infrastructure in rather sobering perspective. Even in major U.S. cities such as New York, he states, within a mere 100 years, oak and maple trees would begin to cover the landscape; it would be another 900 years, however, before landmarks such as the Hell Gate Bridge finally collapsed. But of all the lasting effects our species might have in the long term, Weisman notes that radioactivity leaking from nuclear sites such as the Indian Point nuclear reactors just north of Manhattan could continue for tens of thousands of years.[28] If we once again consider the possibility that someone had nuclear capabilities here on Earth long ago, perhaps it comes as no surprise that the best evidence we have for their existence is measurable level of radiation at those proposed nuclear blast sites, which remain even in the present day.

If we choose to accept the terrifying possibility that there really was a nuclear war on Earth sometime during our prehistory, the potential ramifications can tell us a great deal about our past; however, they also indicate much about who we are today. They indicate an aspect of our human nature—specifically, our propensity to destroy one another—that has been with us since the beginning of time, and though we've managed to evade impending crises and wholesale destruction thus far, the threat of what could await humankind if a full-on nuclear conflict ever occurred still lingers. Despite our certainty that our accomplishments will be remembered for all time, this legacy could very easily be undone, especially if we manage to jump-start the process of erasing ourselves from the geological record through the assured self-destruction that nuclear weapons promise. In a world where the threat of terrorism and dangers of this sort have become all too real, perhaps it is even more critical that we gain a deeper understanding of the mistakes of the past and perhaps even accept the possibility that our existence as we know it may not be the first of its kind.

J. Robert Oppenheimer seemed to know all this, and as we have now seen, it was no coincidence that he was so fascinated with the ancient texts of the *Mahabharata* and the *Bhagavad-Gita*. Similar knowledge has been expressed in other ancient texts, too. Even the great philosopher Plato surmised in his *Critias* dialogue, with the fabled and supposedly highly advanced city Atlantis as its focus, that "nine thousand was the sum of years which had elapsed since the war which was said to have taken place between those who dwelt outside the Pillars of Heracles and all who dwelt within them."[29] Indeed, it seems that wise men of both today and of ages past knew that something remarkable had occurred in our prehistory; but what we choose to do with this same knowledge, bestowed on us by masters such as Oppenheimer and Plato, remains to be seen. Oppenheimer himself must have wrestled with the terrible potentials that came along with the forbidden knowledge he unlocked. The secrets of the ancients—whose very existence here long ago was betrayed by their technology, unearthed in bits and pieces over the years—may also be the keys to a veritable Pandora's box. Unless we use them wisely, they could still unlock the certain destruction of our future and of humanity itself, which by all accounts *may have already been destroyed.*

Notes

1. Walker, Stephen. *Shockwave: Countdown to Hiroshima*. New York: Harper Perennial, 2006.

2. "The Story of Hiroshima: Instant Confusion." *Atomicarchive. com: Exploring the History, Science, and Consequences of the Atomic Bomb.* Web. Accessed June 20, 2011. *www.atomicarchive.com/ History/twocities/hiroshima/page10.shtml.*

3. "Destruction at Hiroshima." *Guardian Century Archives, Japanese reports.* Originally appeared Thursday, August 9, 1945. *http://century.guardian.co.uk/1940-1949/Story/0,127720,00.html.*

4. "The Decision to Drop the Bomb." Fred Freed (producer). J. Robert Oppenheimer (guest). New York: NBC White Paper, 1965.

5. Kolesnikov et al. "Finding of probable Tunguska Cosmic Body material: isotopic anomalies of carbon and hydrogen in peat." *Planetary and Space Science.* 47, 6–7 (June 1, 1999): 905–916.

6. Prashar, Nilesh. "The Bhagavad-Gita, Oppenheimer and nuclear weapons." *Hindu Voice UK.* July, 2006.

7. Ibid.

8. Gorbovsky, Alexander. "Riddles of Ancient History." *The Sputnik Magazine.* (Sept. 1986): 137.

9. Hoerlin, Herman. "United States High-Altitude Test Experiences: A Review Emphasizing the Impact on the Environment." Report LA-6405. Los Alamos Scientific Laboratory, October 1976.

10. Ibid.

11. "Regional Nuclear War Could Devastate Global Climate." *Science Daily: News & Articles in Science, Health, Environment & Technology. www.sciencedaily.com/releases/2006/ 12/061211090729.htm.*

12. Ganguli, Kisari Mohan (Translator). *The Mahabharata of Krishna-Dwaipayana Vyasa.* New Delhi: Munshiram Manoharlal, 2004.

13. "Radiation Exposure and Contamination: Injuries; Poisoning: Merck Manual Professional." Merck & Co., Inc. Pharmaceutical Products Company. *www.merckmanuals.com/professional/sec21/ch317/ ch317a.html.*

14. Lattacher, Siegbert. *Viktor Schauberger: Auf Den Spuren Des Legendären Naturforschers*. Steyr, Austria: Ennsthaler, 2003.

15. Thomson, Peter. "Unidentified Flying Vehicles." *www.peter-thomson.co.uk/anomalies/unidentified_flying_vehicles.html*.

16. Thomson, Peter. "The Record in the Ice: is there evidence for ancient civilization?" *www.peter-thomson.co.uk/anomalies/record_in_the_ice.html*.

17. Ibid.

18. Firestone, Richard B. and William Topping. "Terrestrial Evidence of a Nuclear Catastrophy in Paleoindian Times." *Mammoth Trumpet Magazine* (March 2001).

19. Ibid.

20. Dani, Ahmad Hasan. "Critical Assessment of Recent Evidence on Mohenjo-daro." Second International Symposium on Mohenjo-daro. Author lecture. February 24–27, 1992.

21. "Pakistan floods: World Bank to lend $900m for recovery." BBC News Online. *www.bbc.co.uk/news/world-south-asia-10994989*.

22. Coppens, Philip. "Best Evidence?" *www.philipcoppens.com/bestevidence.html*.

23. Gray, Jonathan. *Dead Men's Secrets: Tantalising Hints of a Lost Super Race*. Bloomington, IN: AuthorHouse, 2004.

24. Ibid.

25. Weisman, Alan. *The World Without Us*. New York: Thomas Dunne /St. Martin's, 2007.

26. Weisman, Alan. "Earth Without People." *Discover Magazine*. http://discovermagazine.com/2005/feb/earth-without-people/.

27. Ibid.

28. Ibid.

29. Jowett, Benjamin (translator). *Critias, by Plato*. MIT Classics Subdomain. http://classics.mit.edu/Plato/critias.html.

From the Pyramids to the Pentagon: The U.S. Government and Ancient Mysteries

By Nick Redfern

That government agencies around the world have, for decades, exhibited deep interest in and fascination with ancient artifacts and religious mysteries, is not a matter of any doubt at all. For example, it is an established and undeniable fact that Adolf Hitler and many of his cronies, including Rudolf Hess, Otto Rahn, Heinrich Himmler, and Walther Darré, were profoundly intrigued by such issues. Hitler himself had nothing less than a full-blown obsession with the fabled spear or lance—the so-called Spear of Destiny—that supposedly pierced the body of Jesus during the crucifixion. The reason for that obsession: to secure the spear and harness its mysterious might as a weapon to use against Allied forces. However, as the account goes, Hitler utterly failed in his quest, and as the conflict of 1939–1945 came to an end, the spear eventually came into the hands of General George Patton. According to legend, attempting to use the spear for negative purposes or even recklessly losing it was to guarantee one's demise—a prophecy that was apparently fulfilled when Hitler killed himself as the Nazi regime collapsed around him in 1945.

The Spear of Destiny, about which Adolf Hitler and high-ranking Nazis during the Second World War were so obsessed. Painting by Fra Angelico, circa 1437–1446.

As for Otto Rahn, who made his mark in a wing of Germany's greatly feared SS, he spent a significant period of time deeply engaged in a quest to find the Holy Grail, which according to Christian teachings, was the dish, plate, or cup used by Jesus at the legendary Last Supper. That the Grail was said to possess awesome and devastating powers spurred the Nazis on even more in their attempts to locate it, and then employ those same powers for their own sinister purposes. Thankfully, the plans of the Nazis did not come to fruition, and the

Allies were not pummeled into the ground by the mighty power of God or of any such artifact.

Acknowledged by many historians as being the ultimate driving force behind such research, Heinrich Himmler was perhaps the only high-ranking official in the Third Reich who was concerned with matters ancient and enigmatic. In 1935, Himmler became a key player in the establishment of the Ahnenerbe, which was basically the ancestral heritage division of the SS. The chief purpose of the Ahnenerbe was to conduct research into religious artifacts; however, its interest and work also spilled over into areas such as the occult—the latter, primarily from the perspective of determining if it, just like the Holy Grail, could be useful in further strengthening the Nazi war machine.

So much for Nazi Germany. Far less well known, however—and certainly barely documented until now—is the profound extent to which the various agencies and military units of the U.S. government exhibited extraordinary interest in puzzles of a distinctly archaeological and historical nature. It is a truly strange story that delves into such intriguing areas as the nature of Noah's Ark; claims that the pharaohs of ancient Egypt may have possessed secret knowledge of levitation; the theory that a number of biblical accounts may actually have had their origins in early visitations from aliens; and much, much more.

Astronauts of the Ancient Variety

Born on March 12, 1910, in Jefferson County, Ohio, George Wellington Van Tassel maintained that he experienced years of face-to-face contact with humanlike alien entities, following a claimed encounter in August 1953 near his Yucca Valley home in California. The complete history of Van Tassel's exploits with apparent extraterrestrials is highly bizarre, involving weird accounts of meetings with imaginatively named aliens, including Numa of Uni; Ah-Ming of Tarr; Rondolla of the Fourth Density [sic]; and Zolton, the Highest Authority in the Sector System of Vela. Van Tassel also suggested that many widely held and cherished beliefs relative to matters of a biblical nature were, in reality, distorted tales of extraterrestrial visitation from a fog-shrouded past. Notably, such beliefs caught the deep attention of none other than the legendary director of the FBI, J. Edgar Hoover.

The intriguing details of Van Tassel's initial encounter of August 1953 were detailed for Hoover in a classified memorandum prepared on November 16, 1954. The report described how, at around 2 a.m. on the day in question, Van Tassel and his wife were camping outdoors in an area near Landers, California—known locally as Giant Rock due to a huge, ancient rock that dominates the desert landscape—when something truly amazing occurred. According to the FBI, Van Tassel was awakened from his slumber by nothing less than an alien entity attired in a one-piece outfit, similar to those worn by fighter pilots at the time. It then invited Van Tassel to tour its craft, which had touched down near Giant Rock. Van Tassel told FBI agents who visited his home in 1954 that the vehicle in question was bell-shaped and around 35 feet (11 m) in diameter. He claimed that the aliens described it as a scout craft.

Giant Rock, California, where George Van Tassel allegedly met aliens who told him that the Bible was based upon distorted tales of ancient alien visitation. Author's photo.

As for the aliens themselves, Van Tassel said they conversed only via telepathy. Their specific purpose for visiting the Earth: to carefully warn humankind that the ever-growing atomic arsenals of the superpowers—the United States and the Soviet Union—posed a direct and catastrophic threat to the future of all life on Earth. Unless the human race changed its ways, he was told, our world would soon be destroyed by our own hands. Galvanized and spurred on by the words of warning and wisdom from his alien visitors, Van Tassel then went out and preached the gospel of E.T. to just about anyone who would listen. And plenty listened: from 1954 onward, Van Tassel elected to hold yearly flying saucer–themed conferences out at Giant Rock, which, at their height in the mid-1950s, attracted audiences in excess of *12,000 people*. His claims provoked as much intrigue and attention as they did rolling of eyes. But what really caught the attention of the FBI were Van Tassel's assertions that Christianity had been borne out of alien visitation—ancient astronauts, as they have come to be known.

On April 17, 1960, Van Tassel gave a lengthy speech at the Phipps Auditorium in Denver, Colorado, having been invited to do so by the local Denver Unidentified Flying Objects Investigative Society. To ensure that the lecture was a resounding success, the society took out advertising time on local radio, which caught the attention of the Denver FBI office, who subsequently directed a special agent to clandestinely attend and report back the details of Van Tassel's speech. The secret FBI summary of Van Tassel's presentation began as follows:

> The program consisted of a 45 minute movie which included several shots of things purported to be flying saucers, and then a number of interviews with people from all walks of life regarding sightings they had made of such unidentified flying objects. After the movie George W. Van Tassel gave a lecture which was more of a religious-economics lecture than one of unidentified flying objects (FBI, 1960).

It was this "religious economics" aspect of the speech that made J. Edgar Hoover's finest sit up and take notice. The special agent in attendance, in a lengthy report prepared two days later, stated:

The major part of his lecture was devoted to explaining the occurrences in the Bible as they related to the space people. He said that this is due to the fact that man, space people, was made by God [sic] and that in the beginning of the world the space people came to the earth and left animals here. These were the prehistoric animals which existed at a body temperature of 105 degrees; however a polar tilt occurred whereby the poles shifted and the tropical climates became covered with ice and vice-versa (Ibid.).

Van Tassel went on to say that alien visitors populated our planet with other species of animals to ensure that life on Earth continued following the Ice Age, and that it was this specific action that gave rise to the legend of Noah's ark. On the issue of other Biblical tales and stories, Van Tassel continued that following the aforementioned polar tilt, aliens from a faraway world established a male-only colony on Earth, intending to bring the females on what were termed supply ships at a later date. This, Van Tassel said, was "reflected in Adam not having a wife. Adam was not an individual but a race of men" (Ibid.). Further, according to the FBI's now-declassified records: "[Van Tassel] said that this race then intermarried with 'intelligent, upright walking animals,' which race was EVE [sic]. Then when the space people came back in the supply ships they saw what had happened and did not land; but ever since due to the origin of ADAM, they have watched over the people on Earth" (Ibid.).

Part of that program of secret surveillance, asserted Van Tassel, included the aliens ensuring that the human race was taught certain rules, regulations, and morals as part of a concerted, purposeful effort to control and manipulate. Those same rules, regulations, and morals, claimed Van Tassel, were in actuality nothing less than the legendary Ten Commandments, as provided to Moses on Mount Sinai by what the Christian faith claims is God. Van Tassel's bold assertion was that the Ten Commandments had nothing to do with any God whatsoever, Christian or otherwise; rather, the Commandments were actually "the laws of the space-people" (Federal Bureau of Investigation, 1960).

Also borne of the very same space-people, Van Tassel told the audience at the Phipps Auditorium, was Jesus Christ himself, whom Van

Tassel described as being the product of Mary, "a space person sent here already pregnant in order to show the earth people the proper way to live" (Ibid.). And it was not just these Biblical narratives that Van Tassel wished to describe and interpret for the benefit of his listeners. In his opinion, the activities of the ancient visiting aliens and their fantastically advanced spacecraft was also the reality behind certain centuries-old Native American Indian stories that suggested that "corn and potatoes, unknown in Europe, were brought here by a 'flaming canoe'" (Ibid.).

It can easily be argued that all of this merely represents Van Tassel's unique personal opinions, and that the FBI's only reason for taking careful, secret notice of the man and his assertions was because he was making a wealth of controversial claims and, in the process, significantly influencing the mindsets of literally tens of thousands of people in a God-fearing, predominantly Christian nation: the United States of America. In other words, perhaps the FBI's interest in Van Tassel only resulted from the fact that he was a subversive who attracted attention wherever he went. There is, however, evidence to suggest that there may have been far more to matters than just that—*much more*, in fact. The U.S. government's secret interest in ancient astronauts, biblical puzzles, and times long past extends far beyond the thought-provoking theories of Van Tassel.

Moon Dust and the Ark of Noah

It is highly intriguing that the FBI took careful note of George Van Tassel's beliefs concerning Noah's legendary ark. More than a decade before Van Tassel began speaking out publicly on this particular matter, senior and powerful elements of the U.S. government were diligently compiling secret files on the mighty and renowned biblical boat. In the Bible, in Genesis chapter 6, verse 13, we read: "God said unto Noah...make thee an ark of gopher wood.... And this is the fashion which thou shalt make it of: the length of the ark shall be three hundred cubits, the breadth of it fifty cubits, and the height of it thirty cubits." So much for what the Bible says, but what, if anything, does the U.S. government know of this particular issue? Let's take a look.

Early on the morning of June 17, 1949, a U.S. Air Force aircraft quietly embarked upon a top secret mission to secure imagery of Soviet missile installations reportedly being constructed near the Turkish border, along with photographs of the 17,000-foot (5-km)-high Mount Ararat in Turkey—the alleged final resting place of Noah's ark. As the pilot took the plane to a height of approximately 15,000 feet (4.5 km), the chief photographer aboard the aircraft was amazed to see what looked like a gigantic, man-made object—possibly 500 feet (152 m) long and partially buried within an ice cap on the southwest edge of the mountain. The astonished crew quickly maneuvered the plane in an attempt to get a better view, which they most certainly did. As the pilot closed in, those aboard the aircraft could now also make out what looked like a second huge object, this one on the western side of the mountain. It appeared to be a massive wing protruding through the ice. It will surely surprise no-one to learn that the photographs, after having been developed, were quickly stamped *Top Secret*. And so the clandestine connections between the ark and officialdom were set in motion.

Gregor Schwinghammer of the U.S. Air Force's 428th Tactical Flight Squadron viewed the first anomalous object while flying adjacent to Mount Ararat in the latter half of the 1950s. Whatever the nature of the massive object, Schwinghammer said its appearance gave every impression of having slid down the mountain before reaching its final resting place. Moreover, he heard that the presumed Ark of Noah had apparently been the subject of another photographic mission around the same time, involving the super-secret U-2 spy plane. It was later revealed in 1997 that at the outbreak of the Yom Kippur War in 1973, a CIA spy satellite secured photographs of a boat-like structure on Mount Ararat. Dino Brugioni, a retired CIA photography specialist who was tasked with studying the photographic evidence at the time, confirmed the authenticity of the pictures, and stated that they showed *something* worthy of study, even if its actual identity remained unclear. Echoing Brugioni's words were those of a Deep Throat–like source—a retired high-ranking intelligence official—who advised the *Washington Times*, also in 1997, that one such picture revealed a trio of huge, curved wooden beams sticking prominently out of the thick ice.

A remarkable and related story came from Don Riggs, whose father worked in the field of photographic analysis for the National

Reconnaissance Office. According to Riggs, just prior to his death in 1997, his father revealed a startling story concerning records and photographs on Noah's ark that had been referred to the NRO for analysis by a small group of personnel stationed at Wright-Patterson Air Force Base in Dayton, Ohio, in the latter part of the 1960s. Riggs added that his father told him the file referred to a secret operation called Project Moon Dust, an organization that Riggs' father was previously unaware of, and how Moon Dust personnel had begun to take a notable interest in the Ararat mystery just prior to the 1970s.

Ostensibly, Project Moon Dust had been designed to acquire and secure for the highest echelons of the U.S. military crashed Russian spy planes, satellites, rocket boosters, and space capsules. The purpose: to further advance U.S. technology, spacecraft, and weaponry. There is, however, ample data to show that Moon Dust was involved in the recovery of far more than mere Earth-based space technology, particularly in the 1960s. Official documents declassified under the terms of the Freedom of Information Act demonstrate that in addition to secretly coordinating the retrieval of Soviet space debris and spy planes, Moon Dust personnel were also mandated to investigate "reliably reported unidentified flying objects" and to recover "other items of great technological interest" of a specifically non-Soviet nature (Redfern, 2007). Certainly, the object in the photographs that Don Riggs' father saw would fall firmly into the latter category. Riggs stated that his father discussed with him his knowledge of seven photographs that appeared to show the ark at very close quarters. He further explained that two of the photographs displayed what was, beyond any shadow of a doubt, a very large, metallic, rectangular object partly protruding out of the ice on Mount Ararat. Whatever the object was, the testimony of Riggs Sr. seems to suggest it was far more than just a large old wooden ship.

Interestingly, Don Riggs' father is not the only person who has claimed a Wright-Patterson Air Force Base link to the story of Noah's Ark. Lieutenant Colonel Robert Livingston was working at Wright-Patterson in 1954 in an office of the Topographic Engineering Center, which had its primary base of operations at Fort Belvoir, Virginia. Livingston revealed that one morning in 1954, an Air Force captain brought into the office a single photograph that had reportedly been supplied by the U.S. attaché at the Turkish Embassy. Livingston recalled that the photograph clearly showed a long, dark, oblong structure that was partially obscured by a sheet of ice. He and his team were ordered to make an evaluation of the dimensions of the strange formation, which they duly did after carefully scrutinizing the photograph. Whatever its true origins, the object was clearly huge. The fact that Robert Livingston's team was linked with Fort Belvoir's Topographic Engineering Center is very notable. It was within the heart of Fort Belvoir's 1127th Air Activities Group that none other than Project Moon Dust personnel had their base of operations.

A NASA photograph of Mt. Ararat, Turkey, the alleged final resting place of Noah's Ark. Photo courtesy of NASA.

Whatever lies buried deep below the ice of Turkey's Mount Ararat, it seems safe to say that it is not merely the broken, weathered remains of a large, ancient vessel. To attract the highest echelons of U.S. Intelligence, the Ararat enigma must have represented something far more significant, perhaps even the long-buried remains of a crashed alien spacecraft that inadvertently led to the formation of the legend of Noah's ark, as postulated by George Van Tassel. And, that Project Moon Dust personnel played an intimate role in the affair strongly suggests that the presumed ark possessed advanced and coveted technologies of an incredible nature.

Pyramid Power

The controversy-filled theory that certain of humankind's most impressive and legendary constructions, such as the pyramids of Egypt, were built by, or with the extensive assistance of highly advanced extraterrestrial entities is one that provokes a great deal of interest and attention. The popular published works of Morris Jessup, Robert Charroux, and Erich von Däniken make that abundantly clear. Far less well known, however, is that the U.S. Intelligence community has also taken a keen interest in matters of such an ancient and enigmatic nature. As prime evidence of this, we have to focus our attention on the groundbreaking work of a man named Bruce Cathie.

Cathie, a retired airline pilot based in New Zealand, presented a theory suggesting that (a) there exists throughout our planet what might be termed a power grid that UFOs, piloted by alien entities, use as a source of energy while traversing the skies of planet Earth, and (b) that technology broadly fitting this particular description was also employed in the movement and manipulation of the gigantic stones of the Egyptian pyramids. It was in the late 1960s that Cathie first began to air his views on such matters. He asserted that it was ludicrous to suggest that the thousands of stone blocks used in the creation of the pyramids were quarried, shaped, and hauled into place by nothing stranger than the brute force strength of thousands of slaves. Perhaps Cathie was right on target: one Abu al-Hasan Ali al-Mas'udi, otherwise known as the Herodotus of the Arabs, was a 10th-century writer who prepared an immense, 30-volume series of texts that recounted the history of the world based upon his extensive travels. Within the pages of these texts, al-Mas'udi noted that in Arab legend there existed an intriguing story suggesting that the creation of the Pyramids had absolutely nothing to do with ropes, pulleys, or prosaic manpower. Rather, centuries-old lore that had come his way during his journeys suggested the pyramids were created by what we would today call *definitive levitation.*

The incredible story that al-Mas'udi uncovered went something like this: when building the pyramids, their creators carefully positioned magical papyrus underneath the edges of the mighty stones. Then, one by one, the stones were struck by what was curiously described as a rod of metal. Lo and behold, the stones slowly began to rise into the air and, like dutiful soldiers following orders, proceeded in slow, methodical, single-file fashion a number of feet above a paved pathway surrounded on both sides by similar mysterious metal rods. For about 150 feet (46 m), Al-Mas'udi recounted, the gigantic stones moved forward, usually with nothing more than a gentle prod from the keeper of the mysterious rod to ensure they stayed on track, and would then softly settle back to the ground. And so the strange task was repeated until all the stones arrived at their final destination. Once the stones were all accounted for, they were struck once more, but this time in a fashion that caused them to rise ever higher into the air. When the stones reached their designated locations, they were carefully (and amazingly easily) manipulated into place, one by one, until the huge pyramid was finally complete.

Were the Pyramids built using the mysterious power of levitation?
Photograph by Eduard Spetterini, 1904.

Such a scenario might sound more suited to a blockbuster sci-fi movie than a historical text. As Bruce Cathie rightly noted, however, the conventional theories for the creation of the Pyramids—namely, that they were solely the work of slaves, using rollers, pulleys, ropes, and constructed ramps—were beset by major, nearly insurmountable problems. For starters, some of the massive stones used in the creation of the pyramids (many of which weighed more than 70 tons) originated in quarries more than 600 miles (966 km) from where the pyramids now stand. Another problem was that literally millions of stones were used, which begs the question of where the massive number of trees came from that had to have been chopped down and converted into rollers? Certainly not from the barren deserts of Egypt, that's for sure! In Cathie's mind, there was one answer and one answer only to explain how the gargantuan stones were moved: levitation by anti-gravity.

All of which brings us to the relationship between Bruce Cathie and the U.S. government. In the 1960s, when Cathie's groundbreaking research was coming to fruition, he contacted U.S. Defense personnel at Wellington, New Zealand, chiefly as part of an effort to have his views heard by officialdom. He hoped this might assist him in his quest to uncover the truth about the so-called Earth grid. Having outlined to U.S. authorities his theories and conclusions, it is eye-opening to note that Cathie was not dismissed by the U.S. Defense Department; in fact, he received the opposite response. Referring to Cathie as a "lean, wiry New Zealander, with an apparently above average knowledge of mathematics," a formerly classified U.S. Defense Intelligence Agency report dated February 1968 reveals that American intelligence agents were not only deeply fascinated by Cathie's theories and findings, but had also secretly undertaken background checks on the man himself: "No adverse reports are known," noted the DIA. And, there is evidence to show that Cathie's digging into such controversial areas as UFO grids and levitating stones attracted even deeper official attention—and possibly secret surveillance of the man himself (Defense Intelligence Agency, 1968).

A recently declassified Department of Defense document dating from May 1968 references complaints the Department received from Cathie to the effect that government personnel were secretly tailing him. According to the story that Cathie told American officials, for some time he had suspected he was being spied on by stealthy government agents, but he was not certain of this until April 1968, when he was accosted in the lobby of the Grand Hotel in Invercargill, New Zealand, by three Americans. Cathie alleged that they attempted to have him accompany them to an unknown location—he had the good presence of mind to decline—which Cathie believed may have been a naval vessel, because he had heard that U.S. Navy personnel were in the area at that time. Cathie wasted no time informing the DoD that his work had been cleared at the highest levels of the government of New Zealand, including the Prime Minister. Cathie added in stern tones: "Call your agents off. I have official approval to continue my work; I don't want them tailing me" (Defense Intelligence Agency, 1968).

Precisely why Bruce Cathie would have been surveilled by elements of the U.S. Intelligence community is, sadly, ultimately unclear. Did he stumble upon the truth behind the UFO controversy and its links to the secrets of how the Pyramids of Egypt were really constructed? It's difficult to say for sure. UFO propulsion systems, long-lost antigravity and levitation technology in the hands of the pharaohs, classified Department of Defense files, and a covert surveillance operation—all key components in the remarkable life and work of Bruce Cathie.

Ancient Artifacts as Weapons

Finally, we come to what might very well lie at the heart of U.S. government interest in bygone eras and their attendant amazing tales of incredible technologies, levitating stones and rocks, mighty and massive arks, and long-dead "astronauts" that were really immortal gods. Just as the Nazis had during World War II, it seems that elements of the American ruling elite had and continue to have vested, secret interest in commandeering the ancient wonders of our world for military gain. It is here that we have to turn our attentions to an entity that inspires as much fear and dread as it does awe and lust for power: the Djinn.

The Djinn are supernatural entities of Arab lore, and key players in the narratives and beliefs of Islam as outlined in the Qur'an. They are said to inhabit a strange and twilight realm that coexists alongside our own—another dimension, one might be very much inclined to suggest. Whereas we are purely flesh and blood, the all-powerful Djinn are the product of flame and fire, and can be as playful and benevolent as they can be malevolent and downright deadly. Indeed, some Djinn are widely believed to have an inexorable and inextinguishable hatred of the human race.

One of the most learned scholars of Djinn lore is anomalies researcher and author Philip Imbrogno. In 1995, Imbrogno made a trip to Saudi Arabia, during the course of which he learned of secret, long-term attempts by an elite, covert unit of the U.S. military to actually try and capture Djinn. The purpose of the program, Imbrogno was told by official sources, was to secure for the U.S. government a highly advanced technological device that permitted the Djinn to pass through solid matter, and also through what were intriguingly described as "dimensional windows." It scarcely needs mentioning that if such phenomenal technology did exist, the possible outcome of its use as a tool of the military would be beyond imagination. To what extent the operation was successful, Imbrogno did not find out, unfortunately. If such an extraordinary goal *had* been achieved, however, Imbrogno was advised it would undoubtedly have been classified at an extremely high level. Similarly, while visiting Oman on the same trip, Imbrogno heard a story of the governments of Oman and the United States trying to make some kind of a deal with Djinn.

Surely no one needs to be told that Faustian pacts involving military personnel and dimension-hopping, ancient Middle Eastern entities bent upon the destruction of the human race should not be entered into lightly, if ever. Even the slightest hint that such pacts may have been initiated is something that may explain why the U.S. government has for decades exhibited a deep and abiding secret fascination for ancient mysteries. That such meddling actions from our military might ultimately prove infinitely disastrous and costly to the entire planet, is something that one hopes officialdom is keeping in mind.

Bibliography

(Note: All Websites were accessed in May of 2011.)

Al-Ashqar, Umar Sulaiman. *The World of the Jinn and Devils.* Boulder, CO: Al Basheer Company, 1998.

Al-Mas'udi, Abu al-Hasan Ali. *Meadows of Gold and Mines of Gems*. (Trans. Paul Lunde and Caroline Stone.) London: Kegan Paul International, 1989.

Berlitz, Charles. *The Lost Ship of Noah*. New York: G.P. Putnam & Sons, 1987.

Cathie, Bruce. *The Energy Grid: Harmonic 695*. Kempton, Ill.: Adventures Unlimited Press, 1997.

———. *The Harmonic Conquest of Space*. Kempton, Ill: Adventures Unlimited Press, 1998.

Defense Intelligence Agency files declassified under the terms of the Freedom of Information Act. *UFO Global Grid Theory*, February 8, 1968.

Federal Bureau of Investigation files declassified under the terms of the Freedom of Information Act. *George W. Van Tassel, Unidentified Flying Objects*, April 26, 1960.

Guiley, Rosemary Ellen, and Philip J. Imbrogno. *The Vengeful Djinn*. Woodbury, Minn.: Llewellyn Publications, 2011.

Kneisler, Matthew. "Noah's Ark: United States Government": *www. arksearch.com/nausgov.htm*.

Navarra, Fernand. *Noah's Ark: I Touched It*. Plainfield, NJ: Logos International, 1974.

Ravenscroft, Trevor. *The Spear of Destiny*. Newburyport, Mass.: Weiser Books, 1982.

Redfern, Nick. "Nazis, Aryans and More..." in *Mystic Utopian "Supermen"* by Edmund Shaftesbury. New Brunswick, NJ: Global Communications, 2008.

———. "Project Moon Dust: How the Government Recovers Crashed Flying Saucers." From the Fifth Annual UFO Crash Retrieval Conference Proceedings. Broomfield, CO: Wood & Wood Enterprises, 2007.

———. *Contactees*. Pompton Plains, NJ: New Page Books, 2009.

Redfern, Nick, and Andy Roberts. *Strange Secrets*. New York: Paraview-Pocket Books, 2003.

The Holy Bible: English Standard Version. Wheaton, Ill.: Crossway Bibles, 2003.

Race, Interrupted: Ancient Aliens and the Evolution of Humanity

By Scott Alan Roberts

The question regarding the origins of humanity has sparked a raging debate that is still ongoing in archaeological and anthropological circles. On one side of the debate you have the religious camp insisting that we descend from a singular act of supernatural creation. On the other side—and many times in direct opposition to the religious camp—is the scientific community, which often insists that *Homo sapiens* came about via several discrete stages of evolutionary ascendancy, before reaching the plateau of our current state of development. But there is a third distinctive camp of thought, which posits the alternative theory that humans are a race interrupted, that somewhere in our primordial past our genetic makeup was altered in so abrupt and swift a fashion, and in such a sweeping manner as to forever change the course of our development and break the known laws of the evolutionary process and natural ascendancy.

The notion of ancient alien interruption is not a new one. Its loudest defenders, a group that includes such notables as von Däniken, Drake, Downing, Sagan, and Sitchin, have been writing and theorizing on the topic for decades. Ever since early humans first gazed up in wonder at the star-blanketed night sky, we have been intrigued by the seemingly unanswerable questions posed by a mysterious and unattainable universe. Early mythologies and legends speak of mysterious objects roaring across the heavens. Shards of ancient tablets and shreds of ancient documents describe phenomenal, unexplained manifestations in the skies. And virtually every culture and religion contains an oral and written history of visitations from

147

angels, demons, devils, and gods who made contact with humanity in ancient times. The human race in its infancy described these visitations from the sky in the only terms it could understand—they were deities.

"Young earth" creationists will tell you that the biblical record accounts for an earth that is a mere 6,000–7,000 years old, whereas science has established a vastly older history of human ascension, going back at least 200,000 years for the beginnings of modern man. The recent discoveries of ancient temple complexes such as Gobekli Tepe near the village of Karapinar, Turkey, which itself dates back to about 12,000 BCE, have turned the established nomenclature of civilized, city-building humanity on its ear.

Creation and the First Family

Taking a biblical story and meticulously unpacking all the elements, whether historical, spiritual, literary, or cultural, is an important process necessary in the understanding of *any* ancient culture, really. Simply put, the Bible is a means for us to enter into and understand the ancient anthropology of humanity itself. Depending on your view of the veracity of biblical scripture, its pages may reveal myths, legends, fables, stories, or real-life accounts that mirror or are mirrored by the various cultures of the ancient world. The importance of the Bible, if not for faith and the practice of any one religion, is that it demonstrates another view of certain events that were experienced and then recounted by ancient historians. When you take a step back from the text, removing the sometimes rose-colored glasses of dogma and systematic theology, you can start to read between the lines and observe the vastness of the ancient world rising up before your eyes.

Most of us grew up learning a spiritual story that explained the creation of the world. And most of us are familiar with that first couple, Adam and Eve, and how God commanded them to not eat any fruit from a certain tree in the Garden of Eden ("lest they die"), and how Eve was subsequently tempted and then persuaded by the Serpent to take some of the fruit from this Tree of the Knowledge of Good and Evil, thus bringing about the introduction of sin into the world and the Fall of humanity. We probably learned how the first couple were then barred from Paradise and given the command to "be fruitful, multiply, and fill the earth with offspring." With the birth of Cain and his twin brother, Abel, the world saw the embryonic stages of humanity itself.

Virtually every culture the world over has some kind of account regarding the creation of the earth and of humanity. Of course, some of these stories border on hyperbole and fairy tale, and include such improbable elements as gods or great human warriors casting beasts and animals into the skies to create the swath of heavenly constellations. For example, certain African and Native American accounts describe subterranean humans coming to the surface of the earth, and "gods" from the heavens impregnating their beautiful daughters with quadruplets.[1] In Lakota accounts of the first human family, for example, Waziya, the Old Man, and his wife, Wakanka, come out into the world from underground. (Compare this narrative to the Genesis account, in which Adam is "formed out of the clay of the ground.") Their daughter, Ite, is so beautiful that she captivates the attentions of Tate, the God of the Wind, who then marries her and fathers quadruplets. Another character, Iktomi the Trickster, tempts the first family with promises of great wealth, power, and beauty. In this way, Iktomi bears great resemblance to the Old Testament's account of Lucifer, who appears as a snake and tempts Eve in the Garden of Eden, promising eternal life and godlike knowledge if she eats fruit from the forbidden tree at the garden's center. In all of these tales, disobedience and treachery against God/the gods results in banishment from an aboriginal paradise. Lucifer and his Lakota counterpart, Iktomi, are exiled and cursed to roam the earth for all time, while the first families go on to bear children and spread their kind throughout the world. The similarities between these disparate versions of creation are obvious. The fact that all such tales of creation are so similar satisfies at least one of the requirements of the scientific method. Rather than requiring the reader or historian to test the authenticity of each individual tale on its own, the improbable similarities—cutting across the lines of race, culture, and even time itself—stand as a corporate monument to a sort of "common law" veracity. In other words, where there's smoke, there's fire.

In the Genesis account of Adam and Eve, the fall of all humanity is a direct result of disobedience. People often ask how the entire human

race could have been cursed for all time because of one small bite from
an apple. My answer to this is that merely eating some fruit (which,
by the way, is never identified as an apple) was not the issue; the issue
was Eve's direct disobedience of a command mandated by the Divine.
As a direct result of this violation, and of luring her husband, Adam,
to share in that disobedience, the Fall comes hammering down with
devastatingly permanent effects.

My Brother's Keeper

After this ostensibly fictional (or at least symbolic) beginning to the
narrative, the story begins to take on the characteristics of direct reportage. In Genesis 4:1–5 we read that Adam and Eve give birth to
two sons, Cain and Abel:

> [1]Adam made love to his wife Eve, and she became pregnant
> and gave birth to Cain. She said, "With the help of the LORD
> I have brought forth a man." [2] Later she gave birth to his
> brother Abel. Now Abel kept flocks, and Cain worked the soil.
> [3] In the course of time Cain brought some of the fruits of the
> soil as an offering to the LORD. [4] And Abel also brought an
> offering—fat portions from some of the firstborn of his flock.
> The LORD looked with favor on Abel and his offering, [5] but
> on Cain and his offering he did not look with favor. So Cain
> was very angry, and his face was downcast.

Even in the original Hebrew, it's not clear whether Abel is born
as a second child, years later, or whether, similar to the African and
Lakota creation myths, this is a multiple birth. But based on what
little evidence can be found in the verbiage of the text, the brothers
are most likely twins.

As the story goes, Cain is a "tiller of the ground," a farmer who
grows the vegetables important to the survival of his family. Abel is a
sheep herder, raising meat for the same purpose. As they go to worship their creator, Abel kills and then sacrificially burns a sheep on
the altar as his offering to God. Cain, on the other hand, a farmer la-
boring in the fields, offers up a percentage of his crop at harvest time,
burning it in sacrifice on the altar in the same fashion as the sheep.
But while Abel's offering is a sweet, acceptable sacrifice to God, Cain's

is not. God rejects Cain's offerings because there is no blood sacrifice involved. In biblical times, blood was considered to be Life itself, and the process of blood sacrifice as described in this passage is a foreshadowing of the Kinsman Redeemer, the Messiah who will one day come and redeem all of humanity by the spilling of his own blood. A system of symbolic sacrifices developed over the millennia and eventually carried into the tabernacle and temple worship in Jerusalem. While Cain's offering appears to be from his heart, apparently it is not what is prescribed or necessary to please Jehovah.

It is very interesting that while God comes down and communicates with his creation, he does nothing to hinder the savage murder of Abel. He speaks plenty to the future murderer, but does nothing—nothing that is recorded in the passage, at least—to warn Abel. While this is a subjective observation, it is noteworthy that the only thing God does to assuage Cain's anger prior to the murder is to warn him that he needs to retain his self-control and not give sin an opportunity to take hold of him. Again, nothing is said to the unwitting Abel:

> [6] Then the LORD said to Cain, Why are you angry? Why is your face downcast? [7] If you do what is right, will you not be accepted? But if you do not do what is right, sin is crouching at your door; it desires to have you, but you must rule over it. (Genesis 4:6–7)

Later there is harsh judgment from God when he talks with Cain face-to-face. Consider for a moment what it would be like if the creator of the universe interacted with you on a personal basis as you proceeded through life, guiding you and warning you of various perils. Cain seems to hold a special place in the eyes of God, for we read nothing of this kind of chummy interaction between God and Abel. Cain is warned to not let sin gain a foothold, but Abel doesn't hear a word about how to protect himself from his brother's anger. If we take this story at face value, this seeming inability to grasp the consequences of sin tells the tale of a very young civilization, indeed, one with very little experience in dealing with the harsh realities of the dark side of human nature. Yet, for some reason, God keeps focusing on Cain, and Cain, in a fit of jealousy over his twin brother's position with God—and in anger over his own rejection by the Divine—takes his brother out into the field and murders him. When God asks Cain where his brother is, Cain replies with the famous question: "Am I my brother's keeper?"

East of Eden

As a result of the murder, God brands Cain with a strange, special mark of some sort and banishes him from the region of Eden, destined to wander as an exile the rest of his days. In the meantime, Adam and Eve have their third son, Seth, and Eve holds him up as a replacement from God for her murdered son. In this account of the aftermath of Cain's murder of Abel, take special note of the emotions of Cain. Then take note of what God does by way of judgment and how Cain reacts:

> [10] The LORD said, "What have you done? Listen! Your brother's blood cries out to me from the ground. [11] Now you are under a curse and driven from the ground, which opened its mouth to receive your brother's blood from your hand. [12] When you work the ground, it will no longer yield its crops for you. You will be a restless wanderer on the earth."

> [13] Cain said to the LORD, "My punishment is more than I can bear. [14] Today you are driving me from the land, and I will be hidden from your presence; I will be a restless wanderer on the earth, and whoever finds me will kill me."

Cain is obviously very concerned that if he is found by other people, he will be executed. While there is no civilized system of jurisprudence in place, Cain believes that his life is in danger for killing his brother. Of course, all of this begs the question of whether any other people existed at the time of the murder. Unfortunately, the meticulous detailing of genealogies found in most other parts of the Old Testament are missing from this account. Was there already some sort of system of laws and rules in place? Were there courts or leaders who judged people for the breaking of societal laws and mores? Was there even a society at all? Who could possibly kill Cain if, indeed, only he and his parents had been left alive after Abel's murder? Again, taken as direct reportage, the story seems to indicate one of two things: either there were other descendants of Adam and Eve not mentioned in the passage, or other people were already living and dwelling in the regions outside of Eden—other people who might be inclined to take Cain's life. Cain was clearly afraid to leave Eden.

God addresses Cain's concerns as follows:

¹⁵ But the LORD said to him, "Not so; anyone who kills Cain will suffer vengeance seven times over." Then the LORD put a mark on Cain so that no one who found him would kill him. ¹⁶ So Cain went out from the LORD's presence and lived in the land of Nod, east of Eden.

Remember, Adam and Eve had been ousted from the Garden of Eden, not the geographical region,² so the first family probably never wandered very far from Jehovah's care and protection. But protection from what or, more probably, *whom*? And what of the "punishment" of the mark of protection placed on him? In the case of Abel's murder, there would be no "eye for an eye," "tooth for a tooth," or "blood for blood." Cain was merely sent away with a mark that would enable him to live out the rest of his days as a wanderer in safety.

It is when we read of Cain's progeny in verse 17 of Chapter 4 that the narrative comes to a screeching halt: "Cain made love to his wife, and she became pregnant and gave birth to Enoch." If Adam, Eve, and Cain were the only three living human beings on earth, who was this woman whom Cain married and where did he find her? She is never mentioned as being part of his family tree. Theological apologists will tell you that this woman and the inhabitants of her region were none other than descendants of Adam and Eve's *other* children, who had migrated away from the Edenic region over the course of many, many years. They will also assert that Cain and Abel may have aged hundreds of years before the events of the first murder and banishment, thus providing an undefined period of time for the branching out and resettlement of an exponentially multiplied tree of Adamic offspring:

¹⁷ᵇ Cain was then building a city, and he named it after his son Enoch. ¹⁸ To Enoch was born Irad, and Irad was the father of Mehujael, and Mehujael was the father of Methushael, and Methushael was the father of Lamech.

¹⁹ Lamech married two women, one named Adah and the other Zillah. ²⁰ Adah gave birth to Jabal; he was the father of those who live in tents and raise livestock. ²¹ His brother's name was Jubal; he was the father of all who play stringed instruments and pipes. ²² Zillah also had a son, Tubal-Cain, who

forged all kinds of tools out of bronze and iron. Tubal-Cain's sister was Naamah.

[23] Lamech said to his wives, "Adah and Zillah, listen to me; wives of Lamech, hear my words. I have killed a man for wounding me, a young man for injuring me. [24] If Cain is avenged seven times, then Lamech seventy-seven times." (Genesis 4:17b–24)

Before we go any further in the text, note the bittersweet, poignant end to this passage in which we learn that Adam and Eve have a third child, a son whom they name Seth. Eve pronounces him a gift from the Lord *to replace her murdered son, Abel.* This would seem to indicate that she had no other male children between the time of Abel's murder and the birth of Seth:

[25] Adam made love to his wife again, and she gave birth to a son and named him Seth, saying, "God has granted me another child in place of Abel, since Cain killed him." (Genesis 4:25)

It is this very same Seth who later dwells in Nod with his older brother, Cain, the murderer of his other older brother, Abel.

What's in a Name?

Other than Adam, Eve, Cain, and Abel, there are no other members of the Adamic family listed in the Hebrew scriptures at the time of Abel's murder. There is no genealogical record, no exhaustive listing of names—nothing. Banished from Eden, Cain leaves behind the only two other people mentioned in the Bible as being on the earth at that time, Adam and Eve. He goes out into a world void of inhabitants and civilization, east to the land of Nod. Once there, the passage tells us that he makes love to his wife, whom he has either brought with him from Eden (meaning it was one of his sisters not named in the account of the first family) or met in his wanderings. She, in turn, bears him a son, whom Cain names Enoch. And there in the land of Nod, Cain builds a city (most likely a wooden enclosure around a few huts) in honor of his new son and names it after him.

Of the actual history of this little city we know very little, but of its name we know a great deal. Without entering into too much detail regarding the changes in pronunciation that occur naturally during the course of the development of a language, the letter N in Hebrew is often pronounced as an R. Likewise, the *ch* sound in *Enoch* may be replaced by either a *k*, *g*, or *gh* sound. These sorts of linguistic changes are very common in ancient tongues, and the names of biblical city mounds—or *tels*—remained virtually unchanged over the passage of millennia. All of this points to an important city in antiquity called *Uruk*. A study of the cuneiform writing of that time reveals that it could also have been pronounced *Unuk*, which is recognized as another iteration of the name *Enoch*.[3]

What is perhaps more interesting is that the name Uruk/Unuk became synonymous with the word "city"—not an average, run-of-the-mill city, but a city of great importance. The root meaning of the word actually translates as "the first city." Although Moses (generally considered to be the author of Genesis) was sometimes guilty of giving ancient places names that were more current in his day, many later scribal changes were also made to his manuscripts. While it is a historical fact that he lived from roughly 1526 BCE to 1406 BCE, he mentions the cities of Pithom and Ramses, which didn't exist until some 200 years after he died. That said, he makes a point to mention that Cain's city was called Enoch/Uruk.

Nod is the Hebrew root of the verb "to wander," and is obviously an etymological nod (if you will pardon the pun) to the wandering, nomadic lifestyle of Cain and his future putative descendants, the Kenites. This sort of play on words is typical of rabbinic writings and suggests that this is a later scribal interpretation, more than likely inserted to suggest that Cain's descendants were "without territory"—in other words, nomadic. Additionally, the Hebrew language did not exist prior to the time of Abraham, who lived some 4,000 years *after* the time of Cain. The language Cain and his descendants would have spoken was probably a Nilotic/Kushitic language closer to Old Arabic (Dedanite).

The Missing Link?

In *Intelligent Life in the Universe* (coauthored with I. S. Shklovski), Carl Sagan asserted that "our tiny corner of the universe may have been visited thousands of times in the past few billions of years. At least one of these visits may have occurred in historical times." Sagan, both an astronomer and exobiologist, as well as an established atheist and reasoned skeptic, theorized that Earth may have been visited by various "galactic civilizations" many times during earth's primordial past. He also insisted that it was not entirely out of the realm of possibility that extraterrestrial artifacts and remnants of visitations and even entire civilizations may still exist, or even that some kind of alien base is still being maintained within our solar system to provide continuity for successive expeditions.

Such a hypothesis coming from a respected scientist such as Carl Sagan acted as a catalyst for many in the ufological community and field to come forward with the idea that humanity may have been the result of alien "seeding" or extraterrestrial genetic interference. Despite conventional scientific theory regarding the origin of species, there is still no real proof as to how we got here in the first place. Moreover, the great Darwinian missing link is still, quite frankly, *missing*. So what scientists are doing, in all reality, is simply indulging in exponential leaps of faith to account for this missing information. In a sense, science is creating a mythology of its very own in that it uses the human imagination to fill in the gaps in the theorized sequence of human ascendancy from primates into higher levels of *sapiens*. Even the similarities that we once thought existed between the DNA of apes and humans has been dramatically reduced due to more recent studies, wherein the once 95 percent similarity has been reduced to a woeful 67 percent and even lower, depending on the study. While the evidence is only circumstantial, it is beginning to look as though the link to primates is becoming less and less an active, provable theory on the genetic level. So let's engage in a little gap-filling exercise of our own: the so-called missing link may very well have been DNA provided by visitors from another world.

The Serpent in the Garden

Despite its ostensibly religious nature and purpose, the biblical account of creation and the first family actually presents a thinly veiled subtext of some kind of interruption in the human bloodline. This happens almost at the very beginning, with the first human offspring, one generation out from the dawn of humanity. A non-human character enters the picture and helps to move the plot forward to its inevitable tragic denouement. This character—an alien in the Garden of Eden who disrupts the serenity of paradise—will forever be known as the Serpent, the seducer of the first mother and, as we shall soon see, the father of an alien seed that perpetuates generations of mixed blood.

Recall the tale of the actual temptation. As the mother of all humanity, Eve seems to be the first cause—the *primum movens*—of the Fall, thus breeding into us all a sinful nature that puts us all in need of a redeemer. But Eve's downfall comes as a result of her encounter with a serpent. To the alert reader of this passage, the subtext is that she had intercourse with the creature. Have you ever encountered a serpent that walked upright? That spoke like a person? The snake that Eve encounters does both of these things. Assuming that Eve knew the difference between a snake and a man, this snake was neither:

> [1] Now the serpent was more crafty than any of the wild animals the LORD God had made. He said to the woman, "Did God really say, 'You must not eat from any tree in the garden?'" (Genesis 3:1)

The Hebrew word used in the Book of Genesis for the word snake is *nachash* (pronounced naw-kawsh), meaning "magician, enchanter; a spellbinder; to illuminate, shine." Interestingly, rabbinic interpretation never posits this creature as a literal snake. Nachash is understood as *a shining being with the power to enchant.*[4] In verse 17 of the same chapter, God curses Nachash, saying: "Thy heart was lifted up because of thy beauty, thou hast corrupted thy wisdom by reason of thy brightness...." In many interpretations this cursed being is none other than Lucifer himself, although the passage never actually uses that name; rather, the reader is forced to extrapolate the connection by referring to other, later biblical texts, such as the writings of Daniel and the Book of Revelation. It is this being that influences (or more accurately, beguiles) Eve into disobeying God and eating the fruit of the forbidden tree:

> [2] The woman said to the serpent, "We may eat fruit from the trees in the garden, [3] but God did say, 'You must not eat fruit from the tree that is in the middle of the garden, and you must not touch it, or you will die.'" (Genesis 3:2–3)

The Hebrew word used here for tree is *ets*, a word that is linguistically linked to the Hebrew word *toledah* (both meaning "generations"). It is from these words that we draw the modern conception of the family tree. Another variation of the word is "the wood of a tree, as an opening and closing of a door." Using some linguistic maneuvering and extrapolation, the same word can also mean "portal; opening of one's mind; enlightenment." For these reasons, it is often suggested that the Tree of the Knowledge of Good and Evil was not a literal tree at all, but a symbol of the pre-Adamic races that lived in the regions surrounding the Garden of Eden. (Some assert that these races were what made up the Atlantean civilization, but that is outside the scope of this essay.) The phrase "fruit of the tree" is actually derived from the Hebrew word *periy*, meaning "fruit: produce of the ground; offspring, children, progeny (of the womb); or figuratively: fruit (of actions)." The phrase "eat of it" is the Hebrew word *'akal* (pronounced aw-kal), which is often used to refer to sexual intercourse. And the word "touch" is the Hebrew word *naga* (naw-gah), which is also sometimes used as a euphemism for sex. Clearly this was no ordinary tree!

Keeping all of this in mind, let's take a look at the next part of the passage:

> 4 "You will not certainly die," the serpent said to the woman. 5 "For God knows that when you eat of it your eyes will be opened, and you will be like God, knowing good and evil." 6 When the woman saw that the fruit of the tree was good for food and pleasing to the eye, and also desirable for gaining wisdom, she took some and ate it. She also gave some to her husband, who was with her, and he ate it. 7 Then the eyes of both of them were opened, and they realized they were naked; so they sewed fig leaves together and made coverings for themselves. (Genesis 3:5–7)

The admittedly controversial definitions of the Hebrew words I am using in this passage are driven by the context in which they appear. While the individual words used do not necessarily have overt sexual meanings, most biblical scholars today agree that the context of the passage clearly points to acts of a sexual nature. Here are a few more words and phrases from the passage, along with their alternate definitions:

- The phrase "pleasant to the eyes" is the Hebrew word *chamad,* meaning "to desire, to covet, to take pleasure in, to delight in, to be desirable, to delight greatly, to desire greatly, desirableness, preciousness."
- The word "desired" is the Hebrew word *ta'avah* (tah-av-aw), meaning "to yearn for; to lust after (used of bodily appetites); a longing; by implication: a delight (subjectively, satisfaction; objectively, a charm): a desire, a wish, longings of one's heart; lust, an appetite, covetousness (in a bad sense); to covet; to wait longingly."
- The Hebrew word for "took" is *laqach* (law-kakh'). It is a primitive root meaning "to take (in the widest variety of applications): to take, to lay hold of, to receive, to marry, to take a wife, to take to or for a person, to procure, to get, to take possession of, to select, to choose, to take in marriage, to receive, to accept."

Given the multiple semantic layers available to the reader, a very different picture of Eve's temptation in the Garden of Eden is beginning to emerge. The parsed passage reveals much more than a disobedient appreciation of fruit! All of the references we hear of Eve eating an apple, all the depictions in religious art of the couple holding or eating a rather large piece of fruit, all of this is merely coded euphemism for the shocking truth of what the passage is really describing. What really happens in this scene in the Garden of Eden is that Eve, the mother of humanity, loses her virginity to the Serpent (it is evident from the passage that this occurs before she ever has sex with her husband). Further on, it is implicit that Eve is impregnated by this encounter, and when she draws her husband into the scenario and he willingly "partakes," she is also impregnated by him. Eve is now bearing the fraternal twins, Cain and Abel, one from the seed of Adam and the other from the seed of the character known as the Serpent! And so, the grand sin that is committed in Eden is not mere disobedience in the eating of a forbidden piece of fruit from a forbidden tree; it is a lurid sexual sin that creates dual bloodlines in the twins conceived in Eve's womb—lineages that would be in constant conflict with one another, starting, of course, with Cain's murder of his twin brother.

Alien Interruption

The Sumerian culture of ancient Mesopotamia is the oldest human civilization known to contemporary science and the archaeological record. The sudden (at least in historical terms) onset of this civilized culture has remained a mystery for many years; clearly, it represented an exponential quantum leap in humanity's intellectual development. As Carl Sagan once remarked, we still have no clear perspective about its origins: "Their language is foreign; it shows no resemblance to Indo-European, Semitic or any other language. We can only map them by the actions of their successors, the Akkadians, who created a voluminous Sumerian-Akkadian dictionary."[5]

It all began about 6,000 years ago when the very first cuneiform writing was developed by the Sumerians to record a dramatic astronomical event—what was likely the creation of Vela X, a star that turned into a supernova about 1,300 light years away from our solar system, and which can still be seen today as a faintly flashing pulsar. Virtually overnight—in evolutionary terms, at least—the Sumerians gave the world written language, the first fundamental character of which was the Sumerian symbol for the word "star," commemorating the astronomical event. The cuneiform word was then linked to the symbol for "deity," and the term "star god" was born.

In the ruined mounds of their ancient cities, the ancient Sumerians left behind cuneiform tablets that listed everything from various forms of worship to mundane business receipts drawn up between merchants. They gave us the first love song, the first pharmaceutical prescription (all without any inclusion of magic or spirituality), the first school system, the first code of jurisprudence, and the first parliament. And we are to believe that this all came out of nowhere, in the twinkling of a bursting supernova? Is it any coincidence that it was during this very same period that Berossus, the Babylonian high priest, wrote of the coming of the half-fish, half-human Oannes, the beast with reason who appeared in their midst and taught the Sumerians letters, sciences, and every kind of art—everything that would essentially civilize them?

Cain, the twin brother of Abel, was fathered by the reptilian serpent in the Garden of Eden. This event was recorded in religious mythology as the Fall at the hands of Eve's temptation and "eating of the forbidden fruit." Cain murdered his twin brother in accordance with the "enmity" that was set between the twin siblings, and after being banished by God from the region of Eden, wandered into Nod, in the region just east of Eden. There he built a city which became known throughout history as Uruk, the "first city." Cain did not encounter any other people; Cain *was* "the other people," and it is clear that he bequeathed to the inhabitants of Sumer a connection to the reptiles from the sea and the dragons from the sky. Humankind was indeed genetically altered by alien intelligences, and we have the Sumer-Akkadian cuneiform texts left as a remnant of those events that so altered the course of human evolution. The question still remains, however, as to whether they are still visiting to this day. I'll leave that for you to decide.

Notes

1. Modupe Oduyoye, *The Sons of the Gods and the Daughters of Men: An Afro-Asiatic Interpretation of Genesis 1-11*. New York: Orbis Books, 1984, p. 21.

2. David J. Gibson. *The Land of Eden Located*. Unpublished manuscript draft dating from 1964, published online by author's family: *http://nabataea.net/eden.html*.

3. Ibid.

4. Rev. Mark Oaks, Copyright 2000, The Bible Church. All Rights Reserved. *www.bibleword.org/genesis5.html*.

5. Shklovski, I. S., and Carl Sagan. *Intelligent Life in the Universe*. New York: Dell Books, 1968.

Other Sources

Drake, W. Raymond. *Gods and Spacemen in the Ancient West*. New York: New American Library, 1974.

Ginsburg, Irwin. *First Man, Then Adam!* New York: Pocket Books, 1978.

Sitchin, Zecharia. *The 12th Planet*. New York: Avon, 1978.

Clash of the Giants: The Untold Story of the Lost Atlantean Race

By Pat Chouinard

Mainstream science teaches us that creatures such as giants, ogres, and other monstrous beings are merely mythical figures out of a remote past, with no basis in reality. Terrified of a world they did not understand and could not control, our ancestors devised these myths to bring order and predictability to a chaotic, primeval world. Such are the viewpoints and conclusions of Academia. But there is much more to these stories. This simplistic conception of an ignorant and credulous human race with no concept of reality is currently in its final death throes. Through archaeology, we are coming to understand that the ancients were actually highly advanced and may have possessed technologies comparable to or even surpassing our own. The ancients were excellent record keepers, and had a significant knowledge of astronomy, medicine, and engineering. Thus it seems that we ought to take seriously these seemingly extraordinary tales of titans, frost-giants, and cyclopes. The ancients knew what they were talking about.

The underlying truth of this omnipresent mythos of giants goes beyond mere ancient record-keeping, however. In order to establish that the giants of antiquity were not the product of the primitive imagination, it is necessary to first establish as fact the feats and wisdom of the ancients. This inevitably leads to a discussion of their pre-modern technological achievements, some far more advanced than even our own today. Once this is established, the giants issue can be addressed more objectively. What we have found is that the civilizations of the ancient world were far more advanced than most archaeologists are prepared to admit.

A deceptively small device found in 1900 on the small island of Antikythera, 25 miles (40 km) northwest of Crete, has helped lend credence to this assertion. Retrieved from the submerged wreckage of a Greek galley by fisherman and sponge divers, the device was actually a working computer, intricately devised not by Apple or Dell, but by the Greeks during Hellenistic times. David Childress, author of *Technologies of the Gods,* rightfully boasts of its discovery as being "tantamount to finding a jet airplane in the tomb of King Tut." Hints of other technological feats from antiquity have survived into the 21st century, as well. For example, texts and detailed drawings of flying craft called *vimana* in the Sanskrit writings of India give us at least some indication that in the remote past, someone—or something— was flying in the skies over our planet. Confucius also records that in China, during the reign of the Five Monarchs, from 2852 to 2206 BCE, there were "flying carriages" (Childress 2000). It is difficult to say with certainty what technological wonders the ancient Chinese possessed because prior to his death, Emperor Chin Shih Huang Ti ordered the burning of hundreds of thousands of books, including all those in the royal libraries; only a few lucky tomes escaped the wrath of the Imperial torches. The secrets contained within the others are now forever lost (Ibid.) Based on these few examples alone, it is clear that our ancestors did, in fact, possess the same intelligence, logic, and rationality as more modern "advanced" cultures, which in my opinion makes it highly probable that there is some truth behind these legends.

Myth as Remembrance

Since the time they walked on earth many eons ago, giants have become a part of our collective unconscious, a terrifying Jungian archetype that captivates the imagination. Giants have become the cornerstone of the myths, legends, and traditions of almost every culture on earth; in many cases, these narratives have continued, unabated and unchanged, for millennia. Such myths often depict a civilization ruled by giants that is destroyed by a global deluge and eventually forgotten. Only myth and legend now survive to help us decode the secrets of that forgotten chapter in human history. As with all mythological accounts, however, these are but blurred images of a far more

profound reality. Indeed, these gigantic inhabitants of our imagination are not mere figments, but rather the cultural "residue" from our
past experiences as a species. They are, in fact, imprints or echoes of
a remote but very real dark age that we have long since forgotten—
until now.

For example, Inca myth describes the Ayar-aucca race, which
includes four twin giants who hold up the sky. In this myth (as in
many others like it), the human race becomes unruly and ungrateful.
Angered by this neglect, the four giants agree to let the sky tumble
down and crash into the sea. The result is a global flood that obliter-
ates much of humankind (Joseph 2005). The idea of the sky crashing
to the earth and destroying virtually all of civilization resonates with
Plato's Atlantis and some of the more recent speculation regarding
its demise. Some theories suggest that a comet or asteroid may have
impacted Earth sometime during our remote history, causing the destruction of these ancient and advanced cultures.

In Irish mythology, we learn of the Formorach, a giant sea people
whose leader, Balor, guides them to the shores of Ireland following
the great flood. They then become the native inhabitants of that island. While some scholars locate the Formorach's point of origin in
Spain or North Africa, others claim that the original homeland of
these pre-Celtic giants was Atlantis, thought to have been located 200
miles (322 km) west of Gibraltar (Joseph 2005).

The natives of the Fijian islands believe that their ancestral land,
called Burotu, sank long ago into the Pacific Ocean. This ancestral
realm was obliterated when the "heavens fell down," and fire and
water melded together to produce the islands of Samoa (Joseph 2005).
The survivors, known as the Hiti, were thought to be a race of giants,
the children of Atlantis. They built a monumental arch standing almost 20 feet (6 m) high.

Arab myth describes a race of giants known as the Adites. These
beings are the equivalent of the Atlantean Titans of Greek mythology, and are described as superior architects and builders. Since their
earliest recorded history, Arabs in the Middle East have associated all
immense structures with these great giants of antiquity.

In a Hittite narrative, a giant originating from the Western Ocean
named Kumarbi places the world on his mountainous neck, thereby

becoming the Anatolian equivalent of the Greek deity and Titan Atlas, the founder of the mighty Atlantean empire (Joseph 2005).

Bochica is a figure in the myths of the Chibcha peoples of what is present-day Colombia. A bearded, white-skinned giant similar to Atlas, he supports the sky on his shoulders. When humankind forsakes his teachings, he eventually drops the sky, causing a series of floods and conflagrations that decimate the planet. This event also destroys the giant's own home, forcing his children to flee and seek shelter elsewhere. In the end, they settle along the coast of Colombia, eventually becoming the country's native Indian inhabitants (Joseph 2005).

As you can see from this small sampling, the sheer number and variety of giant myths and legends is staggering; indeed, they can be found in almost every culture on earth. Many of these mythologies include beings closely related to the Titans, who supposedly once ruled Atlantis. And of course there is also the recurring narrative of a great cataclysm that eventually destroys a lost civilization sometime in the remote past. Such common themes and motifs set a precedent for an even broader discussion.

Giants in Hinduism

In the Sanskrit writings of India, we learn of the Daitya, or the water giants. They are mentioned in the *Vishnu Purana* and the *Mahabharata,* two of the most ancient and highly revered of Hindu sacred texts. The Daitya are the offspring of Vishnu. These water giants are the East Indian equivalent of the Titans of Greek mythology, which includes Atlas and the other kings of Atlantis (Joseph 2005). These writings describe how Vishnu's mother conquers the earth for the gods and becomes the first of the mighty Daitya. This ultimately makes her the upholder of the sky—what Frank Joseph describes as "the moral order of the cosmos"—therefore identifying her with the Greek Titan Atlas, who creates the island of Atlantis and literally bears the burden of the world upon his shoulders (Joseph 2005).

According to the *Vishnu Purana*, these water giants reside in Tripura, the Triple City. This now sunken island metropolis, located far across the impenetrable Western Ocean, echoes Plato's own descriptions of the lost civilization of Atlantis. The immortal Greek philosopher wrote that this submerged land mass was beyond the Pillars of Hercules in the middle of the Atlantic Ocean. The Triple City of the *Vishnu Purana* is clearly emblematic of the trident of Poseidon, the patron god of Atlantis. In a final war both the Daitya and Tripura are destroyed, yet another similarity to the myth of Atlantis (Joseph 2005).

Ancient Greek Mythology

The Greeks had their own giants, the Gigantes—grotesque, humanoid creatures with snake-like legs. In the myth narratives, they attempt to overthrow Zeus and the other gods of Mt. Olympus, but ultimately fail. The Greek saga *The Argonautica* describes the giants in the following manner: "Their bodies have three pairs of nerved hands, like paws. The first pair hangs from their gnarled shoulders, the second and third pairs nestle up against their misbegotten hips...." (quoted in von Däniken 2010). The earliest known Greek deities, the Titans, rule the primordial universe before the coming of the Olympians. This parallels the Biblical Nephilim, who ruled the Earth until their age ends and gives way to the rise of the human race. Atlas, perhaps the most well-known of the Titans, was the ruler of Atlantis and, as Frank Joseph noted in *The Atlantis Encyclopedia* (2005), the founder of astrology and astronomy. Atlas is often depicted in illustrations as a gigantic, bearded man crouching on one knee and bearing the sphere of the heavens upon his massive shoulders. Such imagery has come to signify the Atlanteans' stalwart dedication to celestial and planetary sciences. Perhaps not surprisingly, the Sanskrit word *atl* means "to support or uphold" (Joseph 2005). Interestingly enough, Atlas is also the name of a mountain in Asia Minor not far from the incredible ruins of Çatal-Hüyük, perhaps the oldest city on earth (Joseph 2005) It is more than 9,000 years old, and dates back to the destruction of Atlantis, perhaps even to the very first colony of its fleeing survivors (Joseph 2005).

The Gigantomachy recounts the battle between the giants and their main opponents, the Olympian gods. This is perhaps the most widely depicted struggle in Greek art and literary tradition. In it, the Giants bombard the gods with boulders and the flaming trunks of burning trees. According to the oracle, the gods themselves will be unable to destroy the Giants unless a powerful mortal aids them. Of course, in ancient Greece this could be only one individual, the legendary Heracles (Sacks 1995: 92).

The Gigantes are not the only large beings in Greek mythology. The gods themselves are also giants. Unlike the Gigantes, however, they are blond-haired, fair-skinned, and distinctly Nordic in appearance. This is consistent with the fact that Caucasians (some of whom were depicted as giants in contemporaneous reports) were once dominant and prevalent in areas long thought to be the sole domain of non-European peoples (Sacks 1995: 92).

The Norse Deities and the Giants

The Germanic peoples have a rich mythological tradition filled with supernatural creatures, gods, trolls, elves, half-gods, and, of course, giants. As such, many parallels can be drawn between Teutonic myths and legends and those of other cultures. Take, for example, the striking similarities between the Norse god Odin, and Olle, the tribal god of North America's Tuleyone Indians. Like Odin, Olle is a colossal giant with a horned helmet who is both a god of war and a savior. Olle rescues their people from a fiery demon named Sahte (Joseph 2005). The Norse god Thor is, of course, one of mythology's greatest warriors against the enemies of humanity—the dwarves, dragons, monsters, and, yes, other giants. The German scholar Herbert Kuhn has traced Thor back to perhaps the darkest chapter in human history, the Old Stone Age, when hunter-gatherers living in caves dominated Northern Europe. Thor's weapon of choice is the hammer, which, according to Kuhn, means "stone," and is the basis for a new theory linking the Iron Age god Thor to the Stone Age. In Sanskrit he is called *Tanayitnu*, meaning "the thunderer" (von Däniken 1970).

The sagas tell us of the earliest beliefs and cosmologies of the ancient Norse and other Germanic peoples of northwestern Europe. We have visions of the frost giants and *Jotnar*. According to the *Eddas*, one of these ancient collections of Norse stories, there are two races of giants: the children of Thrud, who descend from the frost giant Ymir; and the children of Bor, who include the Aesir. Though tremendous in size, the Aesir are distinctly Nordic in appearance. For reasons unknown, the giants battle in a protracted, seemingly interminable conflict. Finally, Odin, Vili, and Ve, the first Aesir, ambush Ymir and murder him. When they slit his throat, in yet another allusion to the great flood, a great deluge of blood rushes forth and drowns most of the giants. Some escape in a boat to a new realm called Jotunheim. The world as we know it, Midgard, is formed from the body of Ymir. His salty, watery blood then becomes the oceans, rivers, and lakes; his flesh becomes the earth; his bones, the rocks and mountains; his hair, the forests; and the maggots from inside his stomach, the dwarves. But it was the later descriptions of Aryan warriors and battles between giants that became most deeply engrained in the sensibilities of these Western cultures, and which actually had some foundation in reality.

Gigantopithecus: The Original King Kong

Evolutionary biologists have identified a giant humanoid race that they call *Gigantopithecus blacki*. This early hominid stood some 9.5 feet (3 m) tall. Some believe that this creature may have been the ancestor of the Yeti, or Bigfoot. This colossal, manlike ape, which ruled the forests of East Asia and other parts of the world for about a million years, has been extinct for the past 100,000 years. The species coexisted with our immediate predecessor, *Homo erectus*, before our own species, *Homo sapiens*, made its inevitable appearance. Perhaps, it is argued, our prehistoric ancestors experienced firsthand the awesome power of *Gigantopithecus* and passed down the knowledge of this being through a kind of archetype or collective memory. Perhaps our notion of Bigfoot is just one part of such a collective experience. What we know of *Gigantopithecus* comes from the discovery of more than 1,000 fossilized teeth found in numerous areas throughout Southeast Asia, as well as from a reconstruction performed by the Dutch paleontologist and geologist Dr. Ralph von Koenigswald. He initially discovered the giant molars in 1934 southern China. The Chinese, overlooking them as valuable pieces to our evolutionary puzzle, were selling the teeth (which they called "dragon bones") as cures for various illnesses. After World War II broke out in Europe in September of 1939, local Japanese authorities eventually arrested Koenigswald as an enemy alien, thus ending his research. He was liberated in 1945, but much of his research was destroyed in the ensuing conflict.

Giants in the Bible

From the myths and tribal folklore of primitive aborigines to the hallowed scriptures of our modern-day churches, temples, and mosques, the archetype of the giant is inescapable. The Bible is one of our earliest and most widely read resources for understanding these myths. The Book of Job is considered the oldest book in the Hebrew Bible. Job 26:5–6 reveals: "The Primeval giants tremble imprisoned beneath the waters with their inhabitants. The unseen world [the bottom of the sea] lies open before them, and the place of destruction is uncovered" (quoted in Joseph 2005). Author Frank Joseph links this description to an early reference to Atlantis. The giants here could be construed as the original children of Atlantis, just as the founding fathers of Atlantis were a giant super-race known as the Titans, an earlier population of enormous gods that once ruled the primordial universe.

In Genesis 6:4 we read, "There were giants in the earth in those days; and also after that, when the sons of God came in unto the daughters of men, and they bare children to them, the same became mighty men which were of old, men of renown" (King James Version). This particular verse from the Old Testament is actually one of most enduring controversies of modern Biblical scholarship. The term *giants* is actually a mistranslation of the Hebrew word *nephilim*, which is derived from the Hebrew verb *nafol*, meaning "to fall." Thus, the Nephilim are often conceived of as a fallen race of giants who ruled the world prior to the great flood, the global deluge that engulfed the antediluvian world and finally ended their reign. The descendants of the Nephilim are known as the Emin, who are described in the King James Bible as "a people greater, and many, and tall." These descendants of the Nephilim were also the inheritors of the antediluvian religious practices and rites that were enacted atop Seir, the sacred mountain (Joseph 2005). For many, this whole matter remains an enigma that has provoked rampant speculation. Some claim that the Nephilim were actually greys (aliens), while others contend that the mysterious figures were actually the Neanderthals of Ice Age Europe and the Near East.

One can also find evidence for the presence of a gigantic ruling class of gods on earth in the Torah. As Zecharia Sitchin points out in his book, *There Were Giants Upon the Earth*, "It does not speak of the sons of God, but uses the term the *Bnei Ha Elohim*—'the sons of the Elohim,' a plural term taken to mean 'gods' but literally meaning 'lofty ones'" (Sitchin 2010). Thus even the oldest of the Holy Scriptures tell us of a vanished age in which both giants and gods, along with other fantastic and supernatural creatures, inhabited and ruled the earth.

The story of the flood itself gives us an inkling of what life here on Earth may have been like before the global deluge. The Book of Genesis gives us only brief glimpses of that alternative world history, and so contrasts drastically with the non-Biblical, evolutionary view of history now maintained as the established paradigm. The *non-evolutionary* world history, in contrast, is explored further and in much greater detail in the apocryphal works known as the Book of Enoch and the Book of Giants, two books only recently rediscovered that were not officially canonized as part of the Bible. The Book of Giants is actually a portion of the Book of Enoch that was unknown until the mid-20th century, when excavations at the Qumran caves on the Dead Sea counted them among the Dead Sea Scrolls. This rich treasure-trove consists of a collection of dozens of scrolls and hundreds of fragments. They helped provide insight into Old Testament writings and the relatively new religion of Christianity. The Book of Giants describes the antediluvian world as follows: "[These fallen angels] knew the secrets of [all things]. [At this time] sin was great on the earth. The wicked angels killed many people and begot giants [with mortal women]." These passages are echoed in the remaining portions of the Book. Likewise, in Enoch 7:3–6, the daughters of men

> became pregnant, and they bare great giants, whose height was three thousand ells [a Germanic form of measurement approximating the length of one man's arm]: who summoned all the acquisitions of men. And when men could no longer sustain them, the giants turned against them and devoured mankind. And they began to sin against birds, and beasts, and reptiles, and fish, and to devour one another's flesh, and drink their blood. Then the earth laid accusation against the lawless ones.

According to Enoch at least, it was this course of events that precipitated the great flood.

The Giants Who Traveled East

In their book *Uriel's Machine*, Christopher Knight and Robert Lomas attempt to demonstrate that the Watchers, a race of fallen angels—the Nephilim—who mated with mortal women and produced the giants who came to rule the antediluvian world, were in fact members of the Grooved Ware culture, so named after the grooved markings found on their surviving pottery. Some researchers theorize that this culture was also the progenitor of both the Celtic and Germanic peoples of Western Europe. In the Book of Enoch, the Watchers and their offspring implore Enoch to represent them: "All the giants [and monsters] grew afraid and called Mahway. He came to them and the giants pleaded with him and sent him to Enoch [to speak on their behalf]" (quoted in Knight and Lomas 1999, p. 302). They then beg the god of Newgrange to spare them and the world from the comet about to strike and bring about the mighty deluge. The god responds: "All the mystery had not yet been revealed to you.... You have no peace... behold, destruction is coming, a great flood, and it will destroy all" (Ibid.). Knight and Lomas believed that the Grooved Ware culture—the giants of Biblical fame—knew of the coming catastrophe and felt that they would find safety and salvation only in the Tarim Basin, a high plateau guarded by the mountain ranges of Tibet and Mongolia. What they didn't know, however, was that this mystery was about to be unraveled.

A series of Chinese archaeological excavations in the late 1980s revealed hundreds of mummies along the Western border of China. These unique human remains exhibit clear Caucasian traits. Other ancient corpses in Mongolia, Siberia, and Central Asia were also discovered displaying the same European characteristics. While a fair number of these mummies date back to at least 3500 BCE, others have been determined to be even older, dating to around 4000–5000 BCE. In addition to having European features, they wore Western-style clothing, including plaid twill and the world's earliest known pair of pants. Later, carbon-14 dating provided perhaps the best estimate of the mummies' original age, placing them at 3,500 years before the birth of the Han civilization. Evidence suggests that they are related to an Indo-European–speaking group of Caucasians known as the Tocharians (Baumer 28). These prehistoric Chinese remains were unknown to much of the outside world until a security breach led to the announcement of the discoveries in 1994. When they heard about this, Knight and Lomas made an interesting argument. One of the taller mummies, known as Chechen Man (also called the Ur-David), is about 6.5 feet (2 m) tall. Some of the mummies are even taller. To the Asians who first recorded their encounters with these yellow-haired barbarians, asserted Knight and Lomas, they truly must have seemed like giants. These Tarim Mummies, with their large builds and above-average heights, may have contributed or given rise to some of the rumors of giants and strange, yellow-haired peoples. They did not, however, explain away ancient accounts of monstrous and imposing beings that possessed near-supernatural or even extraterrestrial strengths and abilities.

The Rephaim, the Land of Canaan, and Goliath

On the Web site Giantsinthebible.com, author Peter Chattaway presents a complete inventory of the giant myth as they are described in the Bible. In addition to the ominous Nephilim, Chattaway writes, is a vigorous race of giants known as the Rephaim. The first mention of them appears in Genesis 14:5: "And in the fourteenth year came Kedorlaomer, and the kings that were with him, and smote the Rephaim in Ashtoreth Karnaim, and the Zuzims in Ham and the Emin in Shaveh Kiriathaim." This vastly superior force, led by an alliance of kings, chief among them being Kedorlaomer of Elam, crushed every people they encountered and brutally defeated the Rephaim (Chattaway 1994). The main focus of the king's expedition was to sack and gain control of Sodom and Gomorrah. Again, according to Genesis 14:10:

> the kings of Sodom and Gomorrah fled, and fell there; and they that remained fled to the mountain. And they took all the goods of Sodom and Gomorrah and all their victuals, and went their way. And they took Lot, Abram's brother's son, who dwelt in Sodom, and his goods, and departed.

Chattaway also notes that throughout this earliest account, there is no indication that the armies that Kedorlaomer of Elam and his alliance of kings defeated were actually giants. At this point, the Rephaim are portrayed simply as just another one of the many tribes and na-tions that comprised Canaan and the surrounding territories. But later, when Moses is confronted with the same peoples in Deuteronomy, the description of them is more vivid. When Moses addresses the Israelites on the eve of their invasion of Canaan, he explains that they may not invade the land of the Moabites and Ammonites because those lands had been promised to the descendants of Lot, who, he reminds them, had been liberated from evil forces. These forces were a race of giants, the same people who were defeated and called the Rephaim by the al-liance of the kings described back in Genesis. This task was attributed to the God Yahweh, and was but a prelude to future events.

Of course, while the exploits in the Book of Enoch are certainly fascinating, most people are familiar with the confrontation between David and Goliath, the best-known giant of the Bible who was mas-terfully slain by the humble shepherd and future king. In II Samuel 21:20, we read that David engaged in battle with mighty giants. Not only did they tower above the Hebrew soldiers, but they had extra fingers, as well. In his book *Twilight of the Gods*, author Erich von Däniken devotes several pages to the various Biblical accounts of an-cient giants. He describes this battle in some detail, and explains more fully the awesome size and power of Goliath and his fellow giants. For example, in the fifth book of the Pentateuch the narrative speaks of a gigantic sarcophagus:

> For only Og king of Bashan remained of the remnant of gi-ants; behold, his bedstead was a bedstead of iron; is it not in Rabbath of the children of Ammon? Nine cubits was the length of it [about 8.5 feet; 2.5 m], and four cubits the breadth of it, after the cubit of a man (Deuteronomy 3:11).

The Bible also describes what is perhaps the most famous giant encounter of all:

> And there went out a champion from the camp of the Philistines, named Goliath, whose height was six cubits and a span...and he was armed with a coat of mail; and the weight of the coat was five thousand shekels of brass and the staff of his spear was like a weaver's beam; and his spear's head weighed six hundred shekels of iron (Samuel 7:1–4).

Goliath was the direct descendant of King Og of the Ammonites. I Chronicles 20: 3–8 gives a description of Goliath's lineage and how he came to confront David:

> And he brought out the people that were in it, and cut them with saws, and with harrows of iron and with axes. Even so dealt David with all the cities of the children of Ammon. And David and all the people return to Jerusalem. And it came to pass after this, that there arose war at Gezer with the Philistines at which time Sibbechai the Hushathite slew Sippai, that was of the children of the giant: and they were subdued. And there was war again with the Philistines; and Elhanan the son of Jair slew Lahmi the brother of Goliath the Gittite whose spear staff was like a weaver's beam. And yet again there was war at Gath where was a man of great stature, whose fingers and toes were four and twenty, six on each hand, and six on each foot and he also was the son of the giants. But when he defied Israel, Jonathan the son of Shimea David's brother slew him. These were born unto the giant in Gath; and they fell by the hand of David and by the hand of his servants.

To this day, the Bible offers us some of the most compelling evidence that at one time, giants once existed on this planet—what I call the "race of giants" hypothesis. Biblical sources provide scholars with some of the most culturally and religiously significant accounts of giants available in all the European and Near Eastern traditions. However, there are other accounts that are linked not to the Judaeo-Christian world, but rather to the diverse cultures of the New World.

Giants in the New World

In even the earliest written accounts of almost every culture there can be found descriptions of fierce, light-skinned peoples who were once the central force of a lost civilization. Science writer Terrence Aym described the following series of events in two unpublished articles dealing with the presence of giants in ancient America. He also described some of the encounters between European explorers and various gi-gantic Caucasian aborigines in Central and South America.

The Paiute tribe of present-day Nevada tells of an ancient war they waged against a primordial race of white-skinned, red-haired giants. The Paiute called these imposing Caucasians the *Si-Te-Cah*. This name refers to the *tule*, a fibrous plant that the giants used to construct assault rafts. According to tribal lore, this race was already living in North America when the ancestors of the Paiute arrived 15,000 years previously. The modern scientific dogmatism dismisses these reports as sheer fantasy, but there has to be more to it than just a case of overactive imaginations.

Physical remains of giant-sized Caucasian peoples have been found on almost every continent. In the United States, hundreds of sites have been excavated, including those in Virginia, New York State, Michigan, Illinois, Tennessee, Arizona, and Nevada. Hard sci-entific evidence supporting the Paiute account of a war with gigantic red-haired Caucasians first came to light in 1924 at Lovelock Caves in Nevada. During prehistoric times, a massive freshwater lake called Lake Lahontan covered the region. It was underneath this vast body of water that the original cavern was positioned, and remained under-water until the lake eventually dried up over time. According to the Paiute, the giants practiced cannibalism, much in the same way early Neanderthals did. Indeed, Neanderthal campsite remains include human bones with artificial cut-marks on them. The Paiute claim they were as tall as 12 feet (3.6 m) in height, but these may have been ex-aggerations of a naturally tall Caucasoid race, corresponding to the Nordic height.

According to myth, the Paiute pursued the giants into a cave. There the giants found sanctuary and continued to resist the tribe, ignoring their demands to exit the cave and face the tribe head-on. The enraged tribesman covered the cave with brush and ignited it into flames, hoping this would force the giants out of the cave. The small number of the stalwart giants who ran out of the cave entrance were immediately pummeled by a barrage of arrows. Those who remained in the cave were overcome by the intense fumes and perished.

In 1911, skeletons and fossils were found in the area dating to the time of the legend's origin. More than 10,000 artifacts were unearthed including the mummified remains of two red-haired giants. One of them was a female, 6.5 feet (2 m) tall, and the other a male that towered over 8 feet (2.4 m) tall. These relics proved once and for all that the Paiute myth of a war against a race of giants was not fantasy, but a stark and horrifying reality. Evidence in the form of broken arrows that had been shot into the cave and a dark layer of burned material supports the description of the climactic battle scene that concludes the legend. Two very large skeletons were then unearthed in the Humboldt dry lakebed near Lovelock, Nevada. Among the human remains was one skeleton, wrapped in a gum-covered cloth not unlike those found in Egyptian mummifications and measuring some 8.5 feet (2.6 m) tall. The other was an astounding 10 feet (3 m) tall.

The Book of Mormon, which also speaks of giants, calls these original inhabitants the Jaredites, often considered to be the Olmec of Central America, but it is more likely that the Olmec were just a single part of a much more widely distributed population. In Ether 15:26, the Mormon scriptures claim that they were "large and mighty men as to the strength of men." The 16th-century chronicler Fernando de Alva Ixtlilxochitl wrote:

> In this land called New Spain there were giants, as demonstrated by their bones that have been discovered in many areas. The ancient Toltec record keepers referred to the giants as Quinametzin; and as they had a record of the history of the Quinametzin they learned that they had many wars and dissensions among themselves in this land that is now called New Spain. They were destroyed, and their civilization came to an end as a result of great calamities and as a punishment from the heavens for graves [sic] sins that they had committed (Allen, 124).

I believe that a real race of red-haired giants dominated the Americas at one time, perhaps tens of thousands of years before the arrival of the ancestors of today's Native Americans across the Bering Strait some 13,000–15,000 years ago. In defense of this admittedly controversial statement, I will say that race is a mutable thing, and that the physical appearance of New World humans during the Ice Age may have been quite different; perhaps they were part of a line that left no known descendants. By the same token, the presence of a forgotten Caucasian population in Asia that could have walked across Berengia with the other Asiatics is also a possibility. This would best explain some of the unusual results from recent genetic testing, which has actually confirmed the presence of Caucasoid genes in some of the existing ancient remains.

Western European explorers such as Magellan, Sir Francis Drake, Desoto, and Commodore Byron (the famous poet Lord Byron's grandfather) all reported encounters with living giants—remnants of a once proud and noble race of Caucasian "supermen"—all across the North American continent. A well-documented sighting by Magellan occurred in 1520 near the harbor of San Julian, Mexico. There, Magellan and his crew came upon a red-haired giant that stood nearly 10 feet (3 m) tall and whom Magellan described as having a "voice like a bull" (Aym 2011). Later, Magellan learned from normal-sized natives that the giant belonged to a neighboring tribe (Ibid.). "Remarkably," Aym writes, "Magellan's logs show that he and his crew captured two of these living giants and brought them aboard ship, intending to bring them back to Europe. Unfortunately, the giants grew ill and they both died during the return voyage. Magellan had their remains buried at sea" (Ibid.).

Evidence of ancient giants abounds across the globe, proof of lost civilizations and migrations which are slowly coming to light thanks to a series of chance discoveries as well as the dutiful efforts of today's independent-minded amateur archaeologists and other scientists. This research has lead us into a whole new realm of scientific investigation. Inexplicably, established academia continues to deny their existence, so it is up to each and every one of us to challenge the prevailing paradigm—and perhaps forever change our own history in the process.

Bibliography

Allen, Joseph L., and Blake Joseph Allen. *Exploring the Lands of the Book of Mormon*. Orem, Utah: Book of Mormon Tours and Research Institute, 2008.

Aym, Terrence. Personal e-mail correspondence with the author, Saturday, January 22, 2011.

Baumer, Christoph. *Southern Silk Road: In the Footsteps of Sir Aurel Stein and Sven Hedin.* Bangkok: White Orchid Books, 2000.

Charles, R. H., and W. O. E. Oesterley. *The Book of Enoch.* London: Society for Promoting Christian Knowledge, 1929.

Chattaway, Peter T. "Giants in the Bible." *www.peter.chattaway. com/articles/giants.htm.*

Childress, David Hatcher. *Technology of the Gods: The Incredible Sciences of the Ancients.* Kempton, Ill.: Adventures Unlimited Press, 2000.

Christmas, Jane. "Giant Ape Lived Among Humans." McMaster University, 2005. *www.sott.net/articles/show/105936-Giant-ape-lived-alongside-humans.*

Joseph, Frank. *Advanced Civilizations of Prehistoric America: The Lost Kingdoms of the Adena, Hopewell, Mississippians, and Anasazi.* Rochester, Vt.: Bear & Co., 2010.

———. *The Atlantis Encyclopedia.* Franklin Lakes, N.J.: New Page Books, 2005.

King James Bible (ed. Gordon Campbell). Oxford, UK: Oxford Univ. Press, 2010.

Sacks, David, et al. *Encyclopedia of the Ancient Greek World.* New York: Facts on File, 1995.

Sitchin, Zecharia. *There Were Giants Upon the Earth: Gods, Demigods, and Human Ancestry: The Evidence of Alien DNA.* Rochester, Vt.: Bear & Co., 2010.

Stuckenbruck, Loren T., and Otto Betz. *The Book of Giants from Qumran.* Tubingen: Mohr Siebeck, 1997.

von Däniken, Erich. *Twilight of the Gods: The Mayan Calendar and the Return of the Extraterrestrials.* Pompton Plains, N.J.: New Page Books, 2010.

———. *Chariots of the Gods? Unsolved Mysteries of the Past.* New York: Putnam, 1970.

The AB Intervention Hypothesis: The Truth Behind the Myths

By Paul Von Ward

Whether we believe we are special, privileged creatures from a divine source or a chance spark of life on a small blue planet, most of us think that human beings are unique, living on a lonely planet in a vast, empty universe. Such a belief is neither accurate nor a natural, understandable error; we have been deliberately conditioned to ignore all evidence to the contrary. As it turns out, we are not the product of an accidental chemical interaction in an unlikely universe, nor are we the miraculous creation of a supernatural God (an idea actually concocted by people less than 2,000 years ago): we are self-evolving participants in a marvelously conscious, self-learning, and self-creating universe containing many species of advanced beings (ABs).[1]

An AB is a member of any species more advanced than our own, with the power and independence to decide whether or not to interact with us. We may seek them out, but they are the ones who will control the extent and timing of that contact. ABs include the ancient astronauts I will discuss here, as well as aliens or extraterrestrials (ETs). The acronym[2] also applies to the gods described in early creation stories. It covers beings such as the Annunaki and Elohim, Vishnu and Yahweh, as well as their progeny, who are known by various names but are usually thought of as angels and devils. ABs also include the invisible voices that have spoken to Hindu yogis, Moses, Mohammed, Joseph Smith, and many other founders of the world's religions. ABs also include ethereal beings such as Seth, the Pleiadians, and other self-identified messengers such as spirit guides or channeled ascended masters.

Although ABs are typically more advanced than humans, in some cases a human being may be more moral, may know things that an AB does not know, or may have superior skills in a certain area. However, the very idea of ABs always creates uncertainty and fear: What are their intentions? Are they manipulating us? Can we trust them? What do they want from us? And perhaps most importantly, once we've made contact with them, is this a permanent state of affairs? Such questions unnerve us because our collective memories of earlier AB-human interactions have been suppressed and indeed almost wiped out during the last 2,000 years. Why and how did this happen? To answer this question, let's start with the oldest stories.

Historical Accounts of ABs

Creation myths have been the subject of thousands of tomes, manuscripts, books, articles, and academic papers. Most of these narratives of creation describe what can only be construed as ABs fighting amongst themselves before they insert themselves in the birth and development of humans and their early cultures. In the *Enuma Elish*, for example, the characters Apsu and Tiamat are, in fact, ABs. Another creation myth, this one from China, describes P'an Ku, another AB who instructs primal humans about the universe. An Apache account tells of Hactein, who is the creator of all human beings.[3] Similar themes are found in writings from Egypt, India, Japan, and indeed in practically every other nation and culture around the globe. What are we to make of the universality of these stories? Do they refer to an actual event or events in our history that etched deep images into our memory bank that have survived for 250,000 years or more? Did the ABs who were involved in or knew of these "humanoid creation projects" teach these stories to *Homo sapiens*? Or are they simply delusions, the anxious projections of early cultures at a time when life was "nasty, brutish, and short"?

A brief perusal of the offerings on the Internet reveals more about scholars' beliefs than what the stories actually tell us. What they write reflects a predetermined worldview[4] that denies the existence of ABs despite all evidence to the contrary. Such scholars disparage the very idea of an AB history, dismissing it instead with unsubstantiated assertions, such as that early humans made up stories of the gods because they felt powerless and afraid of the unpredictable forces of nature. Similarly, when psychiatry was in its infant stages, Freud and others explained away the "primitive" idea of a god or gods by saying that adults who were living in such a world ("nasty and brutish") needed to project the idea of a loving, protective father into the unknown, which provided a feeling of comfort and purpose.

While many attribute the universal accounts of a god or gods creating the human race to a childish fantasy or to a spontaneous "short-circuiting" of false memories in the human brain, neither psychological research nor behavioral neuroscience supports such speculations. Despite the fact that they lack robustness as theories, however, these academic pretensions persist in the mainstream. And there is no room for discourse: Anyone who even hints that these stories might have a basis in reality is now quickly censored—and censured—by those who do not share this view. What many of the authors of those learned books and academic papers don't understand, however, is that these myths are actually descriptions of real events when ABs descended from the skies to Earth. If science actually followed its beloved principle of Occam's Razor—in which the simplest answer is generally the correct one, all things being equal—the most likely explanation for these early AB stories is that *they must be based in actual human experience.* Unfortunately, most scientists accept these pseudo-scientific hypotheses as fact and/or are unwilling to challenge the religions that were responsible for expurgating any sign of ABs from the annals of history in the first place. This deliberate erasing of the evidence of ABs from early historical accounts was accomplished via psychological conditioning, religious edict, and, when all else failed, brute force. These efforts by dozens of generations of religious leaders were facilitated by literal armies of political enforcers.

Fortunately, some scientists have had the courage to investigate and even support the AB Intervention hypothesis. For instance, the theory of *panspermia* (the existence of life throughout the universe) suggests that the "seeds" of life may have been purposely spread by an advanced extraterrestrial civilization.[5] The fact that we've discovered virtually hundreds of planets that could support life increases the possibility that a more advanced species may have directed such "seeds" our way, or that they could have visited, deposited simple life forms, and then cultivated the barren Earth to support this new life. A more complex model of intervention, consistent with pre-modern human memories about ancient gods, would have the ABs arriving, establishing bases, having sporadic contact with humans, and then departing. Such a scenario could explain some of the artifacts I will be discussing shortly. This theory is consistent with human observations of ABs on Earth from spaceships, as represented in the drawings and carvings of pre-modern peoples. However, I would like to posit a third and even more complex model. Buttressed by research from the late Zecharia Sitchin, Eric von Däniken, and others, it includes AB genetic invasion and manipulation of Earth's species as well as the exploitation of humans. As grim and terrifying as this sounds, the ABs also provided valuable assistance in our evolution as a species.

Hominids have been around for six million years. *Homo erectus*, still brutish but increasingly civilized, arose less than two million years ago. Due to genetic intervention by ABs, *Homo sapiens* arose in Africa about 200,000 BP (BEFORE THE PRESENT; WITH JANUARY 1, 1950 AS THE ORIGIN, OR "PRESENT" DATE, OF THE TIME SCALE). Under AB colonial rule, *Homo sapiens sapiens* arose by 100,000 BP, quickly branching off into different regions and varying genotypes. With only sparse evidence from the last 250,000 years, we must fill in the gaps as best we can and make certain inferences regarding times, places, and so forth. After the 11,500 BP global cataclysm, however, the record is much clearer. Sophisticated cultures blossomed from survivors in several locations—Mesopotamia, India, the Andes, and so on. The stories that survived (some explicit, others vague) contained memories of AB-human interaction occurring prior to the cataclysm. Some hinted of highly evolved civilizations such as Lemuria[6] and Atlantis, or holy places such as Eden and Shambhala.

The post-cataclysm stories—the tale of Noah, for example—described AB assistance that helped humans rebuild after the catastrophe. The downside of this help, of course, was continuation of the AB colonial rule first hinted at in the story of Adam and Eve. The revival of human culture did not escape the subjugation and sense of disenfranchisement imposed by the ABs. Several survival accounts (Sumerian, Hebrew, Sanskrit, and African, for example) describe conflicts among the gods and with their human tribes. This warring is partly what caused the AB colonizers to quit their overt rule of Earth prior to 4,000 BP. They left humans to their own devices or under kings and queens whose lineages were derived from AB bloodlines. The extant lists of Egyptian rulers actually track this shift: ABs gave way to 5th-millennium hybrid kings, to be followed by the pharaohs, who both imitated and claimed to be descendants of the ABs/gods.

The first priest-kings turned their regencies into sects in order to manipulate people into the continuing worship of their absentee AB forebears. This maneuver only succeeded in stifling intellectual and social progress: multiple civilizations descended into the age of cults, and squabbling priest-kings perpetuated the tribal wars that humans had fought under the flags of their AB overlords for millennia. As centuries passed without a sign of the ABs returning, the priest-kings, with their weakening bloodlines, began to lose the "spell" they once exerted over their subjects. To continue leveraging this control over new generations, royal priests began to reframe the historical facts about ABs into supernatural terms, inventing the idea that the heavenly realm had bestowed upon them a unique and privileged advantage over the masses. Cult leaders such as the Roman popes declared that only they possessed the divine channel to receive messages from the departed AB-gods. In this manner, supernatural religions were created to replace the AB-based cults. This sleight of hand, shifting the human focus from real ABs to false gods, kept humans under the psychological sway of authoritarian leaders who, naturally, had their own political agendas.[7] For two millennia humans have fretted between this supernatural "spell" and the natural, biological impulse to realize their human potential. Mired in an emotional stagnation largely of our own creation, many of us are now (perhaps with the help of input from more enlightened ABs) working to reveal the *real* story behind the cover-up.

Evidence for AB Intervention

The evidence that supports the AB Intervention hypothesis is both direct and indirect. The direct evidence includes artifacts of possible extraterrestrial origins—see the research of Michael Cremo and others—as well as eyewitness reports of AB-related events. The indirect data corroborate postulated timelines, locations, and activities attributed to ABs.

Eyewitness reports with varying levels of detail can be found in early texts recorded on papyrus, copper, clay, stone, wood, and fabrics, found *in situ* or of known provenance. Later interpretations of these texts still reflect that culture's record of its conscious memories. This is clearly illustrated in the Hebrew texts that I will describe in a moment. Sumerian, Egyptian, Hindu, Hebrew, and other records reporting observations of ABs or human interactions with them are credible and reliable pieces of evidence. Examples include the Dead Sea Scrolls,[8] the Nag Hammadi Scriptures,[9] and the Gnostic Gospels.[10] Additionally, an excellent analysis prepared by Roger Voss illustrates the quality of such information found in the oldest publicly available version of the Paleo-Hebrew Torah.[11] Although there are earlier texts that describe ABs interacting with humans, this version shows that about 2,000 years ago, Hebrew scribes still acknowledged the AB reality. Voss cites Deuteronomy 10:17, which states, "For Yahweh your God—He is God of the Elohim, and Lord of the lords; God, the great, the mighty, and the fearful...." The names *Yahweh*, *Lord*, *lords*, *God*, and *Elohim* all refer to ABs. Later versions of these texts were rewritten to distort the facts. By the time of the Nicean Council in 325 CE, which formally institutionalized Christianity, both Jewish and Christian leaders had conflated the absentee Yahweh and Elohim ABs into their notion of a singular god. Why they shifted from reality to fantasy I will reveal a bit further on in this essay. For now, let's review the more indirect evidence for the AB Intervention hypothesis: fossil records, anomalous artifacts (which can also be considered direct evidence, depending on the item or items in question), indirect DNA corroboration, and language patterns. Each one of these exerted an external influence on human physical evolution and social development.

The fossil record shows that our hominid ancestors slowly evolved over a time period of more than six million years. They coped with harsh conditions for a long time and with little genetic mutation. Yet, around 200,000 BP, in what was to be a radical, abrupt change in the *erectus* pace of genetic mutation, a much more nimble and intelligent species (*Homo sapiens*) suddenly appeared in Africa. Multiple sites illustrate this rapid divergence. One is the existence of *erectus*-type stone hand axes and other tools found in south Africa and on Crete (an island separated from Africa for millions of years) that dated to 700,000 BP. They were still in use 130,000 years ago, while *Homo sapiens* was already establishing far-ranging seafaring routes. Again, the genetic changes producing *Homo sapiens* occurred within a very short period rather than hundreds of thousands or even millions of years. Some feel that this "gap" in human evolution requires an extraordinary explanation. The Genesis passage cited previously offers one. As Voss cites from Genesis 1:26, "...the Elohim said, Let us make man in our image...." To achieve that goal would require something akin to genetic manipulation to create an entirely new species—in this case, *Homo sapiens*.

After about 100,000 years, another anomalous gap occurred in the genetic evolution of genus *Homo* development. *Homo sapiens sapiens* fossils dating from that period can be found in Africa and beyond. Armed with complex language skills and tools, these modern humans demonstrated greater mental capabilities with no corresponding increase in brain capacity. This historical reality is consistent with Sumerian and Hebrew texts that describe AB "upgrades" of humans.[12] The rabbinical scribes at the time of the Babylonian exile (6th century BCE) still accepted the historical claims that Elohim (read: the ABs) had raised humans above the other animals on Earth. As Genesis 1:26 states, "let them have dominion over [all animals and the earth]...."

Anomalous artifacts can be either indirect or direct evidence of AB Intervention. The most ubiquitous of these are the pyramidal structures that can be found on nearly every continent. In addition to sharing the same angular shape, their positioning indicates an astral orientation. They are often aligned in the direction of fixed stars thought to be the locations of AB home bases (for example, the Pleiades). Designed by the ABs themselves for only periodic visits, human acolytes maintained them as altars where ABs demanded worship and sacrifices. The AB-gods then enforced these obligations. Most pyramids or ziggurats date from after the Cataclysm (the most obvious exception being the Great Pyramids in Egypt), when some ABs decided to return to Earth and render assistance to the survivors.

During this period, AB interaction with humans continued. Biblical accounts of the gigantic progeny of ABs and humans indicated their presence during the time of King David 3,000 years ago. The structures eventually deteriorated after the complete withdrawal of ABs from Earth. By the 5th century BCE, the ABs had been absent for a millennium or more. The Greek historian Herodotus, describing the cradle of Western civilization, reported that the ziggurats had fallen into ruin. These events and dates neatly coincide with the AB timeline already mentioned here.

Indirect DNA corroboration of the AB Intervention hypothesis comes from more than two decades of genetic research. Using mitochondrial DNA (mtDNA), researchers now believe that *Homo sapiens sapiens* came from one or a few related females in Africa less than 200,000 years ago. This date precedes the estimated date (between 150,000 to 50,000 BP) for the arrival of *Homo sapiens sapiens* in Europe and Central Asia. This so-called Eve Event is consistent with the fossil record and the Annunaki history first publicized by Zecharia Sitchin in his series of books, *The Earth Chronicles*. No male Y-chromosome analysis to date places an "Adam" coexistent with that "Eve." This is consistent with *in vivo* or *in vitro* genetic manipulation of related female ova using multiple sperm donors. (Ancient texts indicate that the AB colonies had more males than females.)

The history of blood-type genes also provides a window into AB involvement in human history. For instance, type-B blood appeared sometime around 11500 BP. This date is associated with the Deluge survivors in the Turkic-Mesopotamian region (believed by some to be the site of the story of Noah's ark). The peoples who currently live in this region have a higher-than-average percentage of type-B than other peoples living in adjacent areas.

As far as language patterns go, stories from many cultures assert that their ancestors received their language or alphabet from the gods. This includes the Egyptians, who claimed that Thoth was the source of their language, and the Hindus, who credit the Sanskrit alphabet to the AB Saraswati. It appears this AB gift of language also involved a genetic upgrade. The FOXP2 gene, which gave *Homo sapiens* control over the muscles of the mouth and throat, appeared about 200,000 BP, coinciding with the leap from *erectus* to *sapiens*. Insertion of this gene could explain how Abs gave humans language skills beyond those of other hominids.

Help From the Starry Skies

In the biblical tale of the flood, God warned Noah of its coming beforehand. He was told to build a special boat (an ark) and gather his family onboard, along with animals to breed after the storm. The Snohomish tribe in the Pacific Northwest believe that ABs warned their ancestors to prepare canoes to ride the coming tide to the mountaintops. More than 500 similar legends have been identified worldwide. Their central theme is a prior warning by ABs to prepare for survival after a widespread flood or other catastrophic event. While this suggests a universal event, specific dates are lacking. Fortunately, dateable evidence indexed by D.S. Allan and J.B. Delair in their book *Cataclysm* places the date of a global catastrophe about 11,500 BP.[13] In it, the authors describe reports of volcanic eruptions, floods, earthquakes, the rising of mountains, dark skies, the sun appearing to stand still, and more. Scattered groups of people who survived this cataclysmic horror were left with varying levels of knowledge and resources. Civilizations that had been thousands of years old no longer existed. For some lucky clusters of survivors, ABs returned to selected areas on Earth and offered their assistance, just as many countries do today after natural disasters. Sophisticated city centers began to rise in Sumer between the Euphrates and Tigris rivers and nearby mountain regions, along the Indus River Valley, in the Tian Shen Plateau in what is now China, and in the Andes region of South America. The surviving cultures became focused on the ABs who had helped them. This period of rebuilding and relearning under the tutelage of the "gods of old" lasted anywhere from 5,000 to 6,000 years.

The Subjugation of Humans

The first phase of AB intervention in the development of *Homo sapiens* was impersonal, technical gene-splicing. But, as *Homo sapiens* quickly evolved, both physically and mentally, its interactions with ABs became more personal and immediate. Cohabitation between the AB colonizers and humans occurred during both the pre- and post-Cataclysm eras. Humans who labored for the ABs or had become members of their households must have learned a great deal from them. That said, the exile from Eden was a turning point. Humans lost their access to AB knowledge and technologies. As Genesis 3:22 states, "And Yahweh [and the] Elohim said, Behold, Man is become as one of us, to know good and evil. And now, lest he stretch out his hand, and take also of the tree of life, and eat, and live forever...." The ABs realized that human mastery of their advanced knowledge was a threat.

After Eden, the most senior Annunaki/Elohim kept their distance from humans, but their sons (the *Bene Elohim*, in Hebrew) practiced miscegenation—in other words, they mixed with humans via inter-marriage, cohabitation, intercourse, and procreation. As Voss cites from the Ethiopic Book of Enoch and Genesis 1:26, "Lamech, the father of Noah, became afraid and fled, and he did not believe that he [Noah] was of him but of the image of the angels of heaven." (According to all accounts, Noah had pale skin, bright eyes, and long, wooly white hair.) These progeny from *Bene Elohim*-human parentage were called *Nephilim*, meaning "demigods" or "giants" in Hebrew. Some contemporaries saw these strange giants as undesirable rejects from both AB and human societies, but the prevailing view was that they were part of a royal bloodline. After the AB abdication of direct rule (which occurred about 4,000 or 5,000 years ago), these royal half-breeds assumed control over the former AB kingdoms in what is now known as the cradle of Western civilization.

Given the present body of evidence, we have no choice but to see ourselves as a hybrid species. While this fact was well-known by humans at the dawn of modern history, the knowledge was then distorted by the ruler-priests—who became pharaohs, popes, and the like—who took advantage of those who were ignorant, psychologically manipulating them to serve their own economic and political agendas. *Unaware of our real history, most of us unwittingly see these kings/priests as our benefactors.*

ABs as Colonizers

This kind of close engagement between two species involves advantages and disadvantages for both parties, some with long-term implications. For this reason, at this point in time we cannot see all the pros and cons of the AB intervention in our own evolution. However, a review of European colonization of lesser developed societies during the past five centuries offers insight into some long-term effects of the Elohim/Annunaki on the plight of modern humans. Their interference in the natural process of human evolution (which included hybridization) left us prone to and easily manipulated by existential fears. The AB legacy, continued by their hybrid descendants, caused psychological damage several orders of magnitude worse than what was wrought by any European colonial regime. Admittedly, this genetic intervention (upgrading hominids to *Homo sapiens*) and technical assistance accelerated our physical evolution, but the colonial strategy warped our view of ourselves and our potential. This closely mirrors the experience of native Africans and Americans colonized and enslaved by so-called advanced European societies.

It's probably best to think about the rule of AB gods in the following terms: European colonists used superior firepower to establish control over native populations. They demanded that the natives bow down (worship) and provide their best offerings to them, their new overlords. They maintained control using the "divide and conquer" principle, setting locals against one another in order to weaken their solidarity. In the same way, European colonials gave special privileges to groups in exchange for manipulation of their own people. These small groups—sycophants to the king, queen, or whatever title the royals used—gained access to new and foreign knowledge. Gifts and special prerogatives ensured their loyalty to the colonial governors. Ties between collaborators and the king's men became stronger than loyalties to even their own families or tribes.

This colonial scenario applies to the extraterrestrial occupation of Earth by ABs. Even if it wasn't done deliberately, the fact that ABs mixed with humans introduced social divisions that further weakened local communities. *Homo sapiens* was seen as a source of labor, considered as a physical resource to be used as the ABs pleased: brute laborers, hewers of wood, drawers of water, miners (in south Africa) of precious metals and stones, foot soldiers, cannon fodder, and even sexual servants. Initially, strong *Homo sapiens* were sent to the mines, some used as a support community to provide foodstuffs and other AB needs. Soon a select few were trained in more personal services.

Those who became the loyal subjects of the ABs were the seeds of technically advanced human cultures. But the aboriginal *Homo sapiens* population continued to grow. Increasing numbers not needed by the ABs gained independence. Free aboriginals with the same mixed AB/hominid DNA would spread over the globe, just as our earlier *erectus* half-ancestors did. This initial AB input is evident in all iterations of *Homo sapiens.*

Some later mutations occurred in *Homo sapiens sapiens* as a result of AB-human miscegenation. As Genesis 6:2 states, "the sons of the Elohim [ABs] saw the daughters of men that they were fair, and took themselves wives of all that they chose." This practice created new genetic combinations and produced new human social classes. The ABs created varying human roles and levels of authority, just as the European colonists did much later on. Interpreters became priests, guards became warriors, and personal aides turned into administrators and professionals.

The Impact of the Colonization Experience

A normally evolving species with the intellectual potential of *Homo sapiens* ought to have continually balanced technical and social change in the interest of its own survival. Yet, inventions in manufacturing, energy, transportation, and weapons today far outpace human capabilities to avoid their self-destructive consequences. Our social sciences offer no plausible explanation for such a discrepancy. We must look elsewhere for an explanation of why humans became so self-destructive, spoiling our "nest" for future generations. Studying AB history reveals the true source of these self-destructive habits and internecine wars during the post-Cataclysmic, Annunaki/Elohim colonization.

Every religion-based culture today operates on the notion that it is special, selected for that honor by a god or gods who is expected to bail it out in the end. This sense of being the *elect* absolves the believers from responsibility for consequences of their thoughts or actions. Believing that they have The Truth leads to habitual ignorance or denial of the facts and an inability to solve self-created problems. However, a subconscious need to fend off religious doubt incites conflict and war with others whose Truth contradicts their own. To maintain this religious sense of being *chosen*, believers must remain blind to the implications of their decisions. How did humans become such a psychological mess?

During the reign of the AB-gods, primitive humans—intimidated by the "shock and awe" factor of AB extraterrestrial weapons and other technologies—would do anything the ABs ordered. It only took a few generations of harsh punishment for humans to become conditioned to the custom of obedience and the rituals of worship. To compensate for humanity's dependent, slave-like status, the AB-gods made promises such as: *We have chosen you. We will protect you from the wrath of another god and his people. You may be rewarded with visits to our kingdom.* And so on. The extreme result of this AB punishment/reward rule was an almost psychopathic willingness to engage in crusades, inquisitions, jihads, and genocide to propagate one's religion or wipe out those of others, preferably both. However, not all is gloom and doom. If we choose to, we can excise these psychological blocks and remove these blinders that separate us from each other and prevent our species from achieving a mature culture among other ABs. The first step to becoming a healthy species is to understand the origin of supernaturalism.

From Real ABs to Supernaturalism

When the AB rulers ended their visible presence here on Earth, they left emotionally dependent humans mourning their absence.[14] Wishing to continue their privileged status, the left-behind priesthood decided to take advantage of the bereaved to keep them worshiping and sacrificing at the AB altars. So they invented a concept of a divine AB realm, claiming only priests could contact the ABs in the heavens. Priests began to supplant real accounts of ABs and humans with fictional supernatural myths. By embracing a principle attributed to the Jewish teacher Jesus—*by their fruits shall ye know them*—we can infer the goals of these early cult leaders by the characteristics they sought in their followers: blind faith in their edicts; obeisance to authority figures; a lack of personal responsibility; and the suppression of independent thinking. Sect leaders distorted or destroyed documentation of AB history to justify this concocted supernaturalism. Using it to gain control of converts, they frightened the faithful into obeying their commandments and paying support to the royal/ priestly elites. (At this point, I wish to make it clear that we learned a great deal from the teachings of Buddha, Lao Tze, and Jesus, for example, and that they embodied the cooperative and nurturing traits necessary for human self-actualization. Fortunately these positive characteristics are widely lauded in virtually every one of today's religions and serve as a counterweight to the negative colonial legacy described previously.)

A 2,000-Year Cover-Up

It should be clear by now that power-hungry descendants of direct AB-human progeny covered up the truth about the role of ABs (the so-called gods) in human history. To hide their agenda they created religious supernaturalism and propagated it through what may be the most comprehensive brainwashing effort in our galaxy. In this they were assisted by a great number of *Homo sapiens sapiens* who were the household intimates of the early AB-hybrid kings and knew the true AB story of colonialism. Their descendants became the Hebrew, Egyptian, and Roman priests who conflated the many ABs into one all-powerful god. Humans long conditioned by AB colonials to depend on and even worship them were easily manipulated by these priest-kings to abdicate any natural impulse toward spiritual and mental freedom. Unfortunately, modern science is not an effective counterweight to this deceit. Caught in their own limited dogma, mainstream scientists neither open themselves to theories that expand their views nor challenge the alleged historical underpinnings of supernaturalism. They learned long ago how to benefit from the naive public's deference to "official" authority and to demonize evidence that might undermine their own godlike powers.

Despite spasmodic periods of intellectual and spiritual renaissance, such as what occurred in Greece during classical times, during the zenith of the Library in Alexandria, during the growth of Muslim cultures in the 11th century, and during Europe's own intellectual awakening in the 15th and 16th centuries, the supernatural worldview has prevailed for more than two millennia. The mind-limiting nature of top-down religions and financially driven science (both controlled by the same circles, in fact) has effectively blocked the "uninitiated" from any access to or discussion of the evidence for natural non-human intelligence and its role in human evolution. Medieval clergy and their cohorts in charge of spreading orthodoxy had an institutional interest in maintaining control of the masses.

As new financial and political power groups arose, they saw the benefits of perpetuating the supernatural god myth to maintain continuing physical and economic dominance over both the workers and consumers. This tradition of priestly and scientific circles manipulating their deviously implanted superstitions has existed since the withdrawal of the AB gods of old. The supernatural and materialistic worldviews are now so deeply embedded in the human psyche that our acceptance of them is as routine as breathing. After two millennia of religious and scholarly deception, the modern continuation of this practice has been easy. Even now, we are still a long way from replacing cult-based theology with fact-based knowledge.

Efforts to create a forum for discussion of all the evidence will never be successful without a reexamination of the AB history outlined here. We must honestly face both the psychological impact of being a hybrid race and the warping of our consciousness by supernaturalism, before society as a whole can deal with current evidence that suggests that the ABs have returned. Uncovering our *true* history is an unavoidable prerequisite for creating a healthy human future among ABs in our galaxy and beyond. I believe that a successful strategy aimed at disclosure or revelation of the cover-up must be based on an understanding of the colonial model described previously. Those who wish to create a more open and mutually beneficial relationship with our AB relatives must see themselves as leaders of an uprising in a colony that no longer serves any purpose. As all successful revolutions do, they will need help. Perhaps we should consider the possibility that help may be available from sympathetic ABs among our former colonizers and oppressors.

Notes

1. Von Ward, Paul. *Our Solarian Legacy: Multidimensional Humans in a Self-Learning Universe.* Newburyport, Mass.: Hampton Roads, 2001.

2. ———. *Gods, Genes, and Consciousness: Nonhuman Intervention in Human History.* Newburyport, Mass.: Hampton Roads, 2004. p xii.

3. Dillon, James J. "The Primal Vision: The Psychological Effects of Creation Myth." *Journal of Humanistic Psychology.* 50, no. 4, (Oct. 2010): 495–513.

4. Further information on the worldview concept and additional research can be found at *http://www.vonward.com/selfassessmenttools.html.*

5. Francis Crick and Leslie Orgel at *www.panspermia-theory.com/directed-panspermia.*

6. Hall, Stan. *Savage Genesis: The Missing Page.* Self-published book, April, 2011. From *www.goldlibrary.com.*

7. Roman Catholic papal edicts granted colonizers the right to invade, capture, vanquish, and subdue all non-Christians, reduce them to perpetual slavery, and take away all their possessions and property.

8. From *www.physorg.com/2010-10-google-dead-sea-scrolls-online.html.*

9. From *www.nag-hammadi.com/manuscripts.*

10. From *www.earlychristianwritings.com/gnostics.html.*

11. The author is indebted to Roger Voss for his meticulous review of transliterations and translations of the 2,500-year-old Hebrew into contemporary English and his permission to use them here.

12. The best explanation geneticists have for these two unexplained gaps or leaps are the meaningless words "punctuated equilibrium."

13. Allan, D. S. and J. B. Delair. *Cataclysm: Compelling Evidence of a Cosmic Catastrophe in 9,500 B.C.* Santa Fe, N.M.: Bear and Company, 1997.

14. The departing ABs deserve their share of the blame for not planning a more constructive transition.

The Micmac and the Picts: Distant Cousins?

By Steven Sora

Christopher Columbus did not have to wait until 1492 to reach America to meet the people he called Indians; *they* had actually visited *him* twice previously. In 1477 he was passing through Ireland on his way home from Thule (now believed to be present-day Iceland or Greenland). There, in Galway, the bodies of a man and a woman washed up on the shore. Presumably they had been drifting across the Atlantic in a boat and did not survive the journey. Because of their skin color and physiognomy, Columbus believed they were from somewhere in Asia. This would not be the last time such an event would take place during the lifetime of the man who believed he discovered the New World. After this voyage to the north, he lived for a short time on Madeira's smaller isle of Porto Santo, where all kinds of debris would regularly wash up the beach. Columbus was told that carved wood was occasionally among the flotsam, which some took as evidence of the existence of an as-yet undiscovered civilization somewhere across the ocean. On the island of Flores in the Azores, a chain of islands in the mid-Atlantic, he encountered two more of these tragic travelers from across the Atlantic.

Although Columbus never did meet one of these living expatriates, others did. Because he made a point to seek out sailors and captains to enrich his studies in cartography and increase his expertise as a map-seller, it is highly likely that he was told they came from *Katai* or *Kait-hikan* (Algonquin for "great ocean" and "great body of water," respectively), which actually might have been referring to Cathay (China) in the East Indies, the ostensible goal of his own travels. He had also read Aristotle, who stated that between Iberia and India there

197

existed a navigable sea—the Atlantic. He was also familiar with Pierre d'Ailly's *Imago Mundi*, and even made a note in the margin stating that *India est prope Hispania* ("India is near to Spain"), thereby indicating that he did not believe that there was any landmass separating Spain from Asia.

Discovering the Old World

Evidence of much older encounters with proto–North Americans crossing the Atlantic existed at that time, although to the Europeans it was uncertain from where these visitors originated. Columbus read of such encounters in *Historia Rerum Ubique Gestarum*, by Aeneas Silvio Piccolomini (who would become Pope Pius II). One such story described a voyage (whether it was accidental or not is unknown) of a handful of visitors who had actually made it to Germany during Roman times. In the margins of the book, Columbus made a notation that they must have been from *Katayo*. He believed that such a journey would have been possible but quite arduous. Quintus Metellus, the Roman historian and proconsul of Gaul, recorded firsthand this extraordinary visit when the group of visitors was brought to him. He, too, believed that their appearance and skin color meant they were of Asian extraction. In his *Historia de las Indias* (published in 1553), Francisco Lopez de Gomara wrote that he believed these visitors were natives of Labrador, and that they were merchants traveling the islands of North America. De Gomara may have been privy to another, earlier text that recorded a voyage of a canoe as large as an ocean-going barge that carried people from the coast of the Baccalaos (present-day Newfoundland) to Lubeck, Germany, in 1153. Justin Winsor's *Narrative and Critical History of America* contends that this voyage was repeated more than once.

It should be noted here that Europeans at that time were aware of the Inuit peoples, who regularly navigated the frigid waters of the north Atlantic. It was understood that their customs and characteristics were different from those of other indigenous peoples of North America. Certainly, people knew enough about their habits and culture to know that the Inuits could not have created the *middens* (piles of discarded oyster shells, fish bones, and other food-related debris) that are still preserved today along the New England coastline. These piles (some of which are as large as 150 feet (46 m) wide and 30 feet (9 m) high) were actually left behind by Algonquin-speaking peoples. Oddly enough, such piles can also be found along the Norwegian coastline, which may indicate some connection between the two cultures.

Long before Europeans started exploring the New World in earnest, Native Americans, most likely Algonquin-speaking tribes, were already exploring the Old World. Cardinal Peter Bembo wrote of seven men reaching Brittany in 1508. Short of stature, with swarthy skin and broad faces, their skin was marked with violet streaks. No one could understand their language. The following year another New World expedition to France brought seven more men who were described as wearing only a sort of belt or loincloth. Most of these journeys were never recorded for posterity, as the travelers did not establish permanent settlements or conquer any territory. Is it possible, then, that an even larger migration from North America to the Old World took place?

New World Seapower

Indigenous North American peoples were likely just as adept at crossing long distances of water as their European counterparts, if not more so. In the North, in present-day Canada, the Inuit navigated icy waters and fished from kayaks and *umiaks* (one-person boats). Off of what is present-day Montauk in Long Island, various tribes used larger craft to hunt for whale. The historian Samuel Eliot Morison wrote that further south of New England, all the way to the Caribbean Sea, travelers used 8-foot (2.5-m)-wide canoes that were as long as European galleys. Protected from the sun under awnings of palm, crews of 25 men carried passengers and their goods to market. Some Carib boats were 80 feet (24 m) long, twice as long as some European ships. Columbus himself recorded seeing fleets of 120 ships with 25 armed men in each. (At that point the sail was already in use by Mayans and Carib peoples.) It is not only possible, then, that Native Americans were able to cross the ocean, but that the inhabitants of the Old World were aware of much earlier crossings. For example, Pausania, a Greek geographer writing in 150 CE, described a group of islands whose inhabitants, he said, were red-skinned and had hair like that of a horse. Rather than being a racial characteristic, this "red skin" might have been the result of some kind of face or body paint. All of this of course begs the question of whether the ancient Greeks were already aware of Native Americans nearly 1,500 years before Columbus would sail west.

In the Northeastern portion of the North American continent there still exist today numerous tribes that share the Algonquian super-group of languages. From the Labrador Peninsula and the Canadian Maritime province to as far west as the Mississippi, numerous tribes still speak variants of this basic language group. These tribal organizations traded with one another extensively via a network of roads extending from modern-day Canada to the Gulf of Mexico, and from the Mississippi all the way to the Atlantic coast. Not all trade was conducted by overland routes, however. The rivers and the coastal Atlantic regions were better served by seagoing traders. The tribe that would have been the most likely to have made this cross-ocean contact was the Micmac—also called the Souriquois by the French. The Micmac territory extended as far north as Maine. Their southern neighbors included the Abanaki, Wampanoag, and the Pennacook, as well as the Lenni-Lenapi group of tribes that extended into Long Island.

The Red Paint People (who called themselves the *Beothuk*) eked out a living in Newfoundland and Labrador for thousands of years. They flourished during the Maritime Archaic period, which lasted from approximately 7000 BCE to the mid-18th century. Living primarily along the coasts, sometimes as far south as New England, they were skilled canoeists. Their vessels, which they made out of birch, were large enough to enable them to catch swordfish and hunt for seal. Fish was the staple of their diet, which they supplemented with shellfish and meat. They used tools for woodworking, fishing, and hunting. They had an elaborate burial culture and worked in stone, as well. Richard Edens was one of the earliest writers to mention them, in his 1555 account of Newfoundland's natives, titled *Gatherings from writings in the New World*. He described the Beothuk as having "tawny" skin and commented that they painted their bodies with red ochre, just as their neighbors, the Micmac, did. They further decorated themselves with bracelets of silver and copper. Remnants of their culture extend as far inland as Lake Champlain.

Advanced Culture in the Americas

Verrazano, the Italian explorer who sailed for the king of France, Francois I, in 1524, might have been the first European to describe the Algonquin tribes he met during his exploration of the area spanning present-day New England. He called the area L'Arcadia, a name close to the Micmac word *akadie*, meaning "place of abundance." In Europe, Jacobo Sannazarro's *Arcadia* was a popular work describing an idyllic ancient area in Greece bearing that name. The coincidence of the very similar Algonquin word might have surprised him. Remarkably, Verrazano recorded bringing a Native American aboard his ship to pilot the vessel into Newport Harbor, which indicates that they must have been able to communicate with one another. He, too, described the people as "russet" in color, and remarked how the queen of the tribe would wait in a boat while the men would come to trade.

Not long after Verrazano explored New England, French adventurers under Jacques Cartier reached the St. Lawrence River, near what would later become Montreal. They made camp and settled in with hopes of surviving the winter of 1534. The cruel weather was not the worst of their worries, however, as scurvy began to take its deadly toll. The hideous disease had taken the lives of 25 men, whose bodies were piled under snow drifts, as the ground was too frozen to properly bury the dead. Among the remaining 125, only 10 men were healthy. In order to prevent the nearby Algonquin tribe from finding out just how weak and vulnerable they were, Cartier and his men attempted to make as much loud noise as they could, in hopes that it would keep them away. When their Algonquin neighbors finally made contact with them, it was actually just in time to save their lives. A medicine man boiled the leaves and bark of a certain tree to make a brew they called *annedda*, and had the men drink it. All of them were saved, their scurvy cured by the concoction. It wasn't until 1795 that the British "discovered" the cure for scurvy—which was based on the same knowledge that the native seagoing peoples of Canada had carried with them for centuries.

That the Native Americans had a cure for the greatest plight of long-distance sailors would not be the last surprise for the French. A planned Native village called *Hochlaga* (which would later grow to become Montreal) had streets emanating from a central square, a relatively modern conception that was only just being incorporated into cities such as London and Paris. Clearly they were not the "savages" that they would become in the historical annals of the New World. Just as the Spanish would find the Aztec City of Tenochtitlan to be greater than their own Seville, the Europeans would discover many surprising things about the Native Americans.

In 1606, the French colonization of Nova Scotia was underway. Lescarbot described the Micmac in his *History of New France*. He commented that the language of the native peoples was half Basque, which, again, goes to this idea of early trans-Atlantic contact. Lescarbot met a Micmac ship with a moose painted on its sail. He assumed they had learned how to sail from fishermen, who by now had become quite numerous in the rich fishing banks of the New World. Other European authors noted that the Micmac decorated themselves with arm and leg bracelets comprised of shells, wampum, quillwork, and beads. They covered their skin in grease to stave off the mosquitoes and help protect themselves against the elements. The French writer Diereville was able to observe their art of tattooing and described the process in great detail. He commented on the courage and patience required to endure hours and hours of being painfully pricked by needles on every part of the body, including the face. Women shared in this art, as well. While the Micmac still used the red ochre paint in their burial rituals, the extensive tattooing gave rise to a new epithet, "Bluenoses." Interestingly, after the Roanoke voyage of Sir Walter Raleigh, John White, a famous illustrator, described the Algonquin speaking tribes he met in Virginia as *Picts*. This shows that actual eyewitnesses connected the American native tribes with the Picts of Scotland, and introduces the next part of this argument.

Distant Cousins?

On the other side of the Atlantic a tribal people had already taken root in the north of Scotland shortly before the first century CE. The Scots called them the "wee dark men." What they called themselves is not known, although many names were later attached to them— one of which, of course, was the Picts. Their name comes from the Latin *picti*, which was a general term for the peoples living north of the Forth-Clyde isthmus. Like the Micmac, the Picts tattooed themselves in blue; thus early writers (including the church historian the Venerable Bede) called them the "painted people." Scottish and Orcadian folklore depicted them as underground dwellers. They often appropriated cairns and ancient *brochs* (structures similar to stone igloos, entered by crawling through a short passageway into a main circular room) as shelter, which is likely what led to that distinction. Unfortunately their language, culture, and writing would not survive 1,000 years before they were assimilated into the Christianized culture of the Celts. Therefore much of what we now know of the history of the Picts comes from outside sources. Perhaps not surprisingly, such sources often depicted them in an unflattering light.

When Rome conquered Britain the Picts were the only people who remained unconquered. Roman writers at the time all seemed to share the opinion that they had been the dominant power in the north for at least five centuries, although they disagreed on how many discrete groups of Picts there were. Some said they were two groups, while others contended there were seven separate kingdoms of Picts. Although the Pictish language has never been interpreted, it is believed that their tattoos designated individual rank. According to Bede, the Picts went into battle naked and in blue paint from head to toe. They were a formidable force, indeed; their dress (or lack thereof) and their reputation for being cannibals kept the Roman legions in fear of them.

Rome's conquest of Britain began in 43 CE. When they finally advanced to the Forth-Clyde line around 90 CE, the Roman general Agricola began erecting forts against the fearsome Picts. The Romans stopped there after defeating a large army of Caledonians and decided they could go no farther. In 142, Antonine Pius connected the forts with a massive wall that bore his name. It was hoped that the Picts could be contained behind the Antonine Wall, but this arrangement only lasted 20 years before the powerful Picts caused Rome to retreat south to Hadrian's Wall. Although Hadrian's Wall was regularly reinforced, Rome was slowly and inexorably defeated in one skirmish after another. Not surprisingly, the Romans regarded their defeat as the end of the world. After the mighty Ninth Legion disappeared beyond the Antonine Wall, no further attempts at conquest were made. In the 4th century the Picts allied themselves with the Scotti immigrant tribes, who themselves had originated in Ireland. Rome then had to contend not only with this northern force but with the Saxon invaders in the south. Two major Pictish raids caused Rome to finally sue for peace with the payment of silver and other commodities. In 412 the final withdrawal of Rome created a power vacuum, which the Picts gladly exploited. When Rome retreated, the Picts were able to break free from their northern confines and the Highlands. When the Britons finally appealed to the Angles and Saxons to help defend against the Picts, the Britons became trapped between the Picts and the Germanic invaders who came not to help, but to conquer.

There is no further established history of the Picts until the 6th century. When they became the subject of serious historical research, writers had to contend with their own prejudice, which often caused them to regard the Picts as savages, as well as with conflicting legends. Gildas, writing in 570 CE, claimed the Picts had come from some other land across the ocean. He was not aware of Greenland or the Americas, so he suggested Scythia was the place of their origin, by which he may have meant the northerly realms of Eurasia, Finland, or Russia. This same period saw the height of their power and culture. The northern areas of Scotland abound with Pictish crosses and inscribed monuments dating from this time. Few of them, however, give even the smallest clues as to what the inscriptions mean. Had the Picts remained a dominant force in history, more might have been learned.

Assimilate and Conquer

What the legions of Rome and the warriors of Scotland could not do in battle, Christianity accomplished peaceably. The Picts, never defeated in war, were assimilated in peace, and inevitably their religion and culture changed. Their original language was lost as it eventually morphed into Scots-Gaelic. As a result, the massive amount of stone carvings found throughout Scotland cannot be translated. Only their place-names remain. John Prebble summed it up best in his book, *The Lion in the North*, saying that the "Picts are a lost race, not remembered with charity." Others, however, were kinder in their estimations. Robert Bain, author of *The Clans and Tartans of Scotland*, credits the Picts as the inventors of the clan system. Because the Picts ruled the Highlands until the Vikings began raiding the joint

Pict-Scot alliance, it is the Picts, then, and not the Scots, who deserve such credit.

Shared Customs

No doubt, mainstream historians would find the possibility of a relationship between a North American indigenous people and a Northern European people remote at best, or simply nonsensical at worst. That said, there are some coincidences and striking similarities between the two groups that are not easily explained away. For starters, both the Micmac and Picts were matriarchal. This meant that individuals traced their family through the mother. The Celts, in contrast, were patriarchal. In fact, matrilineal succession separates the Picts from every other tribe that occupied the British Isles. Interestingly, the thoroughly Scottish surname MacDuff is likely Pictish in origin. The name literally means "son of (or belonging to) the black (Dubh)." Clan expert Robert Bain declared that the MacDuff clan were actually Picts, which was further supported by the fact that their lineage was first traced through the female line.

Families of both Picts and Micmac were organized in a clan system. Males in both groups wore similar loincloths. Unlike those of other Native American tribes, a Micmac's loincloth identified his membership in a particular clan. It bore symbols that were very similar to modern Scottish insignias. The loincloth of the Picts, and of course the later Highlanders, was the kilt, an article of clothing that still allows the wearer to distinguish himself as a part of an extended clan. Early kilts carried the animal name of the clan, along with the color associated with it—the Red Deer Clan, the White Dog Clan, and so on. While family was the primary loyalty, clan was also very important. The Clan Chattan, which means the Clan of the Cat, was at one time the largest in Scotland. With its more modern Viking suffix (-ness), the word yields the name for Scotland's largest land mass, Caithness. Interestingly, there was also a Clan of the Cat among the Iroquois Nations.

The Picts and Micmac also shared similar ways of governing themselves. People had a say in the election of their *sachem* (spiritual leader) and chief, and to depose them if needed, as well as a system of inheritance, obligations of mutual assistance and defense, a council of families, clans, and the tribe itself. As well, women sat on the council in both Pictish and Micmac communities, and it was the women who would determine which man would be the chieftain. On both sides of the Atlantic this custom later gave way to patriarchal customs that were more in accordance with the tenets of Christianity. Micmac and Picts alike elected chiefs who were not succeeded by their sons. Women and men shared in the vote.

The two tribes attired themselves similarly, as well. As previously mentioned, both painted their faces and tattooed their skin, and wore little clothing so as to better display their artwork. The Micmac decorated themselves with earrings, nose ornaments, bracelets (worn on the arms and legs), and necklaces of wampum, shells, quillwork, and bells. Similarly, Pictish women adorned themselves with tattoos and jewelry, which may have been a way of displaying wealth or rank. The Micmac wore feathered headdresses, which announced the wearer's rank based on the amount of feathers. This custom was also embraced among the Picts, the only European people to denote rank in this manner. Algonquin tribes often used two feathers to signify a warrior of rank, and one to signify a sachem.

The shelters of the Picts and Micmac had much in common, as well. Most cultures will use whatever building materials are available and useful in gaining protection from the weather. The Micmac built *wigwams*, which could be above ground or, depending on the climate, partially below ground. The Red Paint People and the Inuit almost always built their living structures, called *gammes*, partially under the ground. The Picts built similar houses, called *weems*, using ditches dug six feet (1.8 m) deep into the ground. Some structures were 50 to 200 feet (15 to 61 m) long and as wide as any modern room. The roofs were then covered with slabs of stone, turf, and dirt. The Vikings used the same method at the L'Anse aux Meadows settlement in Newfoundland. The Iroquois longhouse was very similar except that it was built from timber not found in the more barren north. The word *wigwam* remained in North America, while the Pictish *wee-gamme* took on the meaning of "small house."

When it came time to celebrate, the dances of the Native American Indian are well known. In the British Isles it is the Scots and Irish who are best known for their dancing. The Highlanders were known for an annual Gathering of the Clans, which was also a practice among wider tribal units of Native American Indians. (This is something that is still done today, but from what I have seen it has lost its older significance and has taken on a more commercial function.)

The Picts and Micmac also shared many racial characteristics. They were both shorter than their neighbors, and both had darker complexions. The Celts, in comparison, tended to be tall, with red or blond hair and blue eyes—all part of the genetic heritage left behind by Norse invaders. The expression "dark Irish" or "black Irish" survives today to distinguish the Picts from their Celtic cousins. Anthropologists claim that there must have been a Mediterranean or even African genetic influence here, although there is no proof of that.

Linguistics

Other links are found in the languages of both groups. Though little of the Pictish language survives extant, we now know that the prefix *maqq-* means "son of," but it is not followed by a name, as it is in Scottish. Thus, it was likely meant to designate a member of the tribe or clan that referred to a father. Dr. John Fraser, an Oxford professor of Celtic languages, contends that this is because the Picts placed no importance on the father but a great deal of importance on the clan. They were all sons of a wider clan group. It was actually Celtic and Christian influence that elevated the status of the father. Of course the prefix *Mac-* was and still is always followed by a proper name in Scottish.

There are other linguistic parallels. When Cartier, the man who would be rescued from scurvy by a more knowledgeable "primitive" people, came to North America he met a chief whose name he recorded as Donnacana. He said the name was a title that meant "royal king," and believed that all high chiefs took this title. In Scotland, the Duncan clan received its name originally from Donnacaidh, who was their high chief. This word was also a title of respect, meaning "brown warrior."

Charles Seaholm, author of *The Kelts and the Vikings*, continued the search for the Picts along linguistic lines. He developed his theory by comparing Scottish surnames with place-names found in New England. The first record of the surname Hosack, in 1508, was one

Adam Hosack of Inverness. Inverness was the center of power among the southern Picts. The only other record of that name was found in Caithness, the area named for the Clan of the Cat. There exists the Hossack, a tributary of the Thurso River. Thurso was not the original name, however: the Vikings renamed it after their god Thor long after the Picts became Celts. On the other side of the Atlantic there is the Hoosac tunnel in Berkshire County, Massachusetts; a Hoosac Hill in Rockingham County, New Hampshire; the Hoosac Mountains in Bennington County, Vermont; a Hoosic River, also in Bennington; and several other towns named Hoosic in New York State.

Pennacook was a Pictish settlement that only became a surname much later, when the Normans brought the use of surnames to the British Isles. Pennacook was also a settlement in New England that would later become Concord, New Hampshire, when Europeans settled there. It was also an Algonquin word meaning "sloping down place." In Scotland, the Pennacook clan took their name from a place that bore a similar description. Kinbuck, a village in Scotland, combines the word *kin* with the *-uck* ending, which is generally considered to be Pictish. *Kin* and *ken* often signify a connection to water. In New England, Kennebunkport, Kennebec, and Kennebago are all places that are located near water.

Harvard professor Barry Fell has produced a large list of Algonquin and Scot-Irish names. The Merrimack, a river in New Hampshire, means "deep fishing" in the Algonquin language. In Gaelic, *merriomack* means "of great depth." *Monad* in Algonquin means "mountain", while the Gaelic *monadh* means the same thing. *Nock*, an Algonquin word meaning "hill," corresponds to the Gaelic *cnoc* which, again, bears the same meaning.

There may be less than two dozen surviving inscriptions in the Pictish written language. But from what we can deduce from representative samples, Pictish writing favored double consonants, just as many of the names on the pre-Columbian map of New England did. In the Shetlands, the Lunnasting inscription includes the word *ettocuhetts* showing the double Ts found in Massachusetts and Attaquahunchonett (in Barnstable County in that state). Place names in Scotland often end in *–ach*, -*och* and *–ock*, while Algonquin territory place names such as Potomac, Rappahanock, and Kennebec have similar sounding endings.

Seaholm and Fell's work on place names has uncovered scores of words that have similar or identical meanings on both sides of the Atlantic. Usually these are words that describe features of geography, such as hills, rivers, or arable land. Neither agrees with just who brought these common words to whom. Fell insists that the Celts carried them west, while Seaholm claims the Picts went east. The question of just who arrived first will likely never be solved. However it needs to be answered, particularly by those who feel the need to limit the achievements of so-called primitive peoples.

The Basque Connection

Basque is often described as the sole surviving, ancient non–Indo-European language in Europe. When Lescarbot commented that the language of the Picts was half Basque, he knew this from experience. At that point the Pictish language had already been forgotten, their inscriptions unreadable. The Picts and the Basques are similar in that their genesis remains unknown, and their languages unique. John Rhys, a Welsh scholar and professor at Oxford whose specialty was Celtic civilization, also saw the similarities between the lost language of the Picts and the living Basque language. To that he added one other lost language, the non-Celtic (non–Indo-European) language of the inhabitants of Munster in Ireland. The tendency to accentuate the ending consonants in a place or name were shared by all of these (almost) lost languages and evident across the ocean in North America, as well.

Sometime around the first century CE, a migration took place. Painted and tattooed, covered in animal fat, and sailing in lashed-together, hollowed-out logs, early North Americans crossed the north Atlantic. If they were missed by neighboring tribes, it was never recorded in writing. At the same time a handful of new peoples appeared on the shores of the Old World. They would remain insular in a hostile and incomprehensible world. A large number of these visitors would stay in the north of Scotland, some would settle in Ireland, and still others would reach the Bay of Biscay in France and the Pyrénées bordering Spain and France. They would keep their own customs for centuries as well as their own language. Over time, however, their isolation would not last. As they were exposed to larger populations, they were assimilated by them. They would add new words to their vocabulary and eventually convert to Christianity. Prior to their conversion, this assimilation was a mere trickle; post-conversion, it was a flood that altered their customs beyond recognition. In time the maritime Micmac, along with their Algonquin neighbors, would become patrilinear, as would the Picts, who were assimilated by the Scots and, later, the Norse. Just as their languages were lost to the sands of time, the memory of this past connection between two seemingly disparate groups would be nearly lost, as well. Only time will tell if any new knowledge of this connection will surface, thereby providing greater clarity to this version of history which, unfortunately, still treads outside the margins of accepted knowledge.

Sources

Bailey, James. *The God-Kings and the Titans*. New York: St. Martin's Press, 1973.

Bain, Robert. *The Clans and Tartans of Scotland*. London: Collins Publishers, 1983.

Cohane, John Philip. *The Key*. New York: Crown Publishers, 1969.

Forbes, Jack D. *The American Discovery of Europe*. Chicago: University of Illinois Press, 2007.

Laing, Lloyd and Laing, Jenny. *The Picts and the Scots*. London: Alan Sutton, 1993.

MacDonald, R. Andrew. *The Kingdom of the Isles*. East Lothian, UK: Tuckwell Press, 1997.

Morison. *Admiral of the Sea, A Life of Christopher Columbus*. Boston: Little, Brown and Co., 1942.

Prebble, John. *The Lion in the North*. New York: Coward, McCann and Geohegan, 1971.

Seaholm, Charles H. *The Kelts and the Vikings*. New York: Philosophical Library, 1974.

UFO Cults:
A Brief History of Religion
By William Bramley

Did you know that nearly 70 percent of all human beings belong to a UFO cult?

Really. It's true.

I am not claiming that there is a vast conspiracy in which our spouses, children, and neighbors are sneaking off to the nearest Raelian gathering when they say they're going to Home Depot for light bulbs, nor are they reading the latest missives from Benjamin Crème on the Internet when we're not at home. Nor am I saying that you need to worry that most of your neighbors and loved ones will suddenly be found dead one day after having secretly participated in the mass hysteria of another Heaven's Gate or Solar Temple. The UFO cults I am talking about here are much too big for any of that. In fact, our family and neighbors are probably quite open about their participation therein, and they may have even already invited you to join. But tell them that they are in a UFO cult, and some of them may wind up giving you a black eye for your efforts.

What I am talking about, of course, are the four major organized religions of the world.

I do not much care for the term *cult* because it has a pejorative connotation that is not always deserved. The Quakers, for example, are one of many Christian "cults" (sub-groups), but they are generally respected for their teachings of peace and brotherhood. Some fundamentalist Christians call Catholicism a cult despite the much larger population of Catholics in the world. So when I say "UFO cult," it just means a distinct group that preaches spiritual messages that purportedly come from UFOs.

211

The truth is, religious history is mostly a history of UFO cults. Most UFO cults, of course, begin and remain as marginal "fringe" endeavors. They may make a splash for a while, but most eventually fade into the woodwork. Recent examples are the so-called Three Georges who founded their quirky UFO cults in the 1950's: George Adamski, with his Nordic space alien teachers; George Van Tassel, with his channeled messages from Ashtar and other ETs; and George King, who channeled a space-age Jesus on the "etheric plane" of Venus and founded the Aetherius Society, which still operates today.

There are some people who still hold the mistaken belief that UFOs were first seen and reported in 1947. The theory goes something like this: We began exploding atomic bombs, and this raised a red flag for extraterrestrial neighbors that we did not know we had. So they started to covertly surveil Earth to see what we were up to. They did not want to openly interfere in human affairs or make their presence known to us childish warlike humans lest we target them with our aggressive impulses. So the ETs chose to stay behind the scenes while using contactees and abductees to spread teachings of peace and brotherhood in the hope that humans would one day become fit to join the cosmic community of the Space Brothers.

This is a nice story, but the Ancient Astronaut theory blew a gigantic hole in it. The overwhelming evidence indicates that our Space Brothers have been skulking around Earth long before 1947. We just called them by different names to match our misunderstanding of what they were. They were "gods" in flying vehicles, or "angels" in "clouds." These ancient descriptions were similar, if not identical at times to the UFO reports of today. A rose is still a rose, no matter what you call it. And so today we can identify many ancient cults as actual UFO cults. The Egyptian cults of the pharaoh believed that some of their kings were sired by ET "gods." The Mayans depicted human-like gods in bright flying globes observing and participating in the human warfare below. These ancient UFO cults, some of which go all the way back to ancient Mesopotamia, eventually disappeared along with the civilizations that embraced them. Or did they?

As Exhibit A, I give you a man named Moses. Raised in Egypt under the pharaohs, he grew up to become leader of a tribe that was guided by a UFO cult of its own: the cult of Abraham. The "god" of this cult was called "Jehovah"—a "god" that has provided more fuel for Ancient Astronaut theorists than almost any other. Under the guidance of Jehovah, Moses led his tribe out of Egypt to establish the Jewish religion in the Middle East. Jews still believe in Jehovah as their god, and they still cling to the texts that describe ancient UFOs as the source of their religion, be it the flying vehicle of fire and smoke described in Exodus or the "wheels within wheels" described in Ezekiel. And let's not forget the other Old Testament prophets, such as Elijah, who was supposedly taken up bodily into the sky by this god. Judaism is a UFO cult that made it big. And by "made it big" I mean that it has survived for thousands of years and has achieved great prominence, even if its membership is relatively small (less than one percent of the human population today). Judaism spawned two other UFO cults that became even larger: Christianity and Islam.

I now submit for your consideration Exhibit B: the New Testament. What more can be said about UFOs in the Christian scripture that has not already been expressed many times over? The New Testament is probably *the* most quoted text in Ancient Astronaut literature. Add the remarkable UFO-like episodes in the Christian apocrypha, and we have a veritable buffet piled high with tasty treats that have piqued the palates of ufologists for more than half a century.

Today, about a third of the human population identifies itself as Christian. They still believe in the Jewish Jehovah as their god. They still thrill to the story of the star of Bethlehem, which in the apocrypha is described as an intelligently guided craft that moves across the sky and then hovers. Christians still believe in the vision of Paul on the road to Damascus, which also has elements of a UFO abduction or contactee event. And many Christians long for the commencement of future events predicted in the Book of Revelation, which has Jesus clothed in something that resembles a spacesuit. The experiences of John, the author of Revelation, also seem reminiscent of a UFO abduction. The bottom line is that Christianity in all its guises and incarnations is just a UFO cult, even if many of its members would vigorously deny that they believe in UFOs. The next time you drive by a Christian church, understand that you are driving by a building dedicated in large part to a belief in UFOs and alien entities.

And finally we come to Exhibit C, Islam. It all started with Mohammad sitting in a cave meditating. The Christian "angel" Gabriel suddenly appeared to him on the horizon, put Mohammad into a trance, and relayed a religious message. Mohammad claimed that his new sect fulfilled the promises of two religions (read: UFO cults) that had come before him, namely Judaism and Christianity. Today more than 20 percent of the world's population follows the teachings of Mohammad.

And what of Hinduism? Hinduism is actually a hodge-podge of several different religious beliefs and myths. Its colorful pantheon of gods adorned many a hippie abode during the 1960s, and the artwork is still popular in many parts of the world today. Some of those gods flew *vimanas*—another topic of great interest to Ancient Astronaut theorists—which were armed with weapons that sound suspiciously like high-powered laser beams. There are Hindus today who dream of living with the god Krishna in human-like bodies on another planet. These are all the classic elements of a UFO cult. Currently Hindus represent about 14 percent of the human population.

Does this mean that there is no God? No consciousness separate from the body? No soul? So is it all just about humans and UFOs?

Not necessarily.

UFO cults large and small usually address deeper spiritual questions with an affirmation that there is a spiritual reality that underpins the fabric of the world. This is not surprising given the fact that there is often a spiritual element to descriptions of UFO contacts, especially those involving an out-of-body experience. Ancient and modern abductee stories usually involve being in-body during an abduction event, but there are times when it involves accompanying the ET while out-of-body. ETs are often credited with having the ability to direct a human consciousness out of the body, carry it in some kind of container, and then place it back in the body. These kinds of themes found their origin in ancient Mesopotamian UFO cults, were echoed in the beliefs of the pre-Columbian Americas, continued in some of the Christian apocrypha, and are repeated in a number of modern UFO cases.

Does this mean that ETs were and are more "spiritual" than us mere humans? Again, not necessarily. Maybe they are just better mechanics. The evidence for UFOs suggests that their society is much more technologically advanced than ours, which means that they have had more time to figure out how it all works. They do things that seem magical or mystical to us (including those things relating to matters of biology and consciousness), but which are simply a matter of mechanics to them. This does not necessarily mean that ETs are generally more "evolved" or more ethical than humans. Any moral judgment here would depend entirely on their motives, just as it does in our case. We have learned to split the atom for wondrous or nefarious ends. Likewise, we can use our knowledge of psychology to help or manipulate others. Moral and ethical evolution is a separate process from technological evolution, and this is likely true of the ETs, as well. We should expect any ETs to place first priority on their own needs, just as every living thing does here on Earth.

Where does all this leave us today?

First, we need to appreciate that the impact of human contact with UFOs on our civilization has been enormous. The major religions of today are largely the result of that contact. This means that UFOs are not just a silly little fringe phenomenon that is only of interest to kooks. It is a substantial, significant, and, above all, *real* phenomenon that has been around for a very long time. Just because ETs seem evasive and elusive does not make them any less real; just look at the various creatures and species on Earth that have been difficult to find and track. Clearly, this is a trait that extends across many life forms—and many worlds.

Second, we as the human race need to decide if we should keep participating in UFO cults, including the larger ones. I, for one, remain firmly committed to religious freedom, and I am in no way suggesting that any laws should be passed to ban any form of religious expression or non-violent religious practice. I propose instead only a voluntary "weaning" process. After all, are the beliefs of the major UFO cults really of any benefit to us? Yes, the Jewish, Christian, Islamic, and Hindu scriptures contain some fine teachings, but they also tend to encourage an attitude that fosters division and inflames conflict. The real question, of course, is why ETs would encourage such belief systems in the first place, since UFOs seem to be the source for much of it, but that is a question better left to another essay.

And what about those eschatological promises of a coming apocalypse? Why did so many Biblical prophets, such as Ezekiel and John, receive apocalyptic messages from these ET sources? Why would ETs want to drive humans to the brink of hysteria with teachings about an inevitable violent end to all that is? Again, these are questions best left to another essay—perhaps an entire *book*. Suffice it to say that belief systems that have an apocalypse at their center—eschatology—breed anxiety and encourage radicalism. They hide the obvious fact that if and when something bad happens, it will be because someone planned it, because someone was careless, or because there was a cataclysmic failure of nature that we were powerless to stop. It would have nothing to do with any god.

Many modern scientists have been trying to encourage just such a weaning process. They fail, though, when they become stubborn ideologues for the strictly secular. They would be much more successful by pushing ahead with open minds into the realm of quantum processes and by searching for the secret of consciousness behind the observer phenomenon. If the Catholic Church and Tibetan Buddhists can come around to embracing many elements of science, then science can certainly start taking a better look at the evidence regarding consciousness and UFOs that simply won't go away. When they block academic and scientific research into these topics of popular interest, so-called radical secularists do as much to spread pseudoscience as the goofiest UFO contactee ever has. This, of course, leaves a void that is often filled by people with less vigorous and stringent academic principles.

The world of UFO study today is highly polarized. The field desperately needs pragmatic, nuts-and-bolts scientists to collect reports, regress abductees, and analyze the evidence. Without this kind of groundwork, ufology cannot exist as a legitimate area of inquiry. The people who do this kind of work, however, resent the intrusion of "wackos" and "conspiracy theorists" who at first blush always seem to muddy the waters. This conflict arises from a truth about the UFO phenomenon itself: UFO behavior is sometimes, well, *wacky*. As well, behind the facade of the kindly Space Brothers there is sometimes evidence of less beneficent intent. After all, if a group of human beings were to skulk around abducting other humans, we would look at their motives with great skepticism, to say the very least. So it is natural to feel that kind of doubt—and even fear—regarding an influx of ET visitors that has done and is still doing just that.

UFO researchers are often called on to answer the common question of why the ETs are here in the first place. They are faced with a wide array of often conflicting evidence that has yielded a variety of conclusions. Therefore answers to this question have run the gamut from "They just want to quietly check us out" to "In their minds, they own the joint." As well, we now have ancient creation stories suggesting that ETs genetically engineered the human race in pre-history and have been keeping a watchful eye on their creation ever since. Where does the truth really lie? We have yet to figure it out for sure. We can begin by studying what is in front of us, but in the world of UFOs, even that can lead down some rather strange paths. There is just no getting around that. In the meantime we live with the effects of UFO contact every day, particularly as evidenced in the tapestry of UFO cults that have impacted human society in such a tangible and lasting way.

If we could even imagine a world without UFO cults, what would it look like? If all the large UFO cults were to disappear, I suspect that we would all be able to breathe a big sigh of relief. Most conflicts and wars would end. Religious radicalism would disappear almost entirely. We would still believe in UFOs, but we would stop granting them their undeserved aura of mystery and menace. We would no longer need to worry that there is a God-ordained apocalypse on the horizon, and we could more rationally plan for natural disasters. I believe that we could also more reasonably arrange our global financial structure to end the unnecessary economic problems of today, and solve any overpopulation issues using win-win solutions. Our better understanding of consciousness could also ease the fear and pain of loss that comes with death. Religion would become more about understanding and discovery than about obedience. Life on Earth could become genuinely fun.

Some people might object to this scenario. They would say that the large UFO cults are the basis of human morality, and that we *need* the structure imposed by the directives of scripture to stay civilized. The good news is that people can be quite moral without religion, and usually are. Look at where religion is weakest in the Western world: Scandinavia. The Scandinavian countries still enjoy some of the lowest crime rates and highest standards of living in the world. The character of an individual seems to have more to do with innate morality than any religious affiliation.

But this is not an essay about morality or religion in general. It is about UFOs—more specifically, UFO cults. Much more can be said about these cults, and they make for an interesting study. Whatever you do, just don't underestimate them. A marginalized little UFO cult today could one day surprise us and become one of the world's major religions tomorrow. It has happened before, and it could happen again.

A Symbolic Landscape: The Mystery of Nabta Playa and Our Ancient Past

By Thomas A. Brophy

Where did the ancient Egyptian civilization, home of the greatest monument builders of all time, come from? Will mysterious clues waiting to be deciphered once again revolutionize our knowledge of our distant past? My research into the astronomy of Nabta Playa has led to answers to the first question, and some intriguing hints regarding the second.

In early April of 2008, we—my coauthor Robert Bauval, a small team of intrepid adventurers, a deep desert explorer named Mahmoud Marai, and myself—were four days into a strenuous journey by four-wheel-drive Jeep, through totally desolate terrain in one of the most arid environments on earth, and four days from any hint of modern civilization. Because we had to pack all our supplies, including all our water, with us, once we were at our final destination we would have only a precious few hours to accomplish our goals and also do some exploring. On this particular day we were braving the blazing midday heat to explore the northwest face of a small bluff on the north of a mountain range called Jebel Uwainat. Uwainat is a massive, table-topped mountain range straddling the uninhabited region of the Sahara desert where Egypt, Sudan, and Libya meet. It is so remote and inhospitable that the mere existence of this "Alps of the desert" was not even known to the modern world until the 1920s. On the rock face that contained a faded prehistoric painting of a life-sized giraffe and a hunter (or possibly a shaman-like figure), a member of our team scrambled 12 feet (3.7 m) up the side of the cliff to a small ledge of some natural flow-stone. He excitedly exclaimed that he had found some engravings. When I joined him, I immediately cursed the fact that I didn't have my electronic compass, for there, amongst the strange engraved markings, was a beautifully formed arrow pointing to the west-northwest. After retrieving my compass I had to keep badgering our guide, Mahmoud, to take us back to the rock face so that I could measure it. Marai was eager instead to return us to our camp site, which had been carefully chosen to seclude us from the Sudanese bandits that occasionally pass through this lawless area. Finally I got back to the rock ledge engravings and, sure enough, the finely wrought arrow pointed toward the summer solstice sunset.

Elevated rock ledge, Jebel Uwainat, April 2008. Note the engraved lines and arrow pointing to the summer solstice sunset.

We may well have been the first human beings to see these engravings in thousands of years. Most of the rock art in this region dates from as far back as 12,000 years ago up to the most recent, from about 6,000 years ago, when the region became the extreme desert it is today. The engraved rock art tends to be older than the painted rock art. Did the artist or artists who engraved the arrow actually intend to indicate this yearly astronomical event, or was it only random chance? Did the markings represent some sort of early proto-writing? Who were the people who made them? A clue to these questions can be gleaned from the astronomy at the so-called Calendar Circle of Nabta Playa, some 360 miles (579 km) due east from these engravings, because it, too, indicates the summer solstice. Could the two peoples who created these two artifacts be related? It is my belief that they are not only related to each other, but were in fact the peoples who later moved to the Nile and created the pharaonic civilization of ancient Egypt.

In our book *Black Genesis*, Robert Bauval and I present the evidence that the Neolithic peoples who created the plentiful rock art in the Jebel Uwainat and Gilf Kebir regions of the Egyptian Western Desert (the northeastern Sahara) were of the same culture that built the Neolithic regional ceremonial complex at Nabta Playa. And we show that it was those peoples who moved to the Nile Valley and created the pharaonic civilization, precisely when the region suddenly transitioned from temperate savanna to the extreme desert that it is today.

A Neolithic Astro-Ceremonial Center

In 1973, an international team of anthropologists called the Combined Prehistoric Expedition (CPE), headed by Fred Wendorf and Romuald Schild, were about 65 miles (105 km) west of Abu Simbel, taking a comfort break from their labors. Someone looked down and noticed numerous potsherds and fine stone tools. They had discovered what came to be known as Nabta Playa. It soon became obvious that Nabta Playa was a very important site, and the CPE focused its efforts on excavating there every winter when the heat becomes more bearable. They uncovered, catalogued, and radio carbon–dated numerous layers of artifacts dating from circa 7000 BCE to 3300 BCE. They found tombs of cattle that had been ritually interred. Though no human remains were found at Nabta Playa, a graveyard from the same era was found about 12 miles (19 km) away. They found remnants of jewelry that, because of the shells and materials it was made of, must have come through trade from as far away as the Mediterranean and the

Red Sea. The site was used extensively by peoples from all around the region, and clearly involved important ritualistic activities. Wendorf and Schild began calling the site a Neolithic era "regional ceremonial center" even before they noticed what Nabta Playa would become famous for—the megaliths. It seems strange they didn't notice the megaliths. As Fred Wendorf himself wrote:

> The megaliths of Nabta were not recognized or identified for a long time. We began to realize their significance only in 1992....[1] [I]t is not clear why we failed to recognize them previously, or rather why we failed to understand their significance.... It was not that we did not see them because we did, but they were either regarded as bedrock or, in some instances where it was clear they were not bedrock, regarded as insignificant."[2]

The megaliths and megalithic constructions at Nabta Playa were clearly the most central aspect of the site and the rituals that were conducted there, and they required much effort and social organization to construct. There remain many mysteries about the megaliths, but nearly everyone agrees that they served an astronomical purpose of some sort. There is debate about which specific astronomy is involved, but it seems clear that Nabta Playa was not only a regional ceremonial center, but it was also a regional *astro-ceremonial* center.

The visible portion of the megalith arrangements consists primarily of six alignments of stones that radiate out from one central point like the spokes of a wheel. There are three alignments to the north-northeast direction, and three alignments to the east-southeast. The most robust interpretation is that the north-northeast alignments refer to one or more circumpolar stars, and the east-southeast alignments refer to the brightest star in the sky, Sirius, and the stars of Orion's Belt. Given that Nabta Playa was in use for more than 26 centuries, and given the fact that the megaliths had been constructed during that time frame and possibly even before it, it is likely that the alignments represented celestial events occurring during more than one epoch. Because stars "move" due to the precession of the earth, any single alignment can refer to any given star at only one specific date. Thus the multiple megalith alignments may have been used to refer to certain sets of stars at certain dates long ago.

In 1997, the CPE finally invited Kim Malville, an astronomer, to visit the site during the winter excavations. In 1998, Malville and the CPE mentioned the megaliths in a report published in *Nature*.[3] However, the article focused mainly on the Calendar Circle—a separate device made of small stones, not megalithic ones. They described the megaliths and their alignments but did not associate them with astronomy, except to note that some alignments pointed roughly north, and that one megalith alignment was astonishingly precise to due east, with *azimuths* (increments of direction from due north) of 90.02 degrees"[4] The first mention of the astronomy of the megaliths was in a brief article by Wendorf and Malville within the massive book published by the CPE in 2001.[5] In it, Malville proposed that the three northerly alignments of megaliths tracked the star Dubhe from 4742 BCE to around 4200 BCE, and of the three southeasterly alignments of megaliths, one was aimed at Sirius sometime around 4820 BCE, and the two others tracked the stars of Orion's Belt at two other dates. That article also listed the exact GPS coordinates of each megalith. When I attempted to reproduce their calculations, however, I found that some of the stars had not been at the locations given on the dates claimed. So I tried to simply calculate the megalith alignment azimuths from their raw GPS data, and found several of those calculations could not be reproduced, either. I attempted to discuss the discrepancies with the authors, but to no avail. The logical assumption was that the primary raw GPS data should be the most reliable, while their calculations were in error. So, keen to decipher the astronomy of Nabta Playa, I took their raw GPS measures for the megaliths and attempted to solve the puzzle of the astronomy independently. This I published in *The Origin Map*, believing it was of more service to generate some interest in the site and its intriguing astronomy rather than wait until the CPE responded, which could have been indefinitely. As it turns out, my calculations showed the megalith alignment they had given to the rising of Sirius circa 4820 BCE actually aligned with Sirius circa 6090 BCE, a date that, as we shall see, became problematic.

Meanwhile, the Quickbird satellite had just been launched by Digital Globe corporation, and I estimated its resolution might be able to pinpoint the megalith locations from space. I tasked the Quickbird to acquire image data (surely its first independent use for archaeoastronomy), and I was elated to find that I could identify all of the megaliths described by Wendorf in his 2001 publication.[6] As I expected, the raw GPS data from the CPE seemed to be accurate. But to be certain, I needed to visit the site in person and take measurements on the ground, which I did in October of 2003. I then teamed up with my old colleague Paul Rosen (a leader in space-based radar remote sensing) to georectify the satellite data and vet the scientific reasoning. We presented the results at a conference on ancient megalithic cultures, in Rhodes, Greece, and in a peer reviewed journal.[7] We reported that the date for the Sirius alignment given by Malville and Wendorf would have to be moved all the way back to 6090 BCE. We also contended that the three southeasterly megalith lines could be interpreted as representations of the stars of Orion's Belt and the stars of Orion's head and shoulders, all circa 6200 BCE, while the northerly megalith lines indicated the brightest star in the north at the time, Vega.

Our publication finally prompted a response to my questions about the initial faulty calculations, in the form of a paper by Malville et al. in 2007.[8] In it, they acknowledged our corrected data and calculations, and they reinterpreted the megalith alignments, now asserting that the megaliths they originally associated with Sirius circa 4820 BCE may have been away from the ancient lake, or playa, so they now "decline[d] to interpret them,"[9] suggesting instead that the other southeasterly megalith lines may have indicated the rising of Sirius circa 4500 BCE and 3500 BCE. They also suggested an alignment to Orion's Belt circa 4200 BCE, and possibly Alpha Centauri on another date, and they proposed an entirely new target for the northerly megalith alignments—Arcturus. Finally they rejected any dates circa 6200 BCE because that is "about 1,500 years earlier than our best estimates for the Terminal Neolithic."[10]

By then, I had teamed up with Robert Bauval to further research this and a range of other topics that became our book *Black Genesis: The Prehistoric Origins of Ancient Egypt*. We concluded that the southeasterly megaliths very likely did indicate the rising of Sirius. Furthermore, we remembered that early Old Kingdom Egyptian temples had been aligned simultaneously with the rising of Sirius and with the star Dubhe in the north, and so we decided to test for such simultaneous alignments at Nabta. We were surprised to find very accurate simultaneous markings of the rising Sirius with Dubhe in the sky at both dates, 4500 BCE and 3500 BCE, and these simultaneous alignments also formed very neat right angles. These two sets of alignments thus accounted for four of the six major lines of megaliths at Nabta Playa, as we wrote in *Black Genesis*:

> The findings that emerge from this integrated analysis are:
>
> 1. There are at least nine megaliths that form the three lines—A1, A2, and A3—that point north. These track the star Dubhe in the Big Dipper over a considerable period of time.
>
> 2. There are at least six megaliths that form lines B1 and B2 pointing southeast. These track the bright star Sirius at two epochs.
>
> 3. Sirius also coordinated simultaneously with the star Dubhe in the Big Dipper so that their alignments formed an approximate 90-degree angle. (This curious connection also had been noted by Wendorf and Malville; they commented that the megalith builders of Nabta Playa had 'a fascination with right angles.')[11]

Note that these simultaneous Sirius-Dubhe alignments occur when Sirius is just rising above the horizon, and Dubhe is positioned at a low altitude in the sky, as signified both in the Egyptian temples and at Nabta Playa. At first thought it might seem awkward for naked-eye astronomer-priests to simultaneously note a star (Sirius) breaking the horizon and its partner star (Dubhe) 90 degrees to the north and up in the sky. But Nabta Playa was a seasonal lake during Neolithic times (which is why Wendorf dubbed it a "playa" in the first place). It was filled with shallow water part of the year, and the megaliths that would have emerged out of the still water may well have reflected starlight directly along the sight line to an observer. This would have made the alignments readily apparent for an observer situated at the central megalithic construction. We suggest this ritual of the simultaneous sighting of the rising of Sirius together with a bright star in the circumpolar constellation—in this case, Dubhe in the Big Dipper (which the ancient Egyptians called the Bull's Thigh)—originated at Nabta Playa, and was later taken to the Nile Valley. At Nabta Playa the star sightings were both ritual and actual, involving the megalithic constructions and the giant natural reflecting pool that was the ancient seasonal lake. Later, in the pharaonic culture, the ritual became more stylized and symbolic, embodied in the "stretching of the cord" ceremony that is depicted in temple art. As we describe in *Black Genesis*:

> The ancient Egyptian texts and temple reliefs explain that stretching the cord was carried out by a priestess, who represented a deity associated with the stars, and the pharaoh. Both the priestess and pharaoh held a rod and a mallet, and a rope or cord was looped between the rods. The priestess stood with her back to the northern sky and faced the pharaoh. This scene is depicted on many temples, and the texts alongside it tell us that the pharaoh observed the trajectory of the stars with his eye in order to establish the temple in the manner of ancient times. In the texts we are unequivocally told that the king looked at a star in the Big Dipper (called Mesekhtiu, the Bull's Thigh). Some of the texts, however, mention the star Sirius and imply that it also was somehow involved in the ritual. Exactly how was this stellar alignment ritual performed? [...] A further clue to the ritual is that the pharaoh observed carefully the motion of a star in real time. Inscriptions on the Temple of Horus at Edfu, accompanying portrayals of the ritual, quote the pharaoh: 'I take the measuring cord in the company of Seshat. I consider the progressive movement of the stars. My eye is fixed on the Bull's Thigh constellation. I count off time, scrutinizing the clock...' This is also what might have happened at the ceremonial center of Nabta Playa thousands of years earlier...[12]

Around 3300 BCE, the Nabta Playa area became the uninhabitable, extremely arid desert that it is today. Directly following that date is when the earliest temples of the ancient Egyptian civilization began popping up in the Nile Valley, especially the temple of the goddess Satis on Elephantine Island near Aswan. The first known version of the temple was built circa 3200 BCE, but it was rebuilt several times over 3,000 years, its axis changing to align with the rising of Sirius as the star's declination changed through precession.

In the ancient Egyptian civilization the new year was marked by the *heliacal rising* of Sirius, an astronomical event that also herald- ed the life-giving and civilization-supporting inundation of the Nile river. The heliacal rising of a star is when it first becomes visible, glimmering for a few minutes before the dawning brightness of the sky overpowers the starlight at sunrise. In ancient Egypt the brilliant Sirius would have been invisible to the naked eye for a period of about two months or so every year, when it was too close to the sun. By the time of New Kingdom Egypt, at least from what the great tour- ist Herodotus wrote, the Egyptians had forgotten that the source of the flooding of the Nile was the monsoon rains that engorged the river upstream, but they did remember that the floods were symboli- cally heralded by the heliacal rising of Sirius. Earlier, during the time of Nabta Playa, the megalith builders marked the rising of Sirius simultaneously with the Bull's Thigh constellation (Dubhe) for at least 1,000 years (4500 to 3500 BCE), precisely when the monsoon rains directly fell on the playa and inundated the seasonal lake that would, in turn, reflect the starlight onto the megaliths they had construct- ed. The connection of the heliacal rising of Sirius with the coming of the annual life-supporting rains was direct, obvious, and viscer- al, the heavenly events coinciding with the new year renewal of the playa on earth. When the monsoon rains moved south and left their regional astro-ceremonial complex uninhabitably dry, the people of Nabta Playa moved to the Nile Valley and created the greatest temple- building civilization of history.

We believe the megalithic tracking of Sirius and the circumpolar Bull's Thigh constellation is a very robust and defensible interpreta- tion for the function of some of the megaliths at Nabta Playa. It is the astronomy associated with *earlier* dates, however, that is more con- troversial, because it brings in the more mysterious aspects of the site. Before I discuss these dates, however, I first need to mention the most famous feature of Nabta Playa, the so-called Calendar Circle. The Calendar Circle is made of stones that come up to about one's knee, or a little shorter. As we describe in *Black Genesis*, the Calendar Circle itself has suffered a convoluted history. For some reason, the first mention of it was not until the famous 1998 *Nature* paper, even though the primary mapping and archaeological analysis of the Circle had been done in 1991 and 1992. And surely it was known about in

1974. Meanwhile the whole Nabta Playa site was left unguarded, and the excavation methods used were generally destructive to the site and its environs. The remains of excavations of the megalithic complex structures, for example, were left in a circle of detritus clearly visible in satellite images.

As to the interpretation of the astronomy of the Calendar Circle, there is a non-controversial aspect and a controversial aspect. The non-controversial aspect is this: Eight stones on the circumference of the circle form four gates that create two "sight-line windows"—one window indicates the north-south direction, and the other window indicates the rising sun on summer solstice. Also, the location of the site itself, at about 22.5 degrees north latitude, near the tropic line, means the sun passed exactly overhead twice per year during the weeks surrounding summer solstice, and the standing stones would not have cast any shadows at noon. The solstice gates and the meridian (north-south) gates are approximate alignments spread over a few degrees of arc and thus cannot be used to date the circle from the small changes in the earth's obliquity.

The controversial aspect refers to the actual contents of the circle—six standing stones arranged in two sets of three. My approach was to consider the solstice and meridian gates of the circle as vital clues to its overall function. This interpretation was published in the book *The Origin Map*, and presented at professional conferences in Rhodes, Greece; in Atlanta, Georgia; at general audience conferences around the world; in a TV/DVD graphic animation; and, together with Robert Bauval, in my recent book *Black Genesis*. All of my interpretations refer to the careful original mapping of the reconstructed circle by Applegate and Zedeno in 1991/1992.[13] The solstice gate tells the visitor what time of year is relevant—summer solstice. The meridian gate tells the visitor where to look in the sky—up along the north-south meridian (which is the same standard reference astronomers still use today). Together, the gates also tell the visitor what time of day to look—just before sunrise while the sky is still dark. The contents of the circle form a simple star map that the visitor can then visually translate up into the sky in order to identify the asterism indicated inside the circle. Thus armed with the time of year, the time of night, and the area of sky to look at, the only additional factor (*constraint*, in physics parlance) I needed to consider was which year or years. The radiocarbon dates from a nearby hearth supplied that clue—around 4800 BCE. As I calculated what the sky must have looked like at that time, it soon became apparent that the three stars of Orion's Belt would be good candidates for the lower set of the three standing stones in the circle. Further investigation showed that the Orion's Belt stars generally fit during a window of time from about 6400 to 4800 BCE, with the best fit occurring around 4940 BCE. At this time, just the right altitude was represented, at a special time in the long-term precession of those stars—exactly halfway between southern culmination and northern culmination. I also proposed a more speculative interpretation for the other set of three stones inside the circle—namely, that they match the top part of the Orion constellation (the shoulder and head stars) at the opposite part of the precession cycle (about 12,000 years earlier). So the Calendar Circle was likely constructed and used around 5000 BCE (and certainly *not* in 17000 BCE), and it was a diagram to teach about the long-term trajectories of the stars above. Just as the summer solstice sunrise "sight-line gate" on the outer part of the circle taught about the annual motion of the sun through the sky over one year, the inner stones of the circle taught about the 26,000-year precession of the constellations. In this way the Circle is inextricably linked to the megalithic alignments at Nabta Playa, which also refer to Orion's Belt and the rising of Sirius.

The Mystery of the Bedrock Sculptures

The Calendar Circle also gives us a hint about the more mysterious parts of Nabta Playa. The star-aligned megaliths are embedded in the playa sediments. According to paleo-climatologists and the radiocarbon dates of sedimentary layers, the last period of heavy sedimentation that yielded the final thick layer of sediments ended sometime around 5000 BCE. Therefore the megaliths embedded in that layer must have been placed during or after that time. That is why controversy arose over the megalith alignment that the CPE first ascribed to Sirius circa 4820 BCE, which our measurements and calculations showed actually aligned 1,270 years earlier. But the puzzle is complicated by what is found *underneath* the playa sediments, especially underneath the centerpiece called "Complex Structure A" (CSA). All the megalith alignments radiate out from CSA. CSA is comprised of several parts: on top of the sediments are megaliths arranged in a large oval with a standing stone in the center; under that is some playa sediment and a large sculpted megalith (called the "cowstone"); and then underneath the cowstone lies a sculpted lump of living bedrock (bedrock that is still connected to the original bedrock, not cut off as the Great Sphinx is) about 12 feet (3.7 m) under the surface of the playa sediments. CSA sits in a field of about 30 of these complex structures—all similar except the others don't have the additional cowstone sculpture.

Nabta Playa is a bedrock basin covered by sedimentary layers of various thickness (some several yards deep) that were laid down during a period of about 10,000 years, from 15,000 years ago to 5,000 years ago, mostly during a series of humid interphases from around 9,500 to 7,000 years ago. When the CPE excavated the Complex structures and found that they were actually covering bedrock sculptures under 9 to 12 feet (2.7 to 3.7 m) of sediment, they were at a loss as to how to explain the creation of these structures. The standard conception of Neolithic culture is such structures could not have been built by them. So the CPE theorized that the people of Nabta Playa, sometime after 7,000 years ago, somehow figured out where the bedrock lumps (called *lenses* of quartzitic sandstone) were located, dug through the sediments, sculpted the bedrock lumps, filled the sediments back in, and then arranged the oval of megaliths on top of the sediments, leaving them thus for us to dig up today. Obviously there are several problems with this scenario. For one, CSA is the centerpiece of all the megalith alignments (the oldest of which is at least 6,500 years old), and so it must predate them. Another problem is that there was no possible way the Neolithic peoples could have figured out where the bedrock lumps were, under all that sediment, in order to carry out such a strange series of construction steps. And of course there is the question of *why* they would do such a thing in the first place. We suggested that a more likely solution is the bedrock sculptures actually are older.[14] By the time they wrote their 2007 article, the CPE agreed that the bedrock sculptures must have predated the others, as part of an older symbolic landscape that was marked by *cairns* (burial mounds) and a sequence of constructions leading up to the Complex structures we find today. The megalithic alignments placed on top of the sediments from 5000 BCE to 3500 BCE therefore incorporated, and in fact arranged as their centerpiece, the much older bedrock sculptures.

When were they first constructed, and for what purpose? Why were they so important or sacred that people continued to maintain them and incorporate them into their later ceremonial constructions for thousands of years? Does such fealty imply a greater degree of cultural (or religious or technological) continuity than was once believed? If the later megalithic alignments were primarily astronomical (as well as religious), does that suggest the much earlier bedrock sculptures were also astronomical? The answers to these questions are unknown. The CPE completely excavated only two of these structures, partially excavated a third, and drilled test holes into two more. They concluded that all (approximately 30) of the structures probably have a sculpted bedrock lump underneath. It is interesting that these bedrock sculptures date back to the same earlier epoch as has been proposed for the Great Sphinx at Giza, which itself is a giant bedrock sculpture. Geologist Robert Schoch and others have shown that the Sphinx and its bedrock enclosure were weathered by heavy rains that occurred before the standard dating of Dynastic Egypt. It is essentially the same rainy climate pattern that lay down the sediments on top of the bedrock sculptures at Nabta Playa.

When I first considered the astronomy of Nabta Playa, I approached the interpretation of the Calendar Circle purely as an astronomical puzzle, unfettered by preconceived notions of what the ancient people at the site "should" have been doing. My interpretation involves only "naked eye" astronomy, easily visible to any visitor with only the unaided eye. Similarly, the alignments of megaliths with stars rising over the eastern horizon involve only naked eye observations. The puzzle solution for the bedrock sculpture, "shaped like a mushroom" under CSA, however, produced something amazing. Working with the original archaeological drawings made by the excavators, and assuming that CSA is the centerpiece of all the alignments (and that it may have symbolized the astronomical center), it occurred to me that the disk-like, mushroom shape roughly resembled the shape of our Milky Way galaxy, and that the location of CSA approximated Earth's position in it. Furthermore, the "cowstone" sculpture was found wedged in place on top of the bedrock sculpture, its outer surface sculpted and polished into what appeared to be a cross-section of a sphere. As well, its sides were wedge-shaped such that its placement appeared to angle back to Earth's location in the galaxy sculpture as a sort of symbolic viewing window to subtend the area of the sky that the center of the Milky Way galaxy transits through.

Now if we stop and ask ourselves whether this was, in fact, what these sculptures represented if the people who built them only had naked eye astronomy, the answer is "probably not." But is it still possible? Perhaps. The Milky Way is a prominent feature in the sky. It is possible that some Neolithic genius sky-watchers realized that the Milky Way was a giant structure of which the Earth and sun were just a small part. A facility with the rudiments of geometry could have yielded the notion that the Milky Way was a disk-shaped structure (which it is). And it's entirely possible that these ancient observers of the heavens could have intuited from the *anisotropy* (variation) within the Milky Way that Earth must have been somewhere significantly off center in that disk (which it is). Some researchers suggest that the gleaming white outer stones of the mound at Newgrange were intended as symbolic representations of the Milky Way, so the idea that these Neolithic peoples at Nabta Playa could have represented the Milky Way with a stone disk is not that far-fetched. But could our hypothetical Neolithic geniuses at Nabta Playa have pinpointed Earth's location in the galactic disk so accurately? Probably not. The center of the galaxy is not visible to the naked eye because it is obscured by a dark patch of dust clouds (although that dark patch did have ritual significance in some ancient cultures). So, if these ancient geniuses guessed that this prominent dark patch was also the locus of the center of the galactic disk, and if they happened to guess correctly about how far Earth was from that center, they may have been able to map it onto their bedrock sculpture. But this scenario is unlikely. So why go through such a useless mental exercise, you ask? For one thing, it sharpens one's thinking skills. And clearly there is still much we don't know about our Neolithic ancestors; completely unfettered thinking and problem-solving may just generate some insight.

So if we continue our astronomical puzzle-matching for the bedrock sculptures, next we need to consider the bedrock sculpture under Complex Structure B (CSB) the second biggest complex structure and companion to CSA. The CSB bedrock sculpture is an odd, lumpy, tilted oval shape bigger than the CSA bedrock sculpture (CSB is about 19 feet

(5.8 m) across, to CSA's 12 feet (3.7 m)). So, if we suspend disbelief and consider that CSA is a representation of the Milky Way, the obvious conclusion is that CSB represents our galaxy's much bigger companion nearby, the Andromeda galaxy. The Andromeda galaxy as seen from Earth is a tilted oval or ellipse, and its distance from us (measured in galactic diameters) is roughly analogous to CSB's distance from CSA on the bedrock. Could these Neolithic sky-watchers have mapped the Andromeda galaxy using only naked-eye observation? The Andromeda galaxy *is* visible to the naked eye; normally it resembles a star, although a Persian astronomer misidentified it as a small cloud as early as 964 CE. But there is no way for the unaided observer to estimate the actual dimensions of the Andromeda galaxy relative to the Milky Way galaxy. In *The Origin Map*, I continued my puzzle-solving, identifying other astronomical correspondences for the megalithic structures. However, despite a statement made by Malville et al. that I "propose[d] that the nomads had contact with extra-galactic aliens,"[15] I did not. I did, however, note that the curious sequence of astronomical facts coincided with the megalithic features. I also noted that the knowledge of how to create such structures, if the correspondence was indeed intentional, must have been acquired in one of three ways: 1) it was some method with which we are not familiar or facile today (such as remote viewing); 2) it was gleaned through some kind of technology similar to our own but which has since disappeared from history; or 3) it was acquired from some outside source, such as contact with "aliens" or inheritance from a much earlier lost civilization.

Suffice it to say that no matter how conservative or far-out one's thinking is about the past, the true mysteries of Nabta Playa remain. That is why scientists and laypeople alike are trying to glean more data about what is *really* on the bedrock there. Rosen and I began to collaborate on using space-based, ground-penetrating imaging techniques to investigate the mystery of the bedrock sculptures. We have been limited to space-based remote sensing attempts because we can do it without the onerous barrier of getting permission. Ground-penetrating radar satellite technology isn't quite advanced enough yet to enable us to see the bedrock features at Nabta, but someday it will be. Nabta Playa provided a keystone in our knowledge chain that traces the ancestors of the pharaohs back in time and space to a culture that thrived in the region before it became a desert wasteland. Perhaps, as our own space age progresses, we will find out some astonishing things about our very ancient past, and therefore our own future, as well.

Notes

1. Wendorf, Fred and Romuald Schild. "The Megaliths of Nabta Playa." *Academia, Focus on Archaeology,* no. 1 (2004): 11.

2. ———. *Holocene Settlement of the Egyptian Sahara: The Archaeology of Nabta Playa, Vol 1.* New York: Kluwer Academic/ Plenum, 2001.

3. Malville, J. et al. "Megaliths and Neolithic Astronomy in Southern Egypt." *Nature* 392 (April 1998): 488–91.

4. Ibid.

5. Wendorf, Fred and Romuald Schild, 2001.

6. Ibid.

7. Malville, J. et al. "Megaliths and Neolithic Astronomy in Southern Egypt." *Nature* 392 (April 1998): 488–91.

8. Malville, J. et al. "Astronomy of Nabta Playa." *African Skies/ Cieus Africains,* no. 11 (July 2007).

9. Ibid.

10. Ibid.

11. Bauval, Robert and Thomas Brophy. *Black Genesis: The Prehistoric Origins of Ancient Egypt.* Rochester, Vt.: Bear & Company, 2011.

12. Ibid.

13. Wendorf, Fred and Romuald Schild, 2001.

14. Brophy, Thomas, and Paul Rosen. "Satellite Imagery Measures of the Astronomically Aligned Megaliths at Nabta Playa." *Mediterranean Archaeology and Archaeometry* 5, no. 1 (2005): 15–24.

15. Malville, J. et al., 2007.

The Time Machines

By Erich von Däniken

Translated by Christian von Arnim

One of the most significant of all the ancient puzzles lies in the land of the Nile, the location of the Great Pyramid of the Pharaoh Cheops. We know very little of who Cheops was or when he lived. It is thought that he started to build the giant structure sometime around 2551 BCE. How he accomplished this feat remains just as much a mystery as the man himself. Not one craftsman, priest, architect, or pharaoh recorded as much as a single word about the construction of the Great Pyramid.[1] As well, no inscriptions, such as the Pyramid Texts found at Saqqara, have ever been found in the Pyramid of Cheops. The structure is a mute symbol of anonymity and mystery.

The best-known model that explains the construction of the pyramids is the wooden sledge. It is thought that laborers moved the large and heavy stone blocks on wooden sledges, which in turn rested on and slid along a wooden base.[2] Although this is possible, it doesn't seem likely. Wood was very rare (and still is) in this part of Egypt, and wood on a soft substrate such as sand splinters easily. Furthermore, there had to have been ropes used in this process, but nobody knows what sorts of ropes were used or what their tensile strength was. At what point would the logs have cracked or the roped snapped? At three tons? Five tons? We do not know that, either. Like detectives at the scene of a crime, we can only take what clues are available to us, reconstruct the imagined scenario, reflect on it, and search for possible solutions.

The most reasonable solution—up until now, at least—is that a ramp was used to move the stones into place. That said, such a ramp would had to have been two miles (3 km) long, given the position of the building site relative to the Nile, where the stones were brought in on boats. This means that the ramp would have been 161 yeards (147 m) high at its highest point, and many times the volume of the pyramid itself.[3] Furthermore, the incline of such a ramp would had to have been consistent through its entire length. It would have been impossible to build steps into it, for example. Each increase in height of the ramp had to extend over its whole length. A constant height adjustment over the whole length—week for week! Others assert that a ramp running all the way down to the Nile was not required, and that it could have been accomplished with a spiraling ramp running around the sides of pyramid. This is possible, but it would have to have been a very wide ramp, indeed, because several sledges would have been moving past one another at the same time—those going up and those going down. This ramp also would have had a volume many times that of the pyramid.

Aside from the sheer logistics of building such a ramp—let alone the pyramid itself—there are other factors to consider, such as the peculiar mathematical and geometrical measurements and correspondences associated with the structure. These include the following:

- The pyramid is aligned precisely with the four cardinal points.
- The pyramid lies at the center of earth's land mass.
- The meridian running through the pyramid divides the oceans and the continents into two equal parts. This north-south meridian is also the meridian that crosses the most land on the whole globe.
- The three pyramids of Giza are arranged in a Pythagorean triangle, the sides of which are in a perfect 3:4:5 ratio.
- The pyramid is essentially a giant sundial. The shadows thrown from mid-October to early March indicate the seasons and the length of the year. The length of the stone slabs surrounding the pyramid correspond perfectly to the length of the shadow of one day.
- The length of each side of the square base is 365.342 Egyptian cubits. This number is identical to the number of days in the tropical solar year.
- The distance of the Great Pyramid from the center of the earth is exactly the same as its distance from the North Pole.

The inside of this monumental structure is no less of a mystery. We know of only a few passages and chambers—the Queen's Chamber and, above it, the King's Chamber, for example—and the total volume of these chambers and passages was once thought to comprise just one percent of the total volume of the pyramid. Why build such a mighty building if only one percent of the space was going to used?

To answer this question, a team of scientists from Waseda University in Tokyo came to investigate the structure.[4] Among the advanced equipment they brought with them included a device to x-ray the stones. They discovered that at least three percent of the content of the pyramid was hollow, not one percent as was originally thought. A French team of scientists achieved an even more startling result using the most modern equipment available. They found that at least *15 percent* of the volume of the pyramid is hollow. As scientists and laypeople alike continue to investigate this enigmatic structure, what other secrets will it reveal? Will new passages and chambers be opened up to the light of day? Will there be any new messages encoded in the structure itself or contained within its walls? Will it ever throw any light on our supposed contact with the ancient masters? As strange an idea as this may sound, that is precisely what is claimed in some ancient Arab traditions.

Herodotus is the only classical historian to name Chufu (Cheops) as the builder of this pyramid (in his Account of Egypt). He admits that this is second-hand information, given to him by someone else, but then goes on to assert that 11,340 years ago (from his time), "the gods ruled in Egypt and lived with human beings…. The Egyptians are absolutely sure of that because they have continuously counted and written down the years."[5] No other historian refers specifically to any Cheops or Chufu. Diodorus of Sicily names Chemmis as the builder,[6] and while Pliny the Elder expressly lists all the names of the historians who have reported *before* him about the pyramids, he drily notes, "But none of them can name the actual builder."[7] The most important geographer and encyclopedist of Arabia, Al-Mas'udi (895–956) names an antediluvian (before the Flood) king named Saurid as builder of the Great Pyramid. Taqi al-Din Ahmad ibn 'Ali ibn 'Abd al-Qadir ibn Muhammad al-Maqrizi (1364–1442) does, as well. In his work *Hitat*, al-Maqrizi presents various manuscripts and fragments concerning its construction:

> The teacher Ibrahim Ben Wasif Sah Al-Katib says in News from Egypt and its Wonders, where he tells of Saurid…one of the kings of Egypt before the Flood…he was the builder of the Great Pyramid at Misr…. When King Saurid ben Sahluk died,

he was buried in the eastern pyramid, Hugib in the western one and Karuras in the pyramid which is built at the base with stones from Aswan and on top with Kaddan stones. [8]

Al-Maqrizi also notes that the reason for building all three of the pyramids was the coming Flood, and that they contained several chambers filled with books concerning all that was known of the sciences before the Flood. The builder, Saurid, was the same person whom the Hebrews called Henoch, and others, Hermes. Muhammad ben Abdallah ben Abd al-Hakam states more precisely: "In my opinion the pyramids can only have been built before the Flood; because if they had been built afterwards, people would have knowledge about them."

Virtually every historian who visited ancient Egypt (Herodotus, Diodorus, Pliny, Strabo, and so on) told of gods who visited the earth a long time ago, and from whom the human race had received its original knowledge. Were any identifying traces of these gods and the knowledge they imparted preserved on or inside these monstrous structures? Are there perhaps any older, Stone Age structures that can also speak to this dark period, to which so many of the ancient historians alluded? One of these oft-misunderstood complexes is located in modern-day England. Stonehenge lies in the south of the British isles near the town of Salisbury. The complex consists of giant stones arranged in a circle, and more circles further out (marked with holes), and further out still, larger circles. Stonehenge stretches far back into the past. [9] Construction likely commenced sometime around 3100 BCE. Clever priests, who were also fledgling astronomers, had by that time already started observing the heavens. In their observations, they noted that the moon, the sun, and certain stars rose at very specific times. It is thought that they memorialized these observations by marking them somehow on the ground, possibly with ropes or small stones, because one thing is quite certain—at that time, 5,100 years ago, there was no writing. But what is perhaps most baffling is that the Stone Age planners were able to think abstractly. Who were these planners in the Neolithic age, these builders who, against all odds, were able to look far into the future? And then there is the final question that never lets me go: Why did they do what they did? Is the whole thing really only a calendar? As of this writing, that theory has for all intents and purposes been discounted. You certainly do not need a gigantic complex of megaliths to predict or mark the seasons!

We will likely never be able to know the answers to these questions. But in his efforts to try, the British astronomer Gerald Hawkins fed a total of 7,140 different possible combinations into a computer.[10] He wanted to find out which combinations occurred so far outside the realm of probability that they were random. Stonehenge turned out to be the only planetary and interstellar observatory. Of course this was subsequently disputed. Some academics came along and found things to criticize in the professor's algorithms.[11] Nevertheless there still remained more than 40 ways of looking at the matter which clearly indicated that structure was meant to mark astronomical reference points. What could such an astronomical center be used for?

On June 21, the summer solstice, the sun rises precisely over the so-called heel stone, a monolith that stands outside the primary complex. The sun moves between the gates and grows ever larger, brighter, and more dazzling. On December 21 a similar thing occurs. It almost looks as though the sun stops for a brief moment between the two blocks before continuing to rise and illuminate the cold winter sky. The key factor here is the interplay of light and shadow among the monoliths. A similar spectacle can be observed during moonrise and moonset, as the light of Diana bathes the earth, albeit much less strongly. The phases of the moon are easily observed with the naked eye, so there is no way that the priests could not have known about these seasonal cycles and these interplays of light and shadow.

And there is something else. Consider the basic structure of our solar system: The sun lies at the center, followed by Mercury, Venus, Earth, and so on, with their concentric elliptical paths around the sun. Thanks to the invention of the modern telescope, this model is well-known to most every person on earth. The astronomer Mike Saunders, noticing the obvious that everyone else missed, found that Stonehenge is actually a scaled-down model of our solar system.[12] However, this rough megalithic model only represents the average distances between trajectories, rather than the elliptical ones. At the center with the innermost ring is the sun, then the second ring is Mercury, the third is Venus, and the fourth is Earth. Further out lies the ring for Mars. There is a vast distance between Mars and Jupiter, which is where the hundreds of thousands of rocks making up the asteroid belt are located. The heel stone, which lies still further out, away from the other markers, marks the distance to the trajectory of Jupiter.

All of this is very extraordinary and must have been purposeful. However, it can hardly be assumed that Stone Age peoples were aware of the data for the average trajectories of our solar system. Where did they learn this information, and what were the intentions of their teachers, whoever they were? The Russian geologist Dr. Vladimir Tjurin-Avinsky suspects that Stonehenge was a kind of examination question meant for future generations.[13] In this sense, it, like the pyramid complex in Egypt, is a time machine with a purpose, but what purpose that is remains to be seen.

Notes

1. Eggebrecht, Eva. "Die Geschichte des Pharaonenreiches," in *Das alte Ägypten*. Munich, 1984.

2. Goyon, Georges. *Die Cheops-Pyramide*. Munich: Bergisch-Gladbach, 1979.

3. Ibid.

4. Yoshimura, Sakuji. "Non-Destructive Pyramid Investigation— By Electromagnetic Wave Method." White paper, Waseda University, Tokyo, 1987.

5. Herodotus. *Histories*. Trans. C.G. Macaulay. New York: Macmillan, 1890.

6. Cajus Plinius Secundus. *Die Naturgeschichte*, Book 36. Leipzig, 1882.

7. "Das Pyramidenkapitel" in al-Makrizi's *Hitat*. Translated by Erich Graefe, Leipzig, 1911.

8. von Däniken, Erich. *The Eyes of the Sphinx*. New York: Berkley Trade (The Penguin Group), 1996.

9. ———. *The Stone Was Completely Different*. Munich: Bertelsmann, 1991.

10. Hawkins, Gerald S. *Stonehenge Decoded*. New York: Delta, 1965.

11. Atkinson, R.J.C. "Moonshine on Stonehenge," in *Antiquity*, Vol. 40. 1966.

12. Saunders, Mike. *Planetarium Stonehenge*. Surrey, UK: Caterham, 1980.

13. Avinsky, Vladimir. "New Arguments in Favor of the Reality of Space Paleocontacts." Lecture at the 16th World Conference of the Ancient Astronaut Society. Chicago, Illinois, August 26, 1989.

Glossary

arcane Known or knowable only to the initiate; secret; mysterious; obscure.

astrology The divination of the supposed influences of the stars and planets on human affairs and terrestrial events by their positions and aspects.

astronomy The study of objects and matter outside the Earth's atmosphere and of their physical and chemical properties.

concentric Having a common center or axis.

cuneiform Composed of or written in wedge-shaped characters.

deluge An overwhelming of the land by water; a drenching rain.

druid One of an ancient Celtic priesthood appearing in Irish and Welsh sagas and Christian legends as magicians and wizards.

ecliptic The great circle of the celestial sphere that is the apparent path of the sun among the stars or of the Earth as seen from the sun; the plane of the Earth's orbit extended to meet the celestial sphere.

edifice A building; a large or massive structure.

enigma An obscure speech or writing; something hard to understand or explain; an inscrutable or mysterious person.

equinox Either of the two points on the celestial sphere where the celestial equator intersects the ecliptic; either of two times each year (about March 21 and September 23) when the sun crosses the equator and day and night are everywhere on Earth of approximately equal length.

extraterrestrial Originating, existing, or occurring outside the Earth or its atmosphere.

inundate To cover with a flood; overflow.

levitate To rise or float in or as if in the air in seeming defiance of gravity.

linguistics The study of human speech, including the units, nature, structure, and modification of language.

megalith A very large, usually rough stone used in prehistoric cultures as a monument or building block.

obelisk An upright, four-sided, usually monolithic pillar that gradually tapers as it rises and terminates in a pyramid.

occult Not revealed, secret; not easily apprehended or understood; mysterious; matters regarded as involving the action or influence of supernatural or supernormal powers or some secret knowledge of them.

oracle A person through whom a deity is believed to speak; a shrine in which a deity reveals hidden knowledge or the divine purpose through a person; a person giving wise or authoritative decisions or opinions; an authoritative or wise expression or answer.

portal A door, entrance, especially a grand or imposing one.

primordial First created or developed; existing in or persisting from the beginning; earliest formed in the growth of an individual or organ; fundamental; primary.

provenance Origin; source; the history of ownership of a valued object or work of art or literature.

rune Any of the characters of any of several alphabets used by the Germanic peoples from about the third to the thirteenth centuries CE.

solstice Either of the two points on the ecliptic at which distance from the celestial equator is greatest and which is reached by the sun each year about June 22 (beginning of summer in the northern hemisphere) and December 22 (beginning of winter in the northern hemisphere).

surveillance Close watch kept over someone or something.

trance Stupor, daze; a sleep-like state usually characterized by partly suspended animation with diminished or absent sensory and motor activity; a state of profound absorption.

veneration Respect or awe inspired by the dignity, wisdom, dedication, or talent of a person.

For More Information

American Institute of Parapsychology (AIP)

Executive Center

4131 NW 13th Street, Suite 208

Gainesville, FL 32609

Web site: http://parapsychologylab.com

The AIP is a non-profit research and educational organization. Its studies enable a greater understanding of the anomalous aspects of human experience. Research within the institute covers all topics within parapsychology including (but not limited to): extra sensory perception (ESP), psychokinesis (PK), post-mortem survival (PMS), apparitions, hauntings and poltergeists, hypnosis, paranormal dreams, psychic criminology, out-of-body and near-death experiences, and mediumship/vhanneling. AIP conducts courses on parapsychology, aimed at the general public. AIP maintains a library specializing in parapsychology, abnormal psychology, and occult/mystical studies. This collection includes several hundred books, audio-visual materials, and issues of the main parapsychology journals.

American Museum of Natural History

Central Park West at 79th Street

New York, NY 10024-5192

(212) 769-5100

Web site: http://www.amnh.org

The American Museum of Natural History is one of the world's preeminent scientific and cultural institutions. Since its founding in 1869, the Museum has advanced its global mission to discover, interpret and disseminate information about human cultures, the natural world and the universe through a wide-ranging program of scientific research, education, and exhibition. The museum is renowned for its exhibitions and scientific collections, which serve as a field guide to the entire planet and present a panorama of the world's cultures.

American Society for Psychical Research, Inc. (ASPR)
5 West 73rd Street
New York, New York 10023
(212) 799-5050
Web site: http://www.aspr.com

The American Society for Psychical Research is the oldest psychical research organization in the United States. For more than a century, it's mission has been to explore extraordinary or as yet unexplained phenomena that have been called psychic or paranormal, and their implications for our understanding of consciousness, the universe and the nature of existence. The ASPR library and archives are a leading repository of significant aspects of American and scientific history - including the earliest history of psychology and psychiatry in the United States, early studies of multiple personality, the evolution of mind-body medicine, Eastern and Western religious philosophy, the mental healers movement, and American visionary traditions.

The Atlantic Paranormal Society (T.A.P.S.)
2362 West Shore Road
Warwick, RI 02889
Web site: http://www.the-atlantic-paranormal-society.com

T.A.P.S. investigates homes believed to be haunted, free of charge, using state-of-the-art recording equipment. T.A.P.S. investigators also counsel homeowners, seeking to allay their fears and helping them understand the nature of the problem, why this is happening, and how little danger is actually involved. T.A.P.S. seeks to find good evidence either for or against paranormal activity and then shares its findings with the homeowners and comes to a conclusion.

Canadian Museum of Civilization
100 Laurier Street

Gatineau, QC K1A 0M8

Canada

(800) 555-5621

Web site: http://www.civilization.ca

Canada's national museum of human history and the most popular and most-visited

Museum Of Anthropology

6393 N.W. Marine Drive

Vancouver, BC V6T 1Z2

Canada

(604) 822-5087

Web site: http://www.moa.ubc.ca

The Museum of Anthropology at the University of British Columbia is world-renowned for its collections, research, teaching, public programs, and community connections.

Peabody Museum of Archaeology and Ethnology

Harvard University

11 Divinity Avenue

Cambridge, MA 02138

(617) 496-1027

Web site: http://www.peabody.harvard.edu

The Peabody Museum of Archaeology and Ethnography is steward to one of the oldest and largest collections of cultural objects in the Western Hemisphere. Since the late nineteenth century, the museum has played an active part in the history of American anthropology and in the evolving relationship between museums and native peoples. The collections continue to grow through by gift, fieldwork, and purchase. Today, the Peabody houses more than six million individual objects, 500,000 photographic images, and substantial archival records. The Peabody is caretaker to important collections from Africa, Europe, and Asia. Collection types include Archaeology; Ethnography; Osteology; and Painting, Drawing, and Prints.

Ripley's Believe It or Not! Times Square
234 West 42nd Street
New York, NY 10036
(212) 398-3133
Web site: http://www.ripleysnewyork.com
For over 40 years, Robert Ripley traveled the world collecting the unbelievable, the inexplicable, and the one-of-a-kind. His vast collections are now on display, including hundreds of weird and unusual artifacts.

University of Pennsylvania Museum of Archaeology and Anthropology
3260 South Street
Philadelphia, PA 19104
(215) 898-4000
Web site: http://www.penn.museum
The University of Pennsylvania Museum of Archaeology and Anthropology, through its research, collections, exhibitions, and educational programming, advances understanding of the world's cultural heritage. Founded in 1887, Penn Museum has conducted more than 400 archaeological and anthropological expeditions around the world. Three gallery floors feature materials from Egypt, Mesopotamia, the Bible Lands, Mesoamerica, Asia, and the ancient Mediterranean World, as well as artifacts from native peoples of the Americas, Africa, and Polynesia.

Web Sites

Due to the changing nature of Internet links, Rosen Publishing has developed an online list of Web sites related to the subject of this book. This site is updated regularly. Please use this link to access the list:

http://www.rosenlinks.com/MUSD/Lost

For Further Reading

Adams, Mark. *Turn Right at Machu Picchu: Rediscovering the Lost City One Step at a Time*. New York, NY: Plume, 2012.

Childress, David Hatcher. *Lost Cities & Ancient Mysteries of the Southwest*. Adventures Unlimited Press, 2009.

Chouinard, Patrick. *Forgotten Worlds: From Atlantis to the X-Woman of Siberia and the Hobbits of Flores*. Rochester, VT: Bear & Co., 2012.

Fawcett, Percy. *Journey to the Lost City of Z*. New York, NY: Overlook, 2010.

Grann, David. *The Lost City of Z: A Tale of Deadly Obsession in the Amazon*. New York, NY: Vintage, 2010.

Greer, John Michael. *The Element Encyclopedia of Secret Societies: The Ultimate A-Z of Ancient Mysteries, Lost Civilizations, and Forgotten Wisdom*. New York, NY: Harper Element, 2009.

Joseph, Frank. *Atlantis and Other Lost Worlds: New Evidence of Ancient Secrets*. Edison, NJ: Chartwell Books, 2008.

Joseph, Frank. *Atlantis and 2012: The Science of the Lost Civilization and the Prophecies of the Maya*. Rochester, VT: Bear & Co., 2010.

Joseph, Frank. *The Lost Worlds of Ancient America: Compelling Evidence of Ancient Immigrants, Lost Technologies, and Places of Power*. Pompton Plains, NJ: New Page Books, 2012.

Mann, Charles C. *1491: New Revelations of the Americas Before Columbus*. New York, NY: Vintage, 2006.

Menzies, Gavin. *The Lost Empire of Atlantis: History's Greatest Mystery Revealed*. New York, NY: William Morrow, 2011.

Wilcock, David. *The Source Field Investigations: The Hidden Science and Lost Civilizations Behind the 2012 Prophecies*. New York, NY: Dutton, 2011.

Wingate, Richard. *Atlantis in the Amazon: Lost Technologies and the Secrets of the Crespi Treasure*. Rochester, VT: Bear & Co., 2011.

Index

About the Contributors

Frank Joseph is the author of *The Atlantis Encyclopedia* (2005), *Discovering the Mysteries of Ancient America* (2005), *Opening the Ark of the Covenant* (2007), and *Unearthing Ancient America* (2008), all published by New Page Books. His latest offering, *The Untold Story of Ancient America*, is due for release in spring of 2012.

After completing his education at Southern Illinois University's School of Journalism, he was a reporter for several Chicago-area publications, including the *Winnetka Paper*. Later, Joseph was the marketing director at Galde Press, Inc., in Lakeville, Minnesota, and published dozens of feature articles and book reviews in *Fate* magazine from 1989 to 2009. He served as the editor in chief of *Ancient American* magazine for 14 years, from its inception in 1993, and is currently a feature writer for the *Barnes Review* and *Atlantis Rising*. His series of four Internet broadcast interviews with Shirley MacLaine were among dozens of similar appearances he has made on *Coast-to-Coast AM with Art Bell*, *The Jeff Rense Show*, *Erskine Overnight*, *21st-Century Radio*, *The Whitley Strieber Show*, and others.

A member of Chicago's Underwater Archaeology Society and the Oriental Institute of the University of Chicago, Joseph is a veteran scuba diver with hundreds of sub-surface dives, from the Aegean Sea and Canary Islands to the Bahamas and Polynesia. Since 1983, he has traveled regularly to Asia, Europe, North Africa, and Central and South America, collecting research for his investigation of lost civilizations.

A frequent guest speaker across the United States, Joseph has also lectured in Britain, the Balkans, and Japan, where he was given the honorific title of Professor of World Archaeology by the Savant Institute in 2002. Earlier he received the Victor Moseley Award from Ohio's Midwest Epigraphic Society, the Burrows Cave Society Award, and recognition from the Ancient American Artifact Preservation Foundation "for generous contributions to the diffusion of knowledge, exploration and expertise in the area of research into the mysteries of Ancient America."

Frank Joseph lives with his wife, Laura, and their Norwegian forest cat, Sammy, in the Upper Mississippi River Valley.

Oberon Zell is a renowned Wizard and Elder in the worldwide magickal community. He holds academic degrees in sociology, anthropology, clinical psychology, teaching, and theology. He is an initiate in several different magickal traditions, and has been involved in the founding of several major groups and alliances. In 1962, Oberon cofounded the Church of All Worlds, a Pagan church with a futuristic vision. First to apply the terms "Pagan" and "Neo-Pagan" to the newly emerging Nature religions of the 1960s, and through his publication of the award-winning *Green Egg* magazine, Oberon was instrumental in the coalescence of the Neo-Pagan movement, which for the past half-century has been reclaiming the religious heritage of pre-Christian Europe. In 1970, Oberon had a profound Vision of the Living Earth, which he published as an early version of the Gaea Thesis—that our entire planetary biosphere comprises the body of a single, vast living organism universally identified as "Mother Earth."

Oberon is a theologian and ritualist, creating and conducting rites of passage, seasonal celebrations, mystery initiations, earth healings, and other large rituals. He has traveled throughout the world, celebrated solar eclipses at ancient stone circles, raised living unicorns, and swum with mermaids in the Coral Sea. He also designs jewelry and sculpts figurines of gods, goddesses, and mythical creatures for the Mythic Images Collection (*www.mythicimages.com*).

In 2002, Oberon gathered together many respected mages and sages to form the Grey Council. In 2004, Oberon and the Council published *Grimoire for the Apprentice Wizard*, filled with their accumulated wisdom and insights. That summer, Oberon created his proudest accomplishment, the online Grey School of Wizardry (*www. greyschool.com*). As the school's headmaster, Oberon has been called "the real Albus Dumbledore."

Living in Sonoma County, California, with his beloved wife and soulmate, Morning Glory, Oberon is also the author of *Companion for the Apprentice Wizard*, *Creating Circles & Ceremonies*, *A Wizard's Bestiary*, and *Green Egg Omelette*, all published by New Page Books. Oberon has a weekly show on Blogtalk radio, "Over to Oberon & Ariel," each Wednesday from 9 to 10 p.m., Central Time.

Adrian G. Gilbert is a bestselling British author and independent publisher who lives in England. His books are centered on investigations into ancient esoteric knowledge and religious mysteries. He attended the University of Kent at Canterbury. After extensive travels to the Middle East he entered the world of publishing and, subsequently, computer programming. He returned to publishing in 1986 and afterward set up his own company, Solos Press, in 1991, which specializes in the publication of books concerning gnosticism, Christian mysticism, and hermetic philosophy. His books include *The Cosmic Wisdom Beyond Astrology* (1991), *The Mayan Prophecies* (1995), *Magi* (1996), *The Holy Kingdom* (with Alan Wilson and Baram Blackett, 1998), *Signs in the Sky* (2000), *The New Jerusalem* (2002), *The End of Time* (2006), and *London: A New Jerusalam* (2010). He is perhaps best known for his book *The Orion Mystery*, which he co-authored with Robert Bauval in 1994.

Philip Coppens is an author and investigative journalist, whose topics of interest range from the world of politics to ancient history and mystery. He cohosts *The Spirit Revolution* radio show with his wife, Kathleen McGowan, and is a frequent contributor to *NEXUS* and *Atlantis Rising* magazines. Since 1995, he has lectured extensively and has appeared in a number of television and DVD documentaries, including *Ancient Aliens: The Series* on the History Channel. He is the author of *The Stone Puzzle of Rosslyn Chapel*; *The Canopus Revelation*; *Land of the Gods*; *The New Pyramid Age*; *Servants of the Grail*; *2012, Science or Fiction?* and *The Ancient Alien Question*.

Freddy Silva is one of the world's leading researchers of ancient systems of knowledge and the interaction between temples and consciousness. He is also a best-selling author and film-maker. He lectures internationally, with keynote presentations at the International Science and Consciousness Conference, and the International Society for the Study of Subtle Energies and Energy Medicine, in addition to appearances on the History Channel, Discovery Channel, BBC, video documentaries, and radio shows. He has been described by the CEO of Universal Light Expo as "perhaps the best metaphysical speaker in the world right now."

Marie D. Jones is the best-selling author of *2013: End of Days or a New Beginning?* and *11:11: The Time Prompt Phenomenon* (with Larry Flaxman). She is also the coauthor of *The Resonance Key*; *The Déjà vu Enigma*; and *The Trinity Secret*—all with Larry Flaxman, her partner at ParaExplorers.com, an organization devoted to exploring unsolved mysteries.

Marie has been interviewed on more than 100 radio talk shows, including *Coast to Coast AM*, *NPR*, *KPBS Radio*, *Dreamland* (which she cohosts), *X-Zone*, the *Kevin Smith Show*, *Paranormal Podcast*, *Cut to the Chase*, *Feet 2 the Fire*, *World of the Unexplained*, and the *Shirley MacLaine Show*, and has been featured in dozens of newspapers, magazines, and online publications all over the world. She is a staff writer for *Intrepid Magazine*, and her essays and articles have appeared in *TAPS ParaMagazine*, *New Dawn*, *Whole Life Times*, *Light Connection*, *Vision*, *Beyond Reality*, and several popular anthologies, such as the *Chicken Soup* series. A popular public speaker, she has lectured at major paranormal, new science, and self-empowerment events. She worked as a field investigator for MUFON (the Mutual UFO Network) in Los Angeles and San Diego in the 1980s and, 90s, and co-founded MUFON North County. She currently serves as a consultant and director of special projects for ARPAST, the Arkansas Paranormal and Anomalous Studies Team. Marie is also a licensed New Thought/metaphysics minister.

Larry Flaxman has been actively involved in paranormal research and hands-on field investigation for more than 13 years. He melds his technical, scientific, and investigative backgrounds together in pursuit of no-nonsense, scientifically objective explanations for anomalous phenomena. He is the president and senior researcher of ARPAST, the Arkansas Paranormal and Anomalous Studies Team, which he founded in February of 2007. Under his leadership, ARPAST has become one of the nation's largest and most active paranormal research organizations. ARPAST is also a proud member of the TAPS family (the Atlantic Paranormal Society). Widely respected for his expertise on the proper use of equipment and techniques for conducting a solid investigation, Larry also serves as technical advisor to several paranormal research groups throughout the country.

Larry has appeared on the Discovery Channel's *Ghost Lab*, and has been interviewed for *The Anomalist*, the *Times Herald News*, the *Jacksonville Patriot*, *ParaWeb*, the *Current Affairs Herald*, and *Unexplained* magazine. He has appeared on hundreds of radio programs, including *Coast to Coast AM*, *TAPS Family Radio*, *Encounters Radio*, *Higher Dimensions*, *X-Zone*, *Ghostly Talk*, *Eerie Radio*, *Crossroads Paranormal*, *World of the Unexplained*, and *Haunted Voices*. Larry is a staff writer for *Intrepid* magazine, and his work has appeared regularly in *TAPS ParaMagazine*, *New Dawn*, and *Phenomena*. He is also a screenwriter and popular public speaker, lecturing widely at paranormal and metaphysical conferences and events all over the country.

Micah A. Hanks is a full-time journalist, radio personality, author, musician, and investigator of the unexplained. Throughout his many years studying the world's mysteries, Hanks has visited a number of diverse places, collecting information about not only UFOs and strange phenomenon but also cultural data, folklore, history, and philosophy. He has been featured as a guest on many television and radio programs, including the History Channel's *Guts and Bolts*, National Geographic's *Paranatural*, CNN Radio, and *The Jeff Rense Program*. He is also a staff writer for *UFO Magazine*, *Mysterious Universe*, and regular contributor to *Intrepid Magazine*, with past articles appearing in *FATE*, *Mysteries Magazine*, *New Dawn*, and several other publications. The latest news about UFOs and unexplained phenomena, as well as information about Micah's ongoing projects and appearances, are available at his Web site, The Gralien Report (*www.gralienreport.com*). He can be contacted directly at *info@gralienreport.com*.

Nick Redfern works full time as an author, lecturer, ghostwriter, and freelance journalist. He has written about a wide range of unsolved mysteries, including Bigfoot, UFOs, the Loch Ness monster, alien encounters, werewolves, psychic phenomena, chupacabras, ghosts, the Men in Black (MIB), and government conspiracies. He has written for Britain's *Daily Express* and *People* newspapers and *Penthouse* magazine, and writes regularly for the newsstand publications *UFO Magazine*; *Fate*; *TAPS ParaMagazine*; and *Fortean Times*. His many previous books include *The NASA Conspiracies*; *Contactees*; *Memoirs of a Monster Hunter*; *There's Something in the Woods*; and *Strange Secrets*. Nick Redfern's most recent book, *The Real Men in Black*, was published by New Page Books in the summer of 2011. Nick has appeared on numerous television shows, including VH1's *Legend Hunters*; the BBC's *Out of this World*; the History Channel's *Monster Quest* and *UFO Hunters*; the National Geographic Channel's *Paranatural*; and the SyFy Channel's *Proof Positive*. Redfern is the co-host, along with Raven Meindel, of the popular weekly radio show *Exploring All Realms*. Originally from England, Nick Redfern lives in Arlington, Texas, with his wife, Dana. He can be contacted through his Web site, Nickredfern.com.

Scott Alan Roberts is the founder and publisher of *Intrepid Magazine* (*www.intrepidmag.com*), and is the author and illustrator of *The Rollicking Adventures of Tam O'Hare*. After several years in Bible college and seminary, Roberts spent the bulk of his next 25 years as an advertising art and creative director, and was the editor in chief of *TAPS Paramagazine,* the official publication of SyFy's *Ghost Hunters*. Roberts has written numerous articles and appeared on countless national radio shows, including *Coast to Coast AM*. He is also a well-known public speaker and is currently working on his magazine and future book projects. He lives with his family in

Lost Cities and Forgotten Civilizations

western Wisconsin, not far from the Twin Cities of Minneapolis and St. Paul in Minnesota.

Pat Chouinard was born and raised in Seminole, Florida. He decided to become a professional writer at age 14. Mr. Chouinard has dedicated himself to the study of archaeology, lost civilizations, ancient flood myths, Atlantology, crop circles, and comparative religions. He has been involved with local public television and produced and hosted an award-winning series called Archaeology TV. He has interviewed Graham Hancock, Michael Cremo, John Anthony West, and distinguished LDS archaeologists, taking the viewer on a whirlwind tour from the Middle East and Western Europe all the way to South America and the United States. During this period, he also became a regular contributor to *Ancient American* magazine. He subsequently joined the Central Gulf Coast Archaeological Society and was asked to join their board of directors as a media specialist. He then started his own magazine, *The New Archaeology Review*, which continues to be published in PDF, Kindle, mobile, and print formats. He is currently working on two more books, *Forgotten Worlds: From Atlantis to the X-Woman of Siberia to the Hobbits of Flores* and *Giants of Atlantis: The Legacy of the Fallen Race,* both to be published by Bear & Company.

Paul Von Ward, MPA, MSc, an interdisciplinary cosmologist and independent scholar, is the author of *We've Never Been Alone: A History of Extraterrestrial Intervention* (2011); *The Soul Genome: Science and Reincarnation* (2008); *Gods, Genes & Consciousness* (2004); and *Our Solarian Legacy: Multidimensional Humans in a Self-Learning Universe* (2001). Since 1995, Paul's work has focused on evidence of nonhuman intelligence. His research includes human and nonhuman consciousness (including neuroscience and reincarnation), the influence of advanced beings (ABs) on human development, the role of religious worldviews in societal conflicts, and how to reform social institutions to reflect a vision of human potential through the development of natural spirituality. He studies human psychological reactions to AB intervention and attempts to reestablish humanity's natural spiritual path based in traditional wisdom and natural science.

With degrees from Harvard University and Florida State University, Paul has served as a church pastor; U. S. naval officer (from 1962 to 1965); American diplomat (1965 to 1980) to France, Martinique, Sierra Leone, and the Dominican Republic; and in senior positions in the U. S. State Department. He founded the Washington-based non-profit Delphi International (of which he was CEO from1980 to 1995) to provide cross-cultural citizen exchanges, professional training, and overseas development and to create Soviet- and Sino-American joint ventures.

Paul can be reached at *paul@vonward.com*, or through both of his Web sites: *www.vonward.com* and *www.reincarnationexperiment.org*.

Steven Sora graduated from C.W. Post College with a degree in history. His career began with a stint as a precious metals trader for a New York firm, but he never lost his interest in history. He set out to discover just how extensive transatlantic contact had been before Columbus. This research led to his first book, *Lost Treasure of the Knights Templar*, which documents a 1398 voyage from Scotland to Nova Scotia. This was followed by four subsequent books (which have been reprinted in 12 languages) and more than 200 articles on diverse topics including travel, photography, investing, and non-fiction/mystery. He also made an appearance in the DVD liner notes for the Jerry Bruckheimer film *National Treasure*. He has appeared on several radio shows and in several documentaries, most recently the History Channel's *Holy Grail in America*. He is a regular contributor to *Atlantis Rising* magazine. He lives in Palmer, Pennsylvania, with his wife, Terry, and two large dogs, Ulysses and Jax.

William Bramley is an author who is best known for his book *The Gods of Eden: A New Look at Human History*. His primary interest lies in social dynamics, a fascination which began with a high school sociology class and continued through college, where he received a bachelor's degree in sociology. Bramley has also appeared on radio and television shows, most recently on the History Channel's *Ancient Aliens* series. Although he is no longer engaged in research and writing on this topic, he continues to comment when invited to do so.

Thomas A. Brophy has a PhD from the University of Colorado, was a research scientist at the Laboratory for Atmospheric and Space Physics, Boulder, with NASA interplanetary spacecraft projects, and was a National Science Foundation exchange scientist with the University of Tokyo and Japan Space Program. Interests in fundamental theory led to broader studies involving the non-calculable and immeasurable aspects of the universe, teaching Integral philosophy, and his book *The Mechanism Demands a Mysticism*. Integral philosophy with astrophysical dynamics led to his studies of the astro-archaeology of prehistoric and proto-historic Egypt, and his book *The Origin Map*. He now teaches Integral theory, physics, and archaeo-astronomy, and is proprietor of a consulting business. He has published peer-reviewed scientific articles in premier journals, including *Icarus, Mediterranean Journal of Archaeology and Archaeometry, IEEE Journal*, and *Science*. He has also been a featured presenter at numerous scientific conferences and Integral spirituality meetings in the United States, Europe, and Asia. He is coauthor of *Black Genesis: the Prehistoric Origins of Ancient Egypt*.

Born on April 14, 1935, in Zofingen, Switzerland, **Erich von Däniken** was educated at the College St.-Michel in Fribourg, where he was already studying ancient holy writings. While managing director of a Swiss five-star hotel, he wrote his first book, *Chariots of the Gods*, which was an immediate bestseller in the United States, Germany, and, later, in 38 other countries. He won instant fame in the United States as a result of the television special "In Search of Ancient Astronauts," which was based on the book. His books have been translated into 32 languages and have sold 63 million copies worldwide. In a more recent offering, *Twilight of the Gods: The Mayan Calendar and the Return of the Extraterrestrials*, he meticulously investigates the mysteries surrounding the Mayan calendar, its amazing connection to the Ancient Astronaut Theory, and the tantalizing information on the extraterrestrials' prophetic return to Earth. In 2003 he opened his "Mysteries of the World" theme park in Interlaken, Switzerland, which still fascinates visitors with his research into the various mysteries of the world, including paleo-SETI and the Ancient Astronaut Theory.

Today, Erich lives in the small mountain-village of Beatenberg, Switzerland, with his wife, Elisabeth. Fluent in four languages, Erich von Däniken is also an avid researcher and a compulsive traveler, averaging 100,000 miles each year to the remotest spots on the globe in order to further investigate the mysteries that so intrigue him.